What Others Are Saying about *Mavericks!*

"*Mavericks!* not only demonstrates that the traditional management emperor is naked, but that he is suffering from a skin condition. Fortunately, it also prescribes a healing salve. Don Blohowiak's analysis is both insightful and inciteful with strong doses of cleverness and levity that elevate it from the usual gang of how-to-manage-book suspects. Supervisors, especially middle managers caught between timid, self-protective senior directors and disgruntled or apathetic subordinates, will find *Mavericks!* well worth the investment of time and money."

Gary A. Hengstler, Editor and Publisher, *ABA Journal*

"When I open the pages of *Fortune*, I find problems. When I opened Blohowiak's book, I found some innovative solutions. This is a terrific book, written at the right time, with the right type of author, with the right type of panache. The style is highly readable, the content provocative and the organization of ideas excellent. . . . It fulfills its potential."

Professional Readers, *Reader's Report*

"Don Blohowiak has blown the lid off what it takes to be tomorrow's true business leader, *Mavericks!* defines how to successfully, tactfully and forcefully do the impossible and not hurt anyone in the process."

Al Parinello, Host/Commentator, *Business Radio Network*

"Detroit's Big 3 auto makers should order bulk quantities of Don Blohowiak's *Mavericks!*. It could unleash the productive juices of their managers and might be a first step in cutting the nation's trade deficit with Japan. Not to mention the benefits to all of us motorists."

Morrie Helitzer, Publisher and Editor-in-Chief, *New Accountant*

"Don Blohowiak covers *all* the bases surrounding the mysteries of creativity in business—what gets in the way, and what makes it happen. . . . He understands creativity at the molecular level. . . . Anyone who wants to wrap his or her arms around why creativity does or doesn't work in any organization should read this book."

R. Donald Gamache, Chairman, Innotech, Co-author, *The Creativity Infusion*

"Finally, someone has written the management book *I've* been looking for. . . . I can think of several instances where . . . had I read this book earlier on, I would not have lost some valuable people. . . . *Mavericks!* is immensely interesting to read, easy to absorb and thorough in its coverage. It's a book I know I'll be re-reading."

Dan Katz, President, *LA ads*

"The entire planet could use Don Blohowiak's book to build a smarter, better world. Packed with information, creative juice, procedures and reference material, *Mavericks!* will help anyone who ever hopes to be an effective leader. I am employing philosophies from this book throughout my organization. The results are phenomenal!

Chet Holmes, President, Kaleidoscope Media Group, Author, *SuperMarketing*

MAVERICKS!
How to Lead Your Staff to
Think like Einstein,
Create like da Vinci,
and Invent like Edison

Donald W. Blohowiak

BUSINESS ONE IRWIN
Homewood, Illinois 60430

This publication is designed to provide accurate and
authoritative information in regard to the subject matter
covered. It is sold with the understanding that neither the
author nor the publisher is engaged in rendering legal, accounting,
or other professional service. If legal advice or other expert
assistance is required, the services of a competent
professional person should be sought.

From a Declaration of Principles jointly adopted by a Committee
of the American Bar Association and a Committee of Publishers.

Sponsoring editor:	Cynthia A. Zigmund
Project editor:	Lynne Basler
Production manager:	Ann Cassady
Jacket designer:	Renee Kyczek Nordstrom
Designer:	Maureen McCutcheon
Art manager:	Kim Meriwether
Compositor:	Alexander Graphics Limited
Typeface:	11/13 Palatino
Printer:	R. R. Donnelley & Sons Company

Library of Congress Cataloging-in-Publication Data

Blohowiak, Donald W.
   Mavericks! : how to lead your staff to think like
Einstein, create like da Vinci, and invent like Edison / Donald W.
Blohowiak.
     p.   cm.
   Includes bibliographical references and index.
   ISBN 1-55623-624-7
   1. Creative ability in business. 2. Leadership. I. Title.
HD53.B58   1992
658.4'092—dc20   91–46310

Printed in the United States of America
1 2 3 4 5 6 7 8 9 0 DOC 9 8 7 6 5 4 3 2

For my favorite mavericks,
Susan, Benjamin, and Aaron,
who continue to show me
what is possible.

Preface

WHY WHAT FOLLOWS, FOLLOWS

This is a book of inquiries and actions. And values. And successes. These pages stem from my own need to know what you soon will read. I wrote *Mavericks!* not because I was an expert on its subjects, but because I wasn't.

In part, this book grew out of frustration with other business books. Like you, I face the managerial Gordian knot of the 21st century: How to encourage people on my team to do ever better and more creative work, and more of it in less time. I write these words as a manager responsible for a staff in a real corporation wrestling with real challenges in a highly competitive market. Few management books speak from this perspective. Or to it.

False Promises and Vanilla Solutions

Management tomes tacitly tend to address an elite cadre of chief executives. Often, a business book's advice is accompanied by admonishments to this effect: "Such recommended policies can only be effective when they start at the top." Most stop there, too. And that leaves a great swell of capable managers helplessly pinning their hopes for improving their beloved organizations on someone other than themselves.

Many business books ring hollow because all too often they are written by people who cannot take their own advice. Many books by psychologists, consultants, retired executives, journalists, and academics elicit a chuckle or empathetic nod of the head, but precious few provide practical application value come Monday morning in the pressure cooker.

Leonard Ackerman, himself a Ph.D. and professor of administrative science at Clarion University, finds it amusing, for example, that much of the participative management literature emanates from universities. He notes the incongruity in that people who make their living in "one of the least dynamic institutions—education—should be . . . touting principles that they themselves have been unable to apply." Max DePree, chairman of furniture maker Herman Miller, Inc., and a best-selling management author contends that "being an effective department supervisor on a manufacturing floor is fundamentally different from giving seminars about it." And the same might be said for any other kind of management endeavor.

Many management books also hold out a false promise. Managers, we're led to believe, need only communicate certain things (issue a mission or vision statement, praise achievements, occasionally affirm their warm feelings for the work force) and people on the payroll will fall in line, magically performing to the boss's expectations. Little is said about the boss actually modifying his or her own day-to-day behavior (which may run in opposition to the prescribed platitudes so often repeated emptily to employees).

Another common failing of business books: they imply that employees constitute a homogenous group. You can easily amass a stack of contemporary management books from floor to ceiling and not read a single word about managing people as *individuals*. Management literature's mob-view of employees mirrors education's failed tradition, in which lessons are aimed only at the mythical mainstream. Employees, like students, are people. And people are individuals first, students and employees second.

Points of Departure

In shaping *this* management book, I kept in mind managers who are seated well beneath the throne of power. Still, I'm confident that emperors who choose their own clothes will find much suitable material on these pages. And because they are where they are, they can do the most with it.

Every department in an organization constitutes a subculture within the dominant culture. Usually, that subculture finds its primary identity in the department manager. Regardless of what the corporate policy and procedure manual says, what you as an individual manager do day-to-day has the greatest influence on what and how your people do what they do.

Mavericks! contains neither psychological tricks nor mystical techniques to manipulate people into complying with an agenda.

You won't find any wishful, Oh, wouldn't it be nice if only, stuff in this book. The how-to material draws from the real experience of many managers in many companies, including my own. Unlike many other management books, this is neither an off-the-top-of-the-head book, nor is it an academic treatise (how can people who are so smart write so poorly!).

The informational platform of *Mavericks!* is built on a research foundation with four corners: (1) My personal experiences as a manager and as an employee reporting to both maverick and conventional bosses; (2) My observations, gathered in the companies where I've worked around the country (I've been employed in rural Wisconsin, downtown Detroit, suburban Denver, Southern California, and New York City, in a broad spectrum of corporations: small privately held companies, a publicly held entrepreneurial start-up, a not-for-profit organization, and two divisions of a Fortune 150 firm); (3) Academic and other secondary research on business, psychology, education, and other disciplines; and (4) Primary research—interviews with executives, workers, and consultants.

Good Words, Good Works

For many of us, reading intriguing management material is similar to attending religious services. We clap our hands. We sing praises. We may even shout, "Hallelujah!" And just as with religion, often we fail to grasp its greatest benefits because our emphasis is on belief, not practice. When the fleeting celebration is over, we, return to the world just as we were before.

Believing in managing better doesn't make you a better manager. Lao Tzu, a Chinese philosopher of the sixth century B.C., observed that "the world's hardest work begins when it is easy." Reading a management book is easy. . . .

My hope is that this collection of words will serve as a catalyst for you to convert thought and intent into powerful acts. In the very back of this book are some pages for recording your thoughts and plans—just open the back cover. Fill the blank pages as you read this book. That way, by the time you've finished reading, you'll have written a personal list of action items. Then, come

Monday morning, you can go to the office armed to take careful aim at your own Gordian knot.

If you want more information about the subjects I cover, you can find a starting point between these covers. I compiled a list of resources in the back of the book. As you read the text, you'll occasionally see the name of an organization printed in bold type. That indicates that I've included helpful information about the firm in the special Resources appendix.

For me, *Mavericks!* represents an enriching journey of professional and personal exploration. I hope you find it to be just what you were looking for.

Don Blohowiak

Contents

Introduction:
INDUSTRIAL REVELATION   2

New Age, New Challenges   4
Creative Enterprise   6
Rising Creative Tide   8
Maverick Thinkers   10
Worker as Thinker   11
The Motivation Gap   12
Micromanagement   14

Chapter One:
Yes-Men and the I-I Syndrome   16

Who's Afraid of Whom?   17
Systematically Constrained   19
Social Conformity   20
I-I, Sir   21
Reverse Yes-Man   22
Rewards of Constriction   23
Artificial Innovation   24
Enter the Maverick   25

Chapter Two:
All Progress Depends on People Who Color
outside the Lines   28

Natural Condition?   34
Champion the Maverick   37
The Corporate Contrarian   38
Controlled Anarchy   40
Quiz: Are You a Maverick?   41
The Not-for-Profit Maverick   46

Chapter Three:
360° Vision and Other Maverick
Characteristics   50

Maverick Work Style   54

Maverickese   62
The Perfection Infection   62
Maverick Emotions in Motion   65
Melancholy and the Impostor Syndrome   71

Chapter Four:
The Maverick Manager: Tearing Down Mental
Electric Fences   74

The Trust Barrier   76
To Catch Some Monkeys   78
Management Rehabilitation   79
The Inadequacies of Leadership   81
Methods of the Maverick Manager   82

Chapter Five:
Maverick Motivation: Psychic Paychecks   96

The Reciprocal Motivation Deficit   98
Motivation Is Not Rational   101
In Praise of Praise   102
Think before You Treat   113
The Spirit of Achievement   115

Chapter Six:
Incenting Mavericks: What Price
Compensation?   116

Money Doesn't Motivate   118
Money Does Motivate   119
Pay for Time, Pay for Brains   120
Fixed Pay, Fixed Performance   122
Incentive Increases?   123
Maverick Compensation: Risk, Performance,
and Pay   125
Some Maverick Proposals   129
Bonus on the Spot   133

Chapter Seven:
Stuffing the Suggestion Box:
A Systems Approach   136

From Box to Big-Time   137
Suggestions for Successful Suggestions   139
Variations on the Theme   145

Rewarding Innovation   147
Kaizen and Other Considerations   149

Chapter Eight:
Encouraging Innovation: Evolving a
Maverick Culture   152

Successful Cultures of Innovation   155
Innovation as Group Exercise   161
Educating for Innovation   162
Bureaucracy Busting   168

Chapter Nine:
Conflict, Confrontation, and
Maverick Creativity   174

Real Managers Aren't Afraid of Conflict   176
Compliance Costs   177
Organized Conflict   178
The Conflict in Judgment   181

Chapter Ten:
Brain Gain: How to Think More like
a Maverick   184

Born or Made?   187
Categorizing Creativity   188
Creative Behavior   190
Generating Ideas   201
Costs of Creativity   206
Communicating Creativity   207

Afterword   208
Maverick Resources   210
References   214
Acknowledgments   239
Index   241
Maverick Action Planner

MAVERICKS

How to Lead Your Staff to Think like Einstein,
Create like daVinci and Invent like Edison

Industrial Revelation

The percentage of U.S. patents granted to American corporations and citizens has fallen steadily, from 62 percent in 1980 to 53 percent in 1990, when seven of the top ten corporate recipients were foreigners.

Fortune

When you mention creativity, business people think of fluff. They just can't picture a pragmatic, buttoned-down person as creative.

Raymond A. Slesinski

Americans, in short, must revolutionize the way they organize, manage, and carry out work, or their jobs will disappear in the fast-paced global economy.

Business Week

FADE UP FROM BLACK

College Professor to Class:

"We are entering a whole new era . . . the decade of positive change.

"Around the world, organizations have realized that you cannot intimidate human beings into productivity.

"The key is to let people do what they do best, whatever way works best for them.

"At the same time, fundamental principles of mass production give ordinary people access to powerful technology.

"That which was affordable to the few becomes available to the many. Mass production becomes mass productivity."

"The Industrial Revolution meets the Age of Enlightenment. The walls have come down! Opportunity has gone up! And your

"Gentlemen, if we act quickly, this could be the 'state of the art' product till Thursday – may be even Friday morning!"

only limits will be the size of your ideas and the degree of your dedication!

"People, this is an exciting time to be alive."

FADE TO BLACK

With those inspiring words, this television commercial for Apple Computer—the title of which I borrowed for this chapter's title—announced some new Macintosh computers. The words from that advertisement begin this book because they eloquently (1) sum up *potential* key shifts in the workplace, and (2) hint at fundamental changes in the technologically sophisticated world market.

Both these volatile factors combine to make managing in today's world a distinct challenge to people who supervise others. Managers everywhere must meet the challenge of doing more, doing it faster, doing it better, with fewer resources. *How will you do it?*

Norton Paley, president of a marketing consultancy, articulates the challenge perfectly: "Outwardly, you must continue motivating your staff, encouraging them to introduce new products and to find methods of adding value to existing products. Simultaneously, you must search for techniques to safeguard a viable competitive position—all while you are immersed in cost chopping and people cutting."

Yes, that makes for some exciting living! And some restless nights.

Think of your business as a competitor in a high jump contest. The bar gets raised every quarter by forces inside as well as outside your company. You and your people must run at it full speed all the time. And then go faster and higher the next time, and the time after that and. . . .

NEW AGE, NEW CHALLENGES

Avon president E. V. "Rick" Goings contends that "something might be permanently broken, but nothing is permanently fixed. Everything changes." Indeed.

A Chinese proverb reminds us that when a door opens, light and air move both ways across the threshold. With American doors swung wide open to international markets, ideas and technology move both ways bringing us to the threshold of the most competitive era in our history. Edward L. Hennessy, chairman and CEO of Allied-Signal, surveys the landscape of the global economy and concludes, "It's becoming increasingly clear that the real frontiers are no longer territorial; they are markets and ideas."

Around the world, technology has become the great equalizer. *Machine Design* magazine observes, "Engineers spend a lot of time thinking up better mousetraps. And in today's competitive environment, they must do their thinking fast. They are under increasing pressure to turn out new products in months rather than years."

Businesses pressured by world-class competitors to innovate more in less time are also squeezed by demands for greater productivity and profits on slimmer margins. They've turned to sophisticated machines to improve their operations. But the glow is off the computer screen as rescuer of the bottom line. The *New York Times* reports, "Though corporations continue to spend billions of dollars on technology, white-collar productivity has stagnated." Throwing computers at office staffs no longer results in greater efficiency.

"Why don't we see more improvements in terms of the white-collar work force in this country?" asks Apple Computer CEO John Sculley. "I believe that one of the important reasons for this is that we have taken this new technology, especially over the last decade, and have mapped it on top of an old work model and an old learning model."

In the old work model the thinking was done only at the top, while doing was done at the bottom. Computers and other machines fail to improve productivity at the point at which human ingenuity and judgment must bear on the enterprise. The biggest computers in the world can only tell you what's already happened to a business. What will happen to it is in the hands and minds of all the people in an enterprise. The most advanced computers or robots can't invent new products, can't generate innovative competition strategies, can't make customers feel welcome or served.

The forces of the new economy are the same whether you make automobiles, sell financial services, or build industrial machinery. "How are we going to make any money?" asks a business services franchise owner. "My overhead has risen faster than my competitors or customers will let me raise my prices. My payroll expenses have risen faster than my employees' productivity. How am I going to make any money?"

It's hustle/hustle, go/go to one-up ourselves and our competitors today and the next day. A senior product manager in a Fortune 150 company shares his frustration with me. "They innovate, we match it. We innovate, they match it. The lag-time in this product improvement ping-pong is shorter and shorter—and we're providing these product enhancements without raising prices. I keep pushing people here to run faster toward a finish line they'll never reach. There's no end to this race. The game has higher and higher stakes. I'm just exhausted at the end of the day, and I know it will never get any easier."

Gary Markovits, patent process program manager for IBM's Research and General Technology divisions, makes a prediction both reassuring and frightening. "If you look ahead five or ten years, you can expect to see a very large number of manufacturers capable of doing world-class manufacturing and marketing. That means they've conquered the quality issues, they've conquered the manufacturing issues, and they're capable of marketing anywhere in the

world. IBM, instead of being one of a handful of world-class manufacturers, will be only one of many," Markovits forecasts.

Parity isn't competitiveness; it's stagnation. So how does a company keep up, much less emerge as a market and profit leader, in
this swirling cauldron of competition and productivity pressures
that leaves even Big Blue just another runner in the pack? "Excellence" isn't enough. "Quality" isn't enough. Quality and excellence only buy you equilibrium with competent competitors—they
do nothing to distinguish your company from a cadre of customer-
wooing competitors.

The answer to this confounding conundrum can be put deceptively simply. In the new world competition there are two strategies for beating your competitors. First you out-think them, then
you out-work them. The race belongs not just to the swift, but to
indefatigable marathoners with great imaginations.

"A company is only as good as its last good idea," says Marsh
Fisher, cofounder of Century 21 Real Estate, the immensely successful franchise operation. "The rest that goes on in a company is
only housekeeping." Where will all the good ideas come from to
propel a company to the head of the pack? Business leaders must
create a corporate culture of constant innovation that ingrains
ingenuity into the work force as today's expected work ethic. They
must understand that the most important corporate asset weighs
but three pounds and is invisible to the unaided eye. It's the brain
in every employee's head.

Dominant leaders will not only have the best creative minds
working for them, they will successfully extract extremely high
levels of psychic productivity from the payroll. In our postindus-
trial world, it is not the capital assets or the number of employees
that will determine a company's fate, but rather the intensity of
motivation and innovation of its work force.

CREATIVE ENTERPRISE

Business creativity sounds oxymoronic, soft, even wimpy. In conventional thinking, a business got "creative" when crafting an ad
campaign to convince the masses to desire and acquire a product

for which there may be no demonstrable need. Creativity isn't a word much used by business people. (Even the literature on creativity doesn't list business as an environment where one exhibits creative behavior. Art, music, pure scientific research, education, and writing—those rate as creative endeavors. But business? Doesn't qualify.)

Creativity strikes some executives as unbusinesslike because many associate the word with the "freer spirits" in the fine or performing arts who dress and behave unconventionally. The term is usually associated exclusively with people who demonstrate great artistic or verbal acuity. Creative people are no more all painters or novelists than are all sales people universally gregarious or loquacious. Creative people can be found in all departments in an organization: data processing, engineering, sales, research and development, operations, finance, marketing, and human resources. The ability to generate original thinking has little to do with job function or even formal education (as you will read in Chapter 2).

Of course, no serious businessperson objects to generating profitable business ideas. Yankee ingenuity (What will they think of next?) always has ranked as a prized value. But the need to produce more and more ideas faster and faster means creativity is a term with which more managers need to come to terms. "Ideas have always made the world go 'round," says Marsh Fisher, "but more so today because it's a faster track. The time a company has to take an idea from inception to finished product is getting shorter and shorter."

Mark Sebell, a principal with the consulting firm **Creative Realities** in Boston, points out that "organizations need to differentiate between managing ongoing growth of what is versus the creative problem solving necessary to create what might be." So why the discomfort with the idea of creativity? Managers fear creativity the way they feared computers 15 years ago, says Sebell, a former new ventures specialist with Colgate-Palmolive. Executives resisted computers because they didn't understand computers. Now they still don't understand computers, Sebell says, but they know what computers can do for a business. "The same will be true for creativity and innovation."

RISING CREATIVE TIDE

Some people are starting to see the important role ingenuity must play in succeeding in a highly competitive world. Business consultant Virgil Barry contends, "business advances are being made by people who outthink others, not people who buy twice as many machines." *Time* magazine declares, "In an economy increasingly based on information and technology, ideas and creativity often embody most of the company's wealth." And not just in the high-tech world. An award-winning newspaper advertisement for Perdue chicken featured a photo of sweater-clad company president Frank Perdue, whose hair was fashioned to be reminiscent of Albert Einstein's. The headline proclaimed: "Developing a More Tender, Meaty Breed of Roaster Takes Real Genius." The ad was more than idle play on the genius theme. The copy specified Perdue's innovations in chicken: broader breast, twice the white meat than in the average chicken, cross-breeding birds for tastier roasters, and a pop-up timer for perfect cooking. Those are real innovations for a market hungry for them.

From supercomputers to tender chickens, ideas are the new currency of commerce, the new capital. The very word *capital* has its roots in the Latin *capitalis*, which means "relating to the head." So it is quite natural for capitalists to concentrate on the heady matters of creativity and innovation. With the Information Age now a reality, the creation of wealth is truly a creative activity.

Call it brain power, intellectual capital, creative assets, or whatever, thinking is the new competitive weapon. The United States is putting its money where its brains are. The National Science Foundation reports that the United States invested some $108 billion on nonmilitary research and development in 1990. That's more than the Japanese, Germans, French, and British combined. American companies are also fighting to protect their investments in innovations. Lawsuits over patents, copyrights, and other intellectual property matters rose from 3,800 in 1980 to more than 5,700 a decade later.

When talking about thinking on the job, it's not just what people on the payroll know that counts, it's what they can imagine. Business moves too fast to ever think you know what you need to know. In his book, *Powershift*, Alvin Toffler explains that "in a

---

Brief Aside

Another intriguing testimony to the competitive nature of creativity—and managing for it—was the occasional resistance I ran into while trying to pry secrets of innovative management from the gatekeepers in corporate public relations offices. "We don't talk about the techniques for managing creativity at Microsoft," said a spokeswoman curtly. In an annual report, the company says, "We distribute decision-making responsibility to individual employees throughout the organization, giving people authority in their areas of expertise."

---

turbulent environment filled with revolutionary reversals, surprises, and competitive upsets, it is no longer possible to specify in advance what everyone need to know." Crystal balls tend to fail regarding the future, but America's future depends on well-guided creative might.

Today, it's what you can invent, improve, or modify to stay a step ahead of the other guy. In a *Fortune* cover story about "Brain Power," the magazine declared that "managing know-how is not like managing cash or buildings, yet intellectual investments need to be treated every bit as painstakingly."

Managers should be asking questions like: *What is the value of a useful new idea? If one good idea leads to another, where could thousands and thousands lead us? What is the cost to the organization for not tapping the endlessly renewable resource of ideas in our employees' heads?*

Curiously, in our knowledge-based economy, there's a huge knowledge gap in the heads of people managing corporate enterprises. John Sculley, CEO of Apple Computer, points out that, "Management and creativity might even be considered antithetical states." He laments that "business literature reveals almost nothing about how to manage creativity." Business creativity consultants R. Donald Gamache and Robert L. Kuhn report, "In sessions with executives we have found that all too many lack any understanding of the fundamentals of creativity. This ignorance is excusable given that certainly less than 5 percent of executives have had any, even quasi-formal, training in creativity. So we say they have a 'license to be stupid' about it. . . . Clearly, this puts them in an extremely difficult situation when they are attempting to *manage* it." [emphasis in original]

If managers don't know how to manage the thought function, they must find out, fast. They need answers to questions such as: *How do I get more ideas flowing in my company? Aren't some people just more creative than others? Aren't creative people difficult to manage? Should I compensate employees differently for contributing their ideas? Is managing for thinking different than managing for task? Is creativity tied to motivation? Can people be trained to be more creative? Can ideas come on command? Are there ways to have more ideas in the organization without a lot of "touchy-feely" silliness? Isn't having ideas the boss's job? How can I be more creative myself? Are there special incentives to encourage people to be creative? If I encourage creativity won't all those new ideas throw the organization into turmoil?* This book proposes some answers to these questions.

MAVERICK THINKERS

There is a special group of people who don't need to read creativity research to learn how to generate new ideas, and these people don't require training to learn how to apply their unique concepts to business. These independent, strong-willed individuals seem innately capable of identifying problems in the market or in their own organizations and then manufacturing novel (and often rule-violating) solutions to them. You probably know these people as mavericks, renegades, deviants, hot dogs, hot-shots, or cowboys.

Managers typically refer to this special breed—upon whose inspiration so much of the world's progress rests—as pains in the anatomy. These corporate contrarians are people in constant danger of being fired—or promoted.

Mavericks pose a challenge to the people charged with riding herd over them. When I started this book, I planned to focus almost exclusively on techniques for effectively harnessing mavericks' creative energies without corralling their enthusiasm. But the more I looked at the question, the more I became convinced that the picture was bigger than that—as wide open as the Texas sky, you might say.

Managers do need to know how to get the most constructive creative productivity out of those people who seem compelled to grace the world with their own way of doing things. At the same time, we can't afford to defer to an inspired few to fuel the progress of our simultaneously advanced and troubled world. We must learn how to manage for better thinking by all members of our corporate teams.

As we shall see later in the book, mavericks *do* think differently than most. They *do* require special understanding and care and feeding to contribute in the most meaningful way possible. They also teach us an important lesson. Our organizations need more maverick thinkers—people who come up with ideas for improving products and processes without being told (or in spite of being told not to!).

Really, this book is about managing two kinds of people. Those who already are mavericks and those who aren't yet; I call that very large second group, *achievers-in-waiting*. They are the masses waiting for management to liberate their creative souls so they can make the greatest contributions of which they're capable.

"While it is true that some people seem naturally creative and others not," says Robert H. Waterman, author of *The Renewal Factor*, and coauthor of *In Search of Excellence*, "we are too prone to leap to the conclusion that creativity is the realm of a relative few. That belief is not only wrong but impractical. Look to each person," he advises, "as a well-spring of [corporate] renewal."

WORKER AS THINKER

In this knowledge economy, no longer is there any such thing as "unskilled labor." Even fast-food outlets—one of last few places an uneducated worker can find gainful employment—are successfully replacing workers with robots that do "slicing, dicing, cooking, and delivery of food," the *New York Times* reports. Robotic janitors can't be far behind. Workers increasingly sell their brains rather than brawn to employers, giving more soul than sweat down at the shop.

Tom Stewart, associate editor of *Fortune* magazine and former president of Atheneum Publishers, contends that bosses now say

---

Brief Aside

The decline of the American industrial base is well known. No need
to retrace the steps taken by others who have documented the case.
Still, here's one interesting development to mull. The U.S. Bureau
of Labor Statistics estimates that despite increases in population
and moderate economic growth, the actual number of U.S. manufacturing jobs in the year 2,000 will number fewer than they did in
1970, 1980, or 1988.

---

to workers, "We no longer just want your body, we want your
brains." He also observes, "It's no accident that real estate costs
more in an idea epicenter like Cambridge or Beverly Hills than in
Pittsburgh or Detroit."

In this service/knowledge-driven economy, most people collecting a paycheck do so for "symbolic work" dependent on their
ability to think, to imagine and create alternatives. The effectiveness of the "worker as thinker" evolution will be the result of
skills that have not been formally taught in either traditional education or corporate training.

The quality of this thought-intensive work also depends on the
psychological well-being of the people doing it. Mental health is
influenced in no small way by the conditions of the workplace and
the integrity of the relationship between the worker and her boss.
Unfortunately, there's tremendous room for improvement in this
area. And this book makes some recommendations.

THE MOTIVATION GAP

Despite the popularity of "people management" books and seminars, a number of surveys point to the tremendous chasm between
the ideal and the reality. A poll sponsored by benefit consultants
William M. Mercer, Inc., shows that more than 60 percent of personnel managers believe their greatest challenge is employee motivation. In another survey of nearly 1,000 firms, 7 of 10 companies
reported a lack of motivation among employees.

Not only are bosses disappointed in worker attitudes, employees aren't too thrilled themselves. Peter Gelfond, who directs research for the Hay Group human resource consultants, reports that only 16 percent of employees believe that they are well-managed. That means 84 percent of our employees believe they are poorly managed! *How will you keep your employees motivated in a tough, demanding business climate?*

As business professor Michael LeBoeuf points out, "Our public and private organizations have the highest number of managers per worker of any nation on earth. Yet when asked to name the leading cause of American organizational problems, the overwhelming majority of managers answered 'poor management.' "

It's unanimous. Workers and bosses alike agree: Management stinks. Is it any wonder that companies struggle with innovation and productivity? Is it any wonder that service is so bad in our so-called service economy? (I hired Harvey *"Swim with the Sharks"* MacKay to speak to my company's top salespeople. During the Q&A session, someone asked him what impressed him most during his wide travels promoting his book. Without even drawing a breath, MacKay fired off, "Incompetence! It's everywhere—like I've never seen before—and it's getting worse." Research commissioned by the U.S. Office of Consumer Affairs seems to bear out MacKay's conclusion. It shows that at 200 large companies, customer service departments are contending with more than twice as many complaints as they did seven years ago.)

Here's the irony. People want to work. Really. A Gallup poll shows that 70 percent of the work force would continue working even if they had enough money to retire! Consistent with the unfortunate dislike of current management practices reported just a moment ago, fewer than 40 percent of those people who could retire but would continue to work would do so in their current jobs. Sixty percent want out from under their current bosses!

Maybe workers have always held management in low esteem. And maybe that didn't matter much when they simply followed a plow or turned a bolt. Today, workers must draw on abstract thinking powers that are inextricably tied to their psychological well-being. Someone who hates or fears the boss won't produce ideas of the same caliber as those of one who likes and respects his supervisor. A Wyatt Company survey reported in *Employee Benefit*

News shows that liking the boss and liking the work are equally important to employees. Productivity is no longer about activity but about psychic engagement in work. *What can you do to be a manager for whom people want to give their best?*

MICROMANAGEMENT

Our society is de-massified. Stores so highly specialize their merchandise that some just sell socks (I couldn't make that up). You can buy personally customized products, even those as complex as automobiles. Media now target so narrowly to individual interests that you can buy a full-color magazine produced just for elk aficionados (published by the Rocky Mountain Elk Foundation, it's called *Bugle*).

In this environment, people at work want to be treated as individuals—not as employees, not as the work force or troops or labor. As individuals. As thinking, choice-making, competent people. This has vast implications for management methodology which I'll explore in this book. Mass management is dead. Managers must help an employee realize his or her personal potential, which in turn helps the corporation realize its potential.

Roy Chitwood, president of Max Sacks International, takes issue with the cliche declaration made by so many speechifying executives who prattle that "people are our most important asset." Chitwood proclaims, "A company's greatest asset is not people but their undeveloped potential."

If managers concentrated on helping people fulfill their potential, our companies would be filled, not with workers, but craftsmen. People would concentrate on making better wheels instead of feeling like cogs in one.

Chapter One

Yes-Men and the I-I Syndrome

We are often most in the dark when we are the most certain, and the most enlightened when we are the most confused.

M. Scott Peck, M.D.

Most organizations would rather risk obsolescence than make room for the nonconformist in their midst.

Warren Bennis

New ideas . . . are not born in a conforming environment.

Roger Von Oech

When I want your opinion, Edith, I'll give it to you.

Archie Bunker

We're going to win on our ideas, not by whips and chains.

John F. Welch, Jr., chairman, General Electric

Grab some Kleenex.® What you are about to read is a crying shame. We need to look at the conditions that make managing for innovation seem so innovative—before we launch into an exploration of the psyches of mavericks or detail suggestions for spawning more corporate dissidents.

Do your staff greet you in the morning bursting with enthusiasm, exclaiming, "G'morning, chief! I have a bunch of new ideas for you to consider just as soon as you can see me!"? If they don't, why not?

Isn't the job of a manager to *recognize and choose* from lots of great ideas generated by fellow work associates? Unfortunately,

"Please check your coat, weapons and unsolicited ideas."

most managers—even those who claim they invite suggestions from their people—subscribe to the time-honored myth that a manager's job is to *have* the ideas. If having ideas is my job, managers reason, then someone else coming up with ideas threatens my role and my security within this organization.

WHO'S AFRAID OF WHOM?

Few managers would admit that they feel threatened by a work force with ambitions as benign as generating new ideas, improving processes, or streamlining methods to improve efficiency. But many are.

New ideas carry the risk of failure. People who achieve manager status presumably have already risked some things to get where they are. Protecting the status quo—minimizing risk—protects one's station, perks, and power. Acting on unconventional proposals might advance a manager's career or end it. Managers say to themselves, Why risk it? Bosses preoccupied with maintaining their status instead of improving their operations are, in the words of former IBM marketing chief Buck Rodgers, building themselves "secure cabins on sinking ships."

Interestingly, nonmanagerial employees aren't afraid to admit that *they* are afraid to suggest improvements.

Dr. Michael Markowich, vice president of human resources for United Hospitals, conducted research into employee attitudes about making suggestions. Dr. Markowich writes that employees identified the following risks inherent in giving the boss a good idea:

- Losing my job.
- Being labeled a troublemaker.
- Not getting credit if the idea worked.
- Co-workers not liking the idea.
- The boss feeling threatened.
- Having the idea rejected.

Naturally, employees who perceive risks in sharing their ideas with the boss will not share many. And therein lies a tragic loss of creativity that could solve most business challenges. We hire people who come equipped with brains and treat them like robots, while teams of brilliant researchers spend untold millions working feverishly to teach robots to think like people!

Managers wrestle with problems in a self-imposed creative solitary confinement because they reserve the obligation for generating ideas for themselves. Even managers who earnestly invite innovations from their staff often find them fearfully resistant. Most enthusiastic employees learn early in their careers to restrain the urge to share their thinking. So even genuine refrains of "We want your ideas," fall on deaf ears calloused by false invitations and reprimands for "sticking your nose where it doesn't belong."

In many organizations, managers blithely ignore the gold mine of ideas tucked within the cranium of every person in the shop. Until a crisis strikes. Suddenly, it's time to pan for rich innovations in a river of employee ideas. But the stream is dry, parched by a long drought of managerial interest. When it needs fertile ideas most, management suffers in a creative dust bowl of its own making.

SYSTEMATICALLY CONSTRAINED

Alvin Toffler observes that "millions of intelligent, hardworking employees find they cannot carry out their tasks—they cannot open new markets, create new products, design better technology, treat customers better, or increase profits—except by going around the rules, breaking with formal procedures." In other words, one must risk the consequences of breaking with the corporate code of conduct to effect positive change at work.

Why do employees feel straitjacketed in their own places of employment? Because most managers want it that way. In the industrial factory, bosses were the idea men. The manager's operative thinking was described by Don Marquis: "The successful people are the ones who can think up things for the rest of the world to keep busy at." That philosophy has served military organizations, dictators, and bosses for eons.

The idea men/managers created systems in which they thought, while the work force implemented. A manager became, in his own mind, God the Creator. Powerful managers engineered systems that supported their self-important roles as thinkers and assigners of tasks. Lenin, decried the fact that more than five million Russian managers constituted a class that did not engage directly in productive labor but rather "administers, orders, commands, pardons, and punishes."

Long after Lenin's lament, management as a uniquely privileged (and obliged) class remains a tradition. "What comes through loud and clear from an employee viewpoint is the idea that management is an elite, whether the individual managers portray themselves as tough guys or nice guys," says Robert Levering, coauthor of *The 100 Best Companies to Work For in America*.

Systems of rules and regulations—stated or implied—grant to managers prescribed powers of initiative and approval over the masses. Independent thought by those below the exalted executive ranks is neither expected nor allowed. So whether they toil in factories, insurance companies, or hospitals, workers still sing a familiar refrain: *Ours is not to wonder why, ours is but to do or die.* Signs of discontent appear over desks, on bulletin boards, taped to the wall. They say things like this poem, written by some unknown, that a colleague passed along to me:

I'm not allowed to run the train
  Or see how fast it will go;
I ain't allowed to let off steam
  Or make the whistle blow;
I cannot exercise control
  Or even ring the bell;
But let the damn thing jump the track
  And see who catches hell!

Theologian Harvey Cox: "What dispirits most people today . . . [is] that they live in a world made by someone else. Their inner desires are anticipated and exploited, their daily schedules are printed out for them, their career trajectory is mapped by benevolent institutions. But they are losing, and they know it, because their inherent need to share in the shaping and creating process is being taken from them."

SOCIAL CONFORMITY

Places of business cannot be free-for-alls. The path of anarchy does not lead to profits. Organizations strive for consistency in member behavior by enforcing rules that may be clearly codified or merely implied.

Those expectations exert a powerful force for self-censorship of personal characteristics and thoughts that vary with the prescribed norm. Consistency in dress, speech, hair styles, work space decor, and the like, all in the name of nothing more valid than corporate sameness, stifles expression of individuality and independent thought. People walk through the company door and agree to turn off their brains in exchange for sufficient money.

Companies don't order their employees to surrender their brains at the corporate threshold. Instead they post invisible signs proclaiming, No Original Thinking Allowed. Fertility of thought threatens the secure sterility of corporate consistency.

The coercion to comply turns an otherwise free spirit into the proverbial yes-man. Gerald A. Johnston, president of McDonnell Douglas, tells a story about Air Force General Emmet "Rosey" O'Donnell.

When he was a lieutenant at an airbase near Denver, O'Donnell received an order from the commanding officer and mustered the courage to suggest a better way. That rubbed the senior officer the wrong way and he demanded to know if O'Donnell was proposing to countermand the order.

"General, sir, I'm sure you didn't reach your present rank by being a yes-man," O'Donnell replied.

"No," fired back the commanding officer, "but that's how I made colonel."

I-I, SIR

With a whole organization of yes-men marching in lockstep, a deadly condition arises: the I-I (Idea Inertia) syndrome.

In a company caught in the clutches of the I-I syndrome, employees don't just nod approvingly at the ideas generated by the boss. The sparks of new ideas are quickly smothered by the organizational wet blanket. "Within a lot of big companies, new ideas are like viruses," says inventor Bob Doyle. "They have their own immune system."

Supervisors pounce on suggestions for change. "What do *you* know about shipping product (keeping customers satisfied, organizing reports . . .)!" barks the boss. Translation: Shut up, keep your fresh-eyed insights to yourself. We have enough problems around here without sticking our noses where they don't belong.

Another popular and frustrating retort to an inventive idea is, "We've never done it that way before." Management consultant Chuck Reaves prosecutes the case. "For every undertaking there will be twenty people who will find some reason why it cannot be done. They will identify something that is merely an obstacle, declare it to be immovable, stand by it, and defend it rigidly." In the process, the creative wind is taken right out of a spirited employee's sails.

"Before a company gets into deep trouble, top executives can always point to a few things that are still going all right," says Hank Johnson, former CEO of Spiegel, Inc., "so there's built-in resistance to change." Thinking expert Edward DeBono describes this condition as being "blocked by the adequate." He exemplifies the delusionary quality of this mentality with the story of the man who jumped off the top of a skyscraper. As the man passed the third-floor window, he was heard to say, "So far, so good."

To get past the always-done-it-this-way-before myopia of the I-I syndrome, managers should heed DeBono's contention that the "historical continuity that maintains most assumptions [is] not a repeated assessment of their validity." Ezra Pound expressed it this way, "The tradition is a beauty which we preserve, and not a set of fetters to bind us." When tradition is no longer beautiful, but only binding, we should cast it off.

Managers trapped in the clutches of the I-I syndrome instinctively react to new ideas with what Elizabeth Bailey of Carnegie-Mellon University calls the "Mrs. Thomas Edison phenomenon." She relates this wonderfully illustrative story. "One night, Thomas woke up and said, 'I am so excited. I just had this great idea for a light bulb.' He explained how it works to her. Then she turned over to go back to sleep. He said, 'How can you turn over and go back to sleep with this wonderful idea?' She said, 'To have it work, you would have to wire the world, and that is just ridiculous.'"

REVERSE YES-MAN

In an organization suffering from the I-I syndrome, a kind of "reverse yes-man" mentality takes hold. Employees not only agree with the boss, but censor themselves by sifting all their ideas through a filter of, Will the boss buy this?

The reverse yes-man is most dangerous in an institution that believes itself immune from the I-I syndrome. Such an organization lies to itself: While it *says* it wants ideas from employees, nontraditional notions really aren't welcome. Employees instinctively grasp the gap between proclamation and reality. Innovative ideas never pass through the sieve of self-censorship.

David Ogilvy, the successful advertising executive and best-selling author, achieved legendary status for his renowned creativity. Historian Stephen R. Fox, in his book, *The Mirror Makers,* paints a more complete and instructive picture of Ogilvy, the *manager* of creativity in his ad agency.

"Coming to the agency as a *tabula rasa*, a new employee was then expected to absorb Ogilvy's very specific rules for making ads: include the brand name in the headline, don't try to be clever, avoid analogies and superlatives, write sentences of less than 12 words, make at least 14 references to people per 100 words, avoid humorous copy, use photographs instead of artwork, and so on. Holding his people to these precepts, he was sometimes accused of rigidity and of stifling creativity. He did, however, excel at client contact."

The infestation of the I-I syndrome feeds on the bureaucrat-manager's inclination to codify, compartmentalize, and regulate activities to a numbing paralysis of procedure. Such regimentation confines and controls most people, thereby assuring the controlling manager's monopoly on creative work that condemns everyone else to work without inspiration or psychic pleasure. Leadership expert Warren Bennis relates that, "Routine work drives out nonroutine work and smothers to death all creative planning, all fundamental change. . . .

Raymond A. Slesinski, president of **Genesis Training Solutions**, put into words a question of many workers who marvel at their boss's inexplicable intransigence: "How can someone so narrow-minded be so thick-headed?"

REWARDS OF CONSTRICTION

Because people normally act within the expectations of their culture, conformity becomes comforting—to manager and employee alike—because it is expected and rewarded.

Managers lucky enough to have ideas that fit within the confines of organizational expectation receive bonuses and perks. As managers, we may subscribe to this arrangement not because we are evil but because the corporate pot of gold seduces those of us with potential access to it. In turn, the system tends to reward nonmanagerial employees—with raises, promotions, special favors—who do more bootlicking than boat rocking.

The paradigm of manager-is-thinker is ingrained in generations of adherents. Just as many child abusers were themselves victims of inhumane cruelty, so, too, may many overbearing, confining managers be repeating behaviors they learned from bosses earlier in their careers. Unlike child abuse, restrictive or even cruel behavior by management can be rewarded—and therefore reinforced—by an organization when such behavior results in positive short-term results, such as achieving goals for cost-cutting, profits, or productivity gains. After all, isn't this just what the company expects from us?

When managers have all the ideas—or at least reserve that privilege unto themselves—their co-workers lower in the hierarchy first become discouraged and then incapable of participating. A frustrated customer service manager confided in me, "They [management] have just kept people down so long with so many rules and can'ts that the employees don't even know how to think for themselves anymore!"

Chinese philosopher Lao Tzu knew the risk of that possibility many centuries ago, when he warned, "Too many prohibitions in the world and people become insufficient."

People denied the joy of symbolic creativity in their work become insufficient because they die a little inside. With no need to create at work, routine becomes monotony, and that boredom equates to living death.

The danger is not only the loss of the employees' capacity to think, but also the loss of management's ability to lead. As the English poet Lord Byron reminds those of us who squash creative instincts in people who call us boss, "He who surpasses or subdues mankind, must look down on the hate of those below."

ARTIFICIAL INNOVATION

Some corporations convince themselves that they are innovative because they respond to customer demands. They proclaim, "We are market driven." But that declaration deceives and does not relieve a company of the I-I syndrome malady. Market research is reactive; it tells you only what people think of what exists or what they already want. Reacting to what the market demands is not innovative. It is about as confining as, We've never done it that way before.

Rolf Landauer, an IBM Fellow at the Thomas J. Watson Research Center, reminds us that "the transistor, the laser, the magnetic disk, the PC were not demands articulated by the customer." Neither were a national telephone network, the interstate highway system, enclosed shopping malls, portable stereos, electronic information retrieval, automatic teller machines, VCRs or a million other products of human initiative that improve our lives and make corporations wealthy.

ENTER THE MAVERICK

"What if . . ." are the first words of all progress. As evidenced above, they can be the most frightening words an employee can utter. Still, some people seem genetically compelled to utter them constantly.

The individual we might label "creative" isn't satisfied with the status quo. Ever. And when such individuals exist outside the upper ranks of a company, they assert their creativity within the organizational structure with great risk to their careers.

"Noncreative people see creatives as a threat," asserts advertising executive Ed McCabe. "They think they must guard against rampant creativity."

Tom Stewart of *Fortune* magazine also observes this unfortunate syndrome in corporate America. "I think a lot of the management guys are afraid of the creative guys and the creative guys are contemptuous of the management guys. It's a self-reinforcing cycle of avoidance."

Such a conflict isn't surprising given the attitude toward nonconforming employees that many managers are *taught*. Robert Levering explains that "the burgeoning genre of management literature has an unstated us-versus-them stance: How do we (the managers) get them (the employees) to do something that we want them to do?" A striking contemporary example comes from a book published by the American Management Association in

1991. The book, *Why This Horse Won't Drink*, was written by Ken Matejka, a professor of management at Duquesne University's School of Business Administration.

Matejka devotes a chapter to "managing difficult employees," whom he defines as "subordinates who refuse to 'get on board' with our goals and needs." Oh, oh—people who think for themselves. The professor groups such people into three categories, major, moderate, and minor misbehavers. "Difficult employees are a real challenge to your abilities as a manager," Matejka concludes.

The very notion of "misbehaving" implies a management modality that is self-righteous, paternalistic, and controlling. A misbehaving employee is one who is merely not doing exactly what the boss wants. Matejka postulates that the motivation for such deviant behavior stems from either a manager's failing to specify clearly the expectations for the employee, or an employee's need "to achieve more singularly selfish targets."

Matejka identifies such selfishness as the need to be recognized, to dominate, to secure a little power, to punish the organization, to inject novelty into routine (heaven forbid!), to find comfort in change. The possibilities that contrary acts might be motivated by ineptitude of management or an employee's genuine urge to improve the business don't make Professor Matejka's list.

Maverick behavior in the work force doesn't necessarily equate with a manager's failure as a task master, or employees' personality flaws. In fact, an employee's unconventional acts may clue astute managers to the untapped potential in their associates.

Antistenes, founder of the Cynic school of philosophy, teaches us that "the most useful piece of learning for the uses of life is to unlearn what is untrue." We must unlearn the old management morality that holds that bosses think, while workers do. Peter M. Senge of MIT gives us hope by pointing out. "The nature of structure in human systems is subtle because we are part of the structure. This means that we often have the power to alter structures within which we are operating."

As a manager, an influencer of people, you wield tremendous power to set free the creative energy trapped and untapped in your colleagues. A key to unleashing that power is to understand its nature, its source, and its potential. We'll examine all that in the following chapters.

Chapter Two

All Progress Depends on People Who Color outside the Lines

Beware when the great God lets loose a thinker on this planet. Then all things are at risk.

Ralph Waldo Emerson

With consistency a great soul has simply nothing to do.

Ralph Waldo Emerson

All history resolves itself very easily into the biography of a few stout and earnest persons.

Ralph Waldo Emerson

Forget it Louis, no Civil War picture ever made a nickel.

MGM production executive Irving Thalberg to Louis B. Mayer on buying the rights to the novel *Gone with the Wind.*

MUSIC UP: Theme from *The Magnificent Seven*
　　　Voice-over (deep male voice with slow drawl):

Out on the Texas open range . . . rode a lone cowboy.
Who went his own way.
　The others, they insisted, "Brand your cattle, boy!"
But Sam paid them no mind. . . . And rode his own way.
　He laughed in their faces. And gathered a fortune. The others—
they demanded, "Brand your cattle, boy!"
　But Sam just smiled. And rode his own way.

MUSIC CONTINUES AND OUT

"There's always one in every crowd!"

Sam Maverick was a real Texas cattleman; and real unconventional, the stuff of legends. Before Samuel A. Maverick departed for that big ranch in the sky in 1870, his very name had entered the language. At first, it was synonymous with an unbranded calf; soon it stood as a symbol for nonconformity and individualism.

Sam Maverick refused to brand his calves. When it came time to round up calves or yearlings, Sam gathered for himself all the unbranded little mooers he could find. This did not sit well with his cattle-raising neighbors who occasionally neglected to brand one of their own.

The rugged individualism of 19th century cowboy Sam Maverick is but one example of how determined people resist expectation and make a name for themselves. When you think about it, Sam Maverick's defiant act is consistent with an American Tradition of opposing conformity. America was founded by antitraditionalists—mavericks. Christopter Columbus broke the bonds of prevailing knowledge, risking a fatal plunge off the earth's edge to sail to the New World. Never mind that his point of arrival had nothing in common with his destination. In true maverick fashion, Columbus treated his error as a great achievement.

The pilgrims who later followed the course to the New World, abandoned their homelands for an arduously long and life-threating ocean voyage, coming to American shores to pursue bohemian religious beliefs. In addition to the anti-authority attitude they imported to their new home, these pioneers learned to innovate (a most desirable alternative to perishing). Away from the familiar comforts of home, they developed new systems to put food in their tummies, clothes on their backs, and shelter over their heads.

The English colonists who settled the land at the behest of the King took up arms in revolt, asserting self-proclaimed independence from their benefactor. Our nation's deep-seated disrespect for controlling authority even evidences itself in our national anthem: played to the tune of an old English beer drinking song!

The U.S. Constitution, the best conceived plan in the world for structuring a government, is an inspired creative work developed by freedom-minded mavericks and signed by them. Even our currency bears the mark of the maverick ethic, suggests James L. Dunlap, president, Texaco USA. He points out that on the back of a dollar bill, right above the pyramid with an eye above it, is a

Latin phrase, *annuit coeptis*. That translates to, "be favorable to bold enterprise." Dunlap says that Benjamin Franklin chose that motto "because he believed imagination was the singular characteristic of the people he helped to forge into a new nation."

The United States has been safe haven for mavericks, from Einstein to Solzhenitzyn to Schwarzenegger. American industry always has been the playground of mavericks. Henry Ford, Charles Schwab, Ted Turner, Mary Kay Ash, H. Ross Perot, Famous Amos, Victor Kiam, and the founders of Apple Computer, Steves Jobs and Wozniak all are icons of the American maverick.

Mavericks are known by many names: odd balls, rogues, gadflies, renegades, radicals, pioneers, creatives, eccentrics, geniuses, heretics, individuals, dynamos, and malcontents. They are by no measure strictly an American phenomenon. Jesus was a maverick. So were Luther and Gandhi. And Joan of Arc, Copernicus, Sun Tzu, Archimedes, Napoleon, Marie Curie, Darwin, Newton, Nabokov, Freud, Mozart, Gorbachev, Dickens, Honda, Lech Welesa, Golda Meir, and legions of others.

The masses both loathe and revere mavericks. They loathe them because people who challenge the status quo strike fear into those who are comfortable with it. In their hearts, most people understand Pablo Picasso's postulate that "every act of creation is first of all an act of destruction." The tearing down of the old to make way for the new frightens people, even those in powerful positions. Galileo was jailed and forced to recant his discoveries. As recently as the late 1800s, genius was considered akin to insanity. Invention as an activity *encouraged by society* is a recent development in the millennia-old history of humanity, coming into its own only during the last 500 years.

While mavericks scare many, the masses also occasionally love mavericks because they know that all progress—advances in medicine, economics, and creature comforts—depends on people who blaze new trails around, through and over the old ones. (Popular author and psychiatrist M. Scott Peck took contemplation of antiauthority to its most extreme, pointing out that Adam and Eve "went ahead and broke God's law without ever understanding the reason behind the law, without taking the effort to challenge God directly, question his authority or even communicate with Him on a reasonably adult level.")

Brief Aside

Successful invention is a cultural phenomenon. Historically, the United States has welcomed innovation and exported derivative products around the world. (One could not say the same for the Soviet Union—a nation of immense size, ample natural resources and a huge population.) The success of an invention depends on how well it meets the momentary needs of society: the market for a better mousetrap depends on the severity of rodent infestation. Society's needs—and the aptitude, or genius for meeting those needs—change constantly. (If our civilization only rewarded those who could construct things like bookcases or repair things like plumbing, I would surely starve!)

Some truly inspired solutions to modern problems may have already been proposed and lost because society did not immediately recognize their value. Certainly some have waited a long time to find an appreciative audience. The first vending machine was invented in the first century A.D. by the Greek scientist Hero. In his device, a dropped coin fell on a lever which opened a valve releasing holy water. While Hero invented his machine some 2000 years ago, talking Coke machines came sometime later. Leonardo da Vinci sketched a parachute back in 1485. Three hundred years later, a French hot air balloonist parachuted into the history books using one (a parachute, not a history book) to slow a fall of more than 2000 feet. Though the daring balloonist demonstrated the efficacy of parachutes, demand for them didn't peak for another 150 years, until airplanes replaced balloons as the preferred mode of transportation for skydivers.

Another Frenchman ahead of his time, scientist Blaise Pascal, invented a mechanical gear-driven adding and subtracting machine back in 1642, when he was only 19 years old. Pascal didn't need to manufacture many—no one wanted them. About 50 years later, an enterprising German devised a mechanical math machine that multiplied and divided. *That* found a market. The first electronic caluculator followed Pascal's invention by more than 300 hundred years, weighing 55 pounds and costing

Brief Aside

concluded

more than $4,000. Eventually the devices evolved into versions thin as a credit card, weighing less than a quarter ounce.

The people who created computer spreadsheets like Visicalc or Lotus® 1-2-3® weren't any smarter than Pascal. They just responded to their society's need to crunch more numbers, building on the knowledge left by Pascal and successive thinkers in mathematics and computer science. While they may not have been smarter, they were more prescient than everyone else who didn't seize the opportunity. Patent attorney and engineer Waldemar Kaempffert wrote (back in 1930), that "Meritorious inventions are not inevitably produced when social conditions are right. The proper imagination must respond to the conditions."

The role that conditions of the moment play in genius, gives rise to a flight of fancy: would famous inventors and creators have distinguished themselves had conditions of their day been different? An example. In today's world, musicians increasingly generate popular music with the help of—if not entirely relying on—computers. One can reasonably expect that trend to continue. Let's say Mozart is born 25 years from today. His potential music genius might well depend on his aptitude for computerized sound manipulation. We couldn't expect a 21st century Mozart—a product of his contemporary culture—to compose orchestral symphonies, could we? What if he never quite grasps the intricacies of programming computer music machines? Let's concede that he would still compose the type of music by which we in this century know his genius. His work might never distinguish itself from obscurity because no patron champions it. If no orchestra plays or records Mozart's music, society remains unexposed to it and confers no special status to Mr. Mozart. By economic necessity, he might be forced to pursue some other line of work entirely. And we'd never again hear a high school orchestra fiddle "Eine kleine Nachtmusik."

NATURAL CONDITION?

While mavericks make most people uncomfortable, theirs is not necessarily an unnatural disposition. Have you ever met a child who instinctively obeyed all rules? Children are born explorers. The hardest concept for them to grasp is "no"—the command they hear so frequently in response to their innate testing of the world around them. What is more natural, following rigid conventions or exploring and testing?

A child's natural inclination to test the world's boundaries—even if encouraged in a loving home—usually is defeated after a short time in school. America stands as a steward of knowledge mandating publicly financed education. And it deserves distinction as a crusher of curiosity in the way it fulfills its mission to educate. Wonder is displaced by force-fed irrelevance; explorations give way to prescribed regimen. Marsh Fisher, co-founder of Century 21 Real Estate, laments, "The whole school system discourages looking at things from a different viewpoint which is really what creativity is all about. Our schools teach us to conform—you get an A by coloring the tree green, not purple. After a while, you get the picture of how the system works." Educator Neil Postman succinctly described the tragedy: "Children enter school as question marks and leave as periods."

Before they leave the third grade, kids have been drilled with such maxims as, Curiosity killed the cat, and, Answer true or false, Select the one right answer. Success in this environment owes much less to the quality of one's thinking than to one's ability to recite or choose answers in a fashion that pleases an individual teacher. After enduring many years of this sterile, mind-numbing regimen children grow up to enter the work force devoid of any wonder, curiosity, or enthusiasm for original thinking. (And you wonder why no one ever brings you an unsolicited idea!)

When industry required masses to stand idly performing rote tasks, such machining of youthful minds served society. Now that our progress necessarily derives from inspired free thinking, the old school is dangerously out of place. No longer does our society require mindless deference to organizational authority so well drilled in schools. Now our nation demands innovative free thought on a large scale. "Companies don't invent; countries don't invent," declares Marsh Fisher. "People invent. We are only as good as people's ideas." To meet the global competitive challenge, our educational institutions must find ways of nurturing and taking to a higher order that natural explorer's spirit observable in every child.

"Compared to the decades of research on remedial efforts geared toward bringing people up to average, and the billions spent on training people for competence," argues peak performance consultant Charles Garfield, "there has been precious little systematic study of the upper levels of human achievement."

The title of this chapter, "All Progress Is Made by People Who Color outside the Lines," is a phrase I uttered in frustration during a conference requested by one of my son's teachers. Leading up to that meeting were her complaints about his frequent questions, proposals for projects that were "too elaborate," and his habit of augmenting the standard curriculum with insights gleaned from his extensive outside reading. That well-intentioned teacher had a different idea about learning than my son, my wife, Susan, or I did. Our discussion that morning flooded my mind with vivid memories of my own frustration in grade school where I took raps on the knuckles for coloring poorly and insisting on using my left hand to do so. (No doubt other lefties like Einstein, da Vinci, Napoleon, Michelangelo, Picasso, Alexander the Great, Ronald Reagan, and George Bush also faced some "correction" for their left-handed ways.)

René Dubos, renowned scientist and Pulitzer prize winner, suggests that "human beings are not really free and cannot be fully creative if they do not have too many options from which to choose." Perhaps not surprisingly, a great number of mavericks chose to drop out of school or put little energy into success there.

Albert Einstein bombed in his college entrance tests after a worse than undistinguished high school career. Winston Churchill failed twice on entrance exams to one school, and was at the bottom of his class in another school. Charles Darwin performed poorly in elementary school and failed a university medical course. Charles Dickens never finished grade school; neither did Samuel Clemens. When Pablo Picasso left elementary school at age 10, he could barely read and write; his tutoring for high school preparation failed. Fellow artist Claude Monet also failed to complete grade school.

Even if they survived the primary grades, some mavericks couldn't take the torture through the secondary grades. The Wright brothers both dropped out of high school. So did Will Rogers and George Gershwin. Newsman Peter Jennings also foreclosed on a high school diploma so he could get his education. Auto and motorcycle magnate Soichiro Honda disdained Japanese formal education, calling his certificate from a technical high school "worth less than a movie ticket."

Apple Computer founders Jobs and Wozniak dropped out of college to pursue their more stimulating personal interests. Ironically, the education market became a prime customer of their computers; Steve Wozniak did return to college and received his degree. Billionaire software mogul William H. Gates, founder of Microsoft, dropped out of Harvard when he was 19 to pursue his interest in the emerging computer field.

Like Abraham Lincoln—lawyer, inventor (he received a patent for a boat design), and politician—who sought to educate himself, most of the mavericks described above did just fine despite their classroom troubles. They were among the lucky few who, with access to a good library and enough study, probably can learn just about anything. But our society can't and shouldn't rely on the self-educated. Who wants to volunteer as the first patient of a self-taught heart surgeon? And what becomes of those children who cannot surmount schooling that stifles more than stimulates?

Primary and secondary schools must do more to encourage the explorer and thinker in all children. James R. Delisle, Ph.D., president of The Associaton for the Gifted, writes, "Some nine-year-olds struggle with fractions while other nine-year-olds contemplate whether the universe has an endpoint. Some high school sophomores prefer to read books one chapter at a time, while others devour the same book in one sitting and the following day ask, 'What's next?' These individual talents and stylistic preferences do not imply that some students are intrinsically more *valuable* than others. However, like it or not, students do function on different levels, one from the next." Schools must teach to all God's children in ways that enrich and excite each of them, not constrain

---

Brief Aside

Success in business doesn't correlate too well with formal education, according to a report published by the *Harvard Business Review*. Professor Lewis B. Ward found that salaries earned by Harvard MBA degree holders plateau about 15 years after the newly- minted grads started their business careers. Interestingly, individuals attending Harvard's Advanced Management Program who had about 15 years' business experience, but "who—for the most part—have had no formal education in management, earn almost a third more, on the average, than men who hold MBA degrees from Harvard and other leading business schools."

The conclusion drawn by the article's author, Harvard business professor J. Sterling Livingston: Those "who get to the top in management have developed skills that are not taught in formal management education programs and may be difficult for many highly educated men to learn on the job."

---

them to a compromised curriculum that cheats them. Students must be allowed and encouraged to discover as much as their imagination and stamina will allow. In the meantime, mavericks (see next chapter) progress by bucking rules and the conventional thinking that schools try so hard to ingrain and unimaginative business bosses try to enforce.

CHAMPION THE MAVERICK

Mavericks don't let the rote of the schoolhouse or the confines of the corporation stifle them. They break such bonds with ideas and drive that no rule can hold back.

English poet A. E. Houseman suggests that "creativity grows out of irritation like a pearl secreted from the friction-generating particle of sand in the oyster's shell." For mavericks, this irritation spurs them to generate solutions to the world's problems. They embody what some call "divine discontent," or "positive maladjustment."

An example. Chester Carlson worked in the New York patent department of an Indiana electronics firm in the late 1930s. He became frustrated with the cumbersome process of getting copies of patent specifications and drawings. The young physics graduate had a better idea and invented it—right at the kitchen table in his small apartment. Carlson offered his electrostatic printing process to the top mimeograph companies which received him with "an enthusiastic lack of interest." He tried to sell his device to IBM, GE, and RCA. They slammed their doors in his face. His fledgling enterprise—founded on finding a better way to do what was already being done by more primitive technology—struggled along, eventually evolving into a world leader in document production, Xerox Corporation, making Chester Carlson a multimillionaire.

Carlson's story follows a familiar theme, repeated time after time in this country. The entrepreneur who risks house, car and everything else to pursue a dream of independent work is a familiar American archetype. It's extraordinary in Japan. But one such entrepreneur became wildly successful in the land of the Rising Sun. This man was described by the *New York Times* on its front page as "something of a delinquent" and a "fiery maverick who spoke his mind." The man was Soichiro Honda, founder of the Honda Motor Company. Mr. Honda grew from "a rebellious auto mechanic" who "was always something of an outsider in his own country," to a powerful industrialist, "his success spawning as much jealousy in Toyota City as it did in Detroit."

Honda was a maverick. He refused the Japanese government's edicts to build only motorcycles, not cars. (Honda's first popular motorcycle was called the *Dream*.) Defiant, Honda built cars in Japan and abroad. Honda Motor Company was the first Japanese car manufacturer to build factories in the United States. That presence, and its automobiles' quality, had Honda vying for the number three automaker spot in the United States, frequently outselling Chrysler Corporation in 1991.

THE CORPORATE CONTRARIAN

Henry Riggs, high-tech management expert, points out that "most founders of new high-technology companies were once frustrated champions in larger companies." Still, not all mavericks chose the route of running their own business. Some of that go-your-own-way maverick spirit lives in larger corporations too, in research labs, sales forces, accounting departments, and every other corner of the enterprise. Harvard business professor Elizabeth Moss-Kanter, who studied the dynamics of change in many corporations, found what she called "the quiet entrepreneurs" in every function at larger companies. Such people "do not start businesses; they improve them," says Moss-Kanter.

Mavericks appoint themselves Champions of the Cause to Improve the Business. They look for ways to do new things, and new ways to do old things. Risking repercussions from the powers that be, mavericks wager their very livelihoods to do what they feel needs to be done, challenging, ignoring, or thwarting organizational policies all the way.

Authority neither intimidates nor inhibits them. Mavericks "are more likely to think of authority as conventional or arbitrary, contingent on continued and demonstrable superiority; to accept dependence on authority as a matter of expedience rather than personal allegiance or moral obligation; to view present authority as temporary," wrote Gary A. Steiner of the University of Chicago Graduate School of Business.

To mavericks, most rules apply only to cowardly mortals, not themselves. They flaunt the rules because they must. Mavericks understand former AT&T sales executive Chuck Reaves' observation that "rules are the first step in blocking changes." Not all organizations block change, of course; some champion them.

Porsche parades its prowess for innovation in an ad headlined, "Legend has it that whenever a new Porsche is being created, you can hear the sound of rules breaking." That award-winning ad backed the company's claim by recounting Porsche's history. "In the warm spring sun of 1948, Professor F. Porsche rolled out an automobile which, simply put, ignored virtually every convention of the day. . . ." After detailing those early departures from conformity, the huge double-page ad introduced a new model with 85 percent new components. The ad closed with this enticing call to action: "Experience this latest package of nonconformity at your authorized Porsche dealership. We do not, however, recommend that during your test-drive you break any rules yourself."

Brief Aside

When the organization doesn't guide its mavericks and provide reasonable checks on their boundless enthusiasm, their well-intentioned zest can stray into dangerous territory. One need only recall the case of a certain ambitious Lieutenant Colonel whose zeal for a self-proclaimed righteous agenda cast a dark shadow of suspicion over the world's most powerful institution. Such an incident doesn't nullify the positive contribution a committed and resourceful individual can make, but it makes the case for why management should always monitor an empowered work force.

CONTROLLED ANARCHY

In a maverick's mind, his or her enlightened agenda and priorities are more important than the organization's unfortunately misguided ones. As one manager put it, "They feel the organization is there to serve them." And in a way that's right.

Apple CEO John Sculley knows that a company needs a little unrest to progress. "I would worry if there wasn't always a little bit of anarchy in the organization. It's like arsenic: a little is medical but a lot can kill you. You want to impart medicinal levels of anarchy within an organization so that people feel they are free enough to express opinions without worrying about the implications."

A little of that individually inspired anarchy seems necessary for real progress in a company. Mark Sebell is a principal in the Boston-based consulting firm **Creative Realities**, with corporate clients of every description (Walt Disney World, Citibank, Warner Lambert, Union Carbide, General Mills, and many more). He says, "Creativity and innovation done democratically tends to sink to a very low common denominator. If you're going to get somewhere, it's because some wide-eyed radical jumps up and says, 'I'm going to do that.' As consultants, we help mavericks—we call them champions—succeed by helping to create an atmosphere in the organization that is conducive to change."

Quiz: Are You a Maverick?

The world's great explorers, thinkers, scientists, artists, and leaders made their mark by daring to be different, by questioning and challenging the status quo. Do you embody the personality traits that are the stuff of renegade genius? Take this little quiz to test your Maverick Quotient. *Circle the letter that best corresponds to how you actually behave.*

1. While driving, you become lost, so you:

    a. Never get lost because you always plan thoroughly.
    b. Wander hopefully until your companion insists that you pull over and ask for directions.
    c. Proceed, confident that you'll get your bearings (no matter how long it takes).
    d. Stop and ask directions as soon as you're sure you're off course.

2. You find humor:

    a. Only in your boss's jokes—you know where your next meal is coming from.
    b. In as many things as possible—better to laugh than cry.
    c. In everything—live is absurd, so laugh.
    d. In very few things—life is a very serious subject.

3. Select the description closest to your TV viewing habits.

    a. You watch whatever is on after turning on the TV.
    b. You carefully select the few shows you allow yourself to watch.
    c. You constantly flip between channels.
    d. You have several favorite shows that you almost never miss.

4. Your music and book collections consist of:

    a. All best sellers of one or two types.
    b. Various styles and artists.
    c. An eclectic grab bag of both the conventional and weird.
    d. A little of this, but mostly a lot of that.

Are You a Maverick?   (*continued*)

5. In a department meeting, your boss lays out a plan that strikes you as inadequate. Which of the following do you do?

   a. Say, "Count on me to do whatever you think is best, boss!"
   b. Make a note to send a private memo to the boss suggesting some alternatives.
   c. Blurt out, "You've got to be kidding! That won't work—but this will . . ."
   d. Sit quietly waiting for reaction from all the others.

6. When evaluating the behavior of others, you:

   a. Can't bring yourself to judge others.
   b. Try to be fair and reasonable.
   c. Use yourself as the desired standard.
   d. Ask others for their opinions first.

7. In describing your own creativity, would you say that you're:

   a. Frightened when a new idea crosses your mind.
   b. Capable of having many good ideas.
   c. A self-contained idea *machine*.
   d. Happy that others have new ideas, but you have few of your own.

8. When unexpected change comes into your life, you:

   a. Wonder why God can be so cruel.
   b. Look for ways to make the most of it.
   c. Thrive on seeking out and exploiting the hidden opportunities.
   d. Adjust the best you can.

9. Your thoughts on the purpose of Life can best be summed up by:

   a. There's a purpose to Life?
   b. To make a contribution.
   c. To try seeing, tasting, and doing everything!
   d. Getting through it with as little damage as possible.

10. Your boss criticizes some of your work unfairly. You respond by:

   a. Begging forgiveness and pledging to do the work over to the boss's liking.
   b. Acknowledging the feedback, but doing nothing further.
   c. Justifying your approach and questioning the boss's evaluation criteria.
   d. Saying, "Thanks for your help, I'll do better next time."

11. Your role in social interactions can best be described as:

   a. Wallflower.
   b. Choosey.
   c. Lone Eagle.
   d. One of the gang.

12. Business associates would describe your taste in clothes as:

   a. Fuddy-duddy.
   b. Contemporary.
   c. Individualistic.
   d. Safe.

13. Your boss would describe your work productivity as:

   a. As little as possible to get by.
   b. Sufficient and maybe a little more.
   c. Awesome (for the work you're really interested in).
   d. "Steady Eddy."

14. If you found yourself with an hour of spare time, you'd spend it:

   a. Sleeping.
   b. Flipping through a magazine you'd never seen before.
   c. Hiking in the mountains.
   d. Watching golf on TV.

15. Your colleagues would describe your work personality as:

   a. Bootlicker.
   b. Boat rocker.

Are You a Maverick? (*continued*)

   c. Rebel with a cause.
   d. Teacher's pet.

16. Which best describes your general attitude toward ethical questions?

   a. Might makes right.
   b. Right is relative.
   c. No matter the price, stick to your principles.
   d. Right is in the rules.

17. A friend invites you to dinner at a restaurant with a menu printed in a foreign language. You order:

   a. Macaroni and cheese.
   b. The waiter's choice from the specials of the day.
   c. Something off the menu that has a catchy sounding name.
   d. A steak and a baked potato.

18. When you receive the new company Policy and Procedure manual, you:

   a. Read and highlight it immediately.
   b. Put it on a shelf "for future reference."
   c. Toss it in the roundfile without opening it.
   d. Flip through it and schedule a time to review it more thoroughly.

19. Your energy level throughout the day is best described as:

   a. A notch above dead.
   b. Usually high with occasional dips.
   c. Super-charged, watch out!
   d. Low but steady.

20. You're better at:

   a. Stopping something.
   b. Starting something.
   c. Changing something.
   d. Staying the course.

Scoring

For each "A" you circled, give yourself 0 points; for each "B," give yourself 3 points; each "C" counts as 5 points; and each "D" is worth 1 point. Add up your score (the total should be between zero and a hundred). Your score equals your Maverick Quotient *according to the following scale:*

85 to 100 points: Do you secretly desire to join the Hell's Angels? You are an incurable antiestablishmentarian. A rogue. A swashbuckler. A thoroughbred Maverick. You know a million ways to make the world a better place, and putting your fingerprints all over it is as vital to you as breathing air. Your need for independent thought and action could drive your boss (and your staff) crazy. **Advice**: Be careful. The world fears disruptive people like you— despite all the potential improvements you freely offer it. If you rock the boat so hard that you're pushed off, you won't be able to take it where it needs to go. As a manager, recognize that your mercurial nature can be unsettling to your charges. Work on developing more patience and tolerance than what comes naturally to you.

60 to 84: You're a "corporate contrarian." Your willingness to speak out sometimes has you dancing between the party line and the unemployment line. Some may find you a bit brash, but they don't understand that you're only trying to effect positive change. **Advice**: Use your talents to effect progress. Draw on your social acumen to challenge the system without threatening it. Assure your boss that your intentions are to help the enterprise be more successful. As a manager, extend to your staff the same tolerance for creative malcontent that you hope your boss would extend to you.

16 to 59: You're an "achiever-in-waiting." You defer to authority, but not hopelessly. Don't be a slave to convention. Try new things. Trust yourself, then give of yourself. **Advice**: Discover the unique person you keep hidden below your obedient exterior. Act not so that the world approves of you but so that you improve the world. Make a suggestion here and there. Don't be discouraged by naysayers, not even your boss. Not everyone will appreciate what you offer, but everyone loses if you offer nothing. As a manager, recognize that innovative thinking by your

---

Are You a Maverick? (*concluded*)

staff isn't a sign of mutiny but rather interest and concern for the success of the enterprise.

0 to 15: Did you work in the Nixon White House? You are a "yes-man" personified. If the Soviet bureaucracy weren't collapsing, you'd be perfect for it. Your boss wants to fire you, your staff wants to undermine you. **Advice**: Get help before it's too late.

THE NOT-FOR-PROFIT MAVERICK

Many who push against the rules do so outside business, in university research labs, charitable organizations, and government offices. The frontiers of science routinely move farther out as maverick thinkers challenge accepted knowledge, pushing it beyond known boundaries. According to psychologist Howard Gardner at Harvard, half of all Nobel laureates in science actually invented their fields of study.

Throughout this book, we'll catch glimmers of innovative management methods from many different kinds of organizations including government agencies (yes, government agencies!). While publicly funded institutions typically bring to mind images of bloated bureaucracy and agonizing inefficiency, mavericks occasionally influence progress in public organizations. Sandra Hale headed a procurement operation as commissioner of administration for the state of Minnesota—a bureaucratic job if ever there were one. But with vision and a pioneering spirit, Hale turned her office into what *Fortune* magazine called "a source of innovation." She improved services and cut costs, saving Minnesotans a billion dollars. How did she do it? By encouraging civil servants to think for themselves and run the state government like an entrepreneurial business. Among the innovations: Accepting credit cards at campgrounds, which boosted attendance and revenues. Banking a million dollars in interest by processing financial transactions faster. Self-funding a half-million dollar laundry facility at a medical center by making it a profit center that does wash for other organizations. Hale is now trying to bring her methods to other public institutions as an independent consultant.

Two civilian employees of the U.S. Army in Tooele, Utah, came up with a five-minute procedure to fix a chronic problem in the fuel control units of some Army trucks. They submitted their idea to the Army Ideas for Excellence Program, which adopted the procedure to save taxpayers nearly a half-million dollars in replacement parts.

The Ford Foundation sponsors an annual Innovations in State and Local Government Awards Program to recognize and promote imaginative programs and policies that tackle social and economic issues. Hopeful contestants for the awards bring their thinking to bear on vexing problems in fields such as education, housing, economic development, environment, and health care. Here, briefly, are a few stories of innovation by mavericks at work on the public payroll.

Robert Fahey faced a jammed, methane gas-oozing landfill in Collier County, Florida, that threatened local water supplies. As director of solid-waste management for the county, Fahey designed a process where machines could mine the buried refuse in the landfill to reclaim recyclable materials. This innovation recovers millions of dollars worth of discarded aluminum, glass, and plastic. Some of the unearthed garbage goes to commercial recyclers, some (composted earthen material) is used as cover for local landfills, saving half the previous costs for such material. Maverick Fahey pioneered a workable system now under study for application at solid-waste sites across the nation.

In Tacoma, Washington, a community organization hires homeless people for jobs that benefit others in need. These newly employed workers help homeless veterans, the mentally ill, and they work at shelters for others down and out. Those with the new jobs develop skills, get a boost in self-esteem, and provide useful services to society.

In Georgia, the state set up a network of "dry hydrants"—nonpressurized pipe systems installed in lakes and streams. The water system serves rural firefighters with quickly accessible water to extinguish blazes—which helps them get into action quickly—and lowers insurance premiums for local residents. The water system also helps road crews maintain the state's many gravel roads, cutting upkeep time in half and improving local drivers' fuel economy.

Arcata, California, confronted a waste-water problem. The state mandated a costly, traditional treatment system, but the locals had a better idea. They built a model plant using new technology that not only cleaned up the water, but improved the quality of life in the area as well. They reclaimed wetlands, creating a 170 acre wildlife sanctuary for waterfowl. The marsh also provides the town with a new recreation area, and an aquaculture center where salmon are raised. How did the townspeople pioneer this idyllic solution? They asked the staff of the local state university for technical advice and then followed up on it.

In Newport News, Virginia, police officers receive training as problem solvers. They learn a four-step process to solve problems at virtually no cost to the city. Surveys indicate that the training improves the officers' job satisfaction, and that they believe it's made them more efficient and effective on the street.

These programs vary in their design and impact, but they're each innovative. All, in the words of Franklin A. Thomas, president of the Ford Foundation, are "stories of extraordinary individuals who wanted their government to work better and who, stubbornly and tirelessly, pursued the necessary program and policy changes."

Thomas points to the magic ingredient. "The development of human potential, as exemplified in these innovators, appears to be as important to innovation as sound program design." Indeed. Mavericks show us the reaches of human potential as we shall see in the next chapter.

Chapter Three

360° Vision and Other Maverick Characteristics

All of our greatest heroes seem to have some component of the overgrown teenager. We like the freshness, and we admire the rebels, but, boy, are they a problem to supervise.

Albert J. Bernstein and Sydney Craft Rozen

Innovators, like all creative people, see things differently, think in fresh and original ways. They . . . are seldom seen as good organization men or women and often viewed as mischievous troublemakers.

Warren Bennis

Creative individuals as a rule live at a level of intensity unknown to the rest.

Michael M. Piechowski

Great spirits have always encountered violent opposition from mediocre minds.

Albert Einstein

It ain't easy being green.

Kermit the Frog

A small crowd gathered near the lectern as it always does after a speaker says something relevant to an audience. "You told my life story up here," a man related to me quietly, a sigh of relief in his voice. "Hey, you made me naked in front of all these people," joked another. "I didn't know anybody else had my strange experiences," exclaimed a woman. Each of these business people is a self-confessed maverick, and each had a moving reaction to my speech on common maverick idiosyncrasies.

If you even suspect you might be a maverick, or if someone who works for you is, spending a few minutes in this chapter will help you understand why rebellious high-achievers do the things they do. In my experience, high-achievers share many of these commonalities, *though not every one of them exhibits every trait*. You'll find these characteristics in everyone who thinks like a maverick: aggressive scientists in R&D, tireless salespeople, constant improvers in manufacturing, deal-doers in law, imaginative marketers, and innovating individuals in accounting, human resources (HR), and management information systems (MIS).

There is no owner's manual for extraordinary people. Consider this chapter an attempt to write but a page in such a book. As Dr. Charles Garfield pointed out in the last chapter, comparatively little research has gone into studying the outer reaches of human potential. Linda Kreger Silverman charges that "at least 42 divisions of the American Psychological Association currently exist, none of which focuses on the gifted."

In addition to my own experiences and observations, I've drawn on several sources for the information you'll read concerning maverick individuals: most notable is educational literature discussing gifted children. While it is not always the case, many high-achieving, innovative adults were also exceptional children. (Billionaire William H. Gates, the founder of Microsoft, was 14 when he founded his first two companies.) Mavericks relate to the world in ways that differ significantly from "normal" people's experiences, in youth and later in life.

Throughout this chapter, and the rest of this book, I'll use the terms *mavericks, creatives,* and *high-achievers* interchangeably. Mavericks aren't just people who challenge authority (then crooks and anarchists would qualify). Mavericks embody a constructive quality—they challenge the system to improve. And improving something is a creative act. Creative acts require two components: ideas and action. The action component invokes the concept of achievement—getting something done instead of just dreaming, wishing, or complaining.

Mavericks don't simply respond to their environment, they shape it. Knowing that the world that exists is far from what could be, mavericks possess a drive to seek and act on new and unconventional ideas. They cannot not initiate. When they wake up in the morning, often at dawn or before, their insides scream, How can I improve the world today!

The triad of maverick characteristics—create, act, and accomplish—sounds deceptively simple. Such traits rarely occur simultaneously in one person. That's what gives rise to a term like *gifted.* But such qualities aren't presents from heaven; usually they're hard and painfully earned. We're all recipients of talents, aptitudes and predispositions (from our progenitors and our surroundings). We each receive different "gifts" in different measure. As with everything in life, it's not what we have but what we do with it that counts. As John Briggs, author of a book on creativity put it, "Talent is at some levels indistinguishable from intensity and passion." The merely imaginative see what could be. The maverick, the high-achiever, sees and makes it so by the force of his or her will—a quality I call potency. Determination and productivity augment curiosity and imagination in potent people.

By definition, high-achievers rank as capable people. While their individual talents and skills vary widely, all potent people might be described as smart. Are mavericks and other creative people more intelligent than most people? (Ask most mavericks and they'll tell you they're forever cursed to work for people who aren't as smart as themselves.) The true answer is: it depends on how you measure smart.

A high score on an IQ test will make you neither innovative nor successful. Intelligence tests only measure a narrow range of skills; "*School aptitude tests* might be a better term for them than intelligence tests," contends James J. Gallagher at the University of North Carolina, Chapel Hill. Indeed. And even that may have little meaning. As Abraham J. Tannenbaum reminds us, those who are successful in school may be "masters of trivia . . . straight A retrievers and dispensers of other people's knowledge, who masquerade as gifted even though they can never generate a worthwhile idea of their own."

Performing well on an IQ test doesn't mean one embodies insight, drive, savvy, perseverance, personality, ethics, skill, knowledge, or ideas.

Harvard psychologist Howard Gardner theorizes that at least seven kinds of intelligence exist. The first two are those commonly measured in the familiar intelligence tests: linguistic and logical-mathematical intelligences. The others he describes are spatial (perceiving relationships between shapes; architects are good at this), bodily-kinesthetic (e.g., dance and athletics), musical, interpersonal (social skills), and intrapersonal (knowledge of self).

To Gardner's list, I would add at least six more. *Mechanical intelligence*—the folks who fix my car deserve and receive my deep admiration for their abilities. *Time sensitivity* is a kind of intelligence. Individuals highly skilled in this aptitude include restaurant servers or busy nurses who proficiently juggle the many needs of their many patrons or patients, and capable managers who execute competing tasks in the right priority to meet both explicit and undefined deadlines. *Curiosity* is an intelligence. Understanding concepts is one thing, wondering *why* is quite another (and a very common trait of mavericks). *Street smarts* is a real intelligence—some people just have an insight into the way people operate in the world's very dirty realms. Add *nurturing intelligence*—giving parents, teachers, and farmers have a way with living things that others do not. Finally, *moral intelligence*, which is not dogma-spewing or ritual-adhering, but thinking and living ethically. This intelligence may be most easily evidenced in its absence.

Creativity expert Roger von Oech says he believes that "much of what is called 'intelligence' is our ability to recognize patterns." And the type of patterns to which each high-achiever is sensitive varies by individual. Some perceive patterns in many aspects of life—high marks in several different intelligences—while others may have extreme concentrations in just a few. Intelligence, then, is a highly personal mixture of perceiving and interacting with the world. Who is smarter: Henry Kissinger or Carl Sagan, Lee Iacocca or John Updike, Frank Sinatra or Pope John Paul II? The vice president of finance or the vice president of marketing?fmShould we rely on academic records, scores on intelligence tests, or other performance measures to screen applicants for positions in our companies?

An individual achiever may just get by using a small percentage of his or her potential, while others squeeze every bit of performance from their innate abilities. "Peak performers are not people with something added," says Charles Garfield, "rather they are people with very little of their potential taken away." Let's look now at some of the qualities high-achieving mavericks bring to their work.

MAVERICK WORK STYLE

Most people respond to a boss's instructions with a grunt and more or less carry out the assigned task. A maverick hearing "Do this," responds twice. First he asks, *Why?* Then, upon hearing the answer, offers, "I think I know a better way—my way." Such a response typifies mavericks and tells us much about them.

How is it that these independent-minded people always feel confident and competent enough to suggest alternatives? At a conference sponsored by the University of Chicago's Graduate School of Business back in 1962, Gary A. Steiner, a professor there, summarized some maverick characteristics:

Everyone agrees that the more creative individual is different from other people and that he knows it . . . he says to himself: I am not just one of the crowd. . . . He is independent plus something else. He is a hard worker. . . . At once he is more impulse-ridden, more irrational in a sense, *and* he has superior controls. . . . He has higher schizoid tendencies and more ego strength—which is a terribly rare combination. . . . He often appears wasteful to the outsider when he is working.

That blend of the practical and intuitive is sometimes metaphorically referred to as left-brain, right-brain. A maverick isn't split down the middle; rather, he or she is a whole-brained individual, sensitive to life's subcontext with practical application in mind. Mavericks trust their instincts and put them to work in the real world.

Research psychologist Frank Barron says, "Creative people are both able to and want to transcend the usual bounds of conscious experience, yet they have the ability to behave in a 'realistic' fashion while doing so." Executive recruiter John Wareham says there's a word for it, *fingerspitzengeful*. "This is a wonderful German word meaning sensitivity—a synthesis of intuition, creativity and judgment—in the tips of the fingers: The Midas touch."

The high-achieving mavericks possess what Robert J. Sternberg of Yale University calls "practical giftedness." Such a person, Sternberg says, "can go into an environmental setting, figure out what needs to be done to succeed in that setting, and then do it." This kind of a person doesn't need to wait for instructions from the boss. "If there is a pinnacle of practical intelligence," Sternberg suggests, "it is in the ability of an individual to shape an environment . . . a practically gifted person is able to set standards, not just conform to them."

One way that mavericks develop the indefinable competence to "shape an environment" is by their uncanny ability to fully comprehend their surroundings. They feed their insatiable curiosity with an acute awareness of what their senses detect, quickly absorbing and recording everything. "My imagination has been overstimulated all my life by life itself," confessed master storyteller Isaac Bashevis Singer, author of 30 books and many short stories.

I think of creative individuals' heightened sense of awareness as 360-degree vision. That diffuse awareness may on occasion make potent people appear scattered. However, these people concentrate intently *on things that interest them*; like Robert Heinlein's *Stranger in a Strange Land*, they *grok* their work. If the building caught fire while they were working on a pet project, they wouldn't notice until their papers started smoldering.

Mavericks have eclectic tastes and interests. Many are well read and well rounded. In describing great scientists, author Arthur E. Bostwick noted that they share "a passion for the truth, a life-long effort to get at new facts to explain old ones, a 'divine curiosity' pursued for its own sake and not for that of any personal advantage."

Interest in life's diversity becomes appetite. Mavericks long to drink from the firehose of life. Many potent people are self-described "news junkies," hooked on information stimulation. (A maverick acquaintance who owns a data processing company goes to the extreme of sleeping in a room with both a radio tuned to an all news station and a television turned to CNN. "I fill my subconscious with ideas all night," he explains.)

Many potent people become "questors" seeking new thrills— they'll try new things just to try them—avoiding (maybe even sabotaging) routine or repetitive tasks. Mavericks bore easily; they seek stimulation, some compulsively. "Boring, monotonous busywork is very stressful for individuals who prefer thinking and reasoning activities. Boredom may result in anger, resentment," and setting personal achievement goals that far exceed others' expectations, reports Leslie S. Kaplan, Director of Guidance for York County Public Schools in Virginia.

Philip A. Perrone, at the University of Wisconsin at Madison, has studied gifted persons' career development for 30 years. He compiled a list of their traits that I've excerpted and intermingled with characteristics of giftedness derived from other educational and creativity research along with my own comments.

Work is central to their lives.   To a creative person, work is not a means to pay the bills, it's an inextricable part of themselves. The sentiment is: "It's not what I do, it's what I am." Given the chance to do work that "turns them on," mavericks greet each week with a cry of joy, "Thank God it's Monday!"

This strong work ethic poses a problem of its own for mavericks, "ironitis," too many irons in the work fires. Because they want to extend themselves to all of creation—and meet everyone's high expectations of them—high-achievers sometimes spread themselves too thin.

Achieving mastery in work is a strong need. Because mavericks identify strongly with their work, they feel compelled to be the best at what they do. It matters deeply to their sense of self. No matter how expert high-achievers become, they simply never believe they know all they need to know. They adopt Michelangelo's personal motto, "I am still learning."

With a library full of books and tapes on their chosen topics, they still feel the need to acquire the latest works on the subject. Assimilating all that information in their tireless minds, creative people reduce complexity to order, and synthesize their own original insights. Working in one's chosen field becomes a joyful, self-reinforcing exercise: the more one does the more one knows, the more one knows the more one can do.

They desire or need to make an *impact* on society. The question, Why are we here? haunts potent people. They cannot bear the thought of walking the earth without leaving a constructive mark on it. These thoughtful go-getters heed William James's advice: "Let everything you do be done as if it makes a difference."

Effecting change becomes for some an obsession, transforming them into what Chet Holmes, former associate publisher of *California Lawyer* and a real maverick himself, calls "nut case believers." Some cause-struck mavericks evangelize for their cause with great intensity. "The more radical the idea, or the more it flies in the face of conventional wisdom . . . the more zealous—and even obnoxious—the champion must be," allows Henry E. Riggs, high-technology management expert.

Apple Computer cofounder Steve Jobs is said to be quite the proselytizer for causes he champions. The *New York Times* reported that Jobs seems endowed with a "reality distortion field," an ability "that makes people see things his way, at least while they are in his presence."

The worst curse for a high-achiever—laid to rest beneath a headstone reading:

Here lies
Just another
Of the guys.

They feel exhilarated rather than exhausted when pursuing their goals. Because so much of life's meaning comes from their work, creatives draw sustenance and energy from it. That's why we hear stories reminiscent of tireless Edison: computer programmers or composers or writers sequester themselves for days (or longer) with little or no sleep or food while they work on their labors of love. Food and sleep—mere animal maintenance—offer little to compete with the stimulating psychic joy delivered by works that erupt from one's soul.

While they're tireless when "on a roll," that energy and drive can't be sustained constantly. Few deliver unrelenting brilliance; for most, the inspired work tends to come in spurts. During the apparent "down time," these creative people aren't stagnant, they're gestating. Fertile ideas incubated in the quiet moments hatch later, bigger than life.

Even when they're not in the midst of an epiphany, their minds are buzzing. These people are perpetually "on"—they're always in motion; they walk with a spring in their step and a snap on their fingers; they sit bobbing their legs and drumming the table.

Occasionally, that energy and enthusiasm translate into impatience. Their minds are so quick, mavericks finish others' sentences, and interrupt slow or meandering trains of thought. They want to move the world at their supercharged rate. Often they feel like a powerful, high-performance sports car trapped behind slow-moving traffic on a one-lane road.

Potent people pursue their work with great determination. Not only will they go for long stretches without rest, they may pursue their work against all odds. Dr. E. Donall Thomas pioneered transplanting bone marrow from one person to another—an experimental procedure that held out hope of recovery for children suffering from leukemia. When the Seattle physician began his work in the field in the 1960s, initial results were discouraging—fewer than 10 percent of the patients survived.

Many medical people declared that there was little more progress that could be made. "Most people left the field," explains Dr. Thomas. "They felt that this couldn't be done." Along with a few other persistent hopefuls, Dr. Thomas pressed on, learning to match tissue types, experimenting with different drugs to suppress his patients' immune systems. Because Dr. Thomas persisted, children diagnosed with leukemia now have an impressive 70 to 80 percent chance of a cure.

Physicians from all over the world have journeyed to train under Dr. Thomas' guidance. For his dedication and subsequent success conquering the child killer, Dr. Thomas won the Nobel Prize for medicine in 1990.

Mavericks constantly test limits, questioning others and themselves, challenging the status quo. Mavericks must pour themselves out into the world. They are vessels with no bottom, yet constantly spilling out over the top, compelled to share with the world the ideas and energy within them that holds such great potential to make our planet a better place, even if the world doesn't respond to their initiatives.

Just because a company isn't ready to adopt a maverick's ideas doesn't make those innovations invalid. One truly can be ahead of one's time. A smart company, suggests maverick Marsh Fisher, cofounder of Century 21 Real Estate and founder of **Fisher Idea Systems,** will develop a system for capturing, storing, and later retrieving ideas. "Can you imagine the reservoir of ideas GM would have," he asks. "Disney and Mattel don't have anything like that, and they have all those high-paid idea people who come and go by the thousands over the years. Ninety-nine percent of those ideas—corporate assets—are not captured and leave when those people leave. Even they may not think of them again." At least one company stores some of the not-immediately useful ideas its employees generate. Honda keeps an idea bank for the 90 percent of experimental research that fails the first time around but which might prove useful in future products.

They are risk takers. Mavericks happily challenge convention, sometimes risking their own future and fortunes. Sam Walton, who sits atop the Wal-Mart retail empire ($26 billion in annual sales; nearly $100 more per square foot than rival K mart) built his success story challenging the conventional wisdom. While most retailers build their stores and then erect a distribution center to serve them, Walton did the opposite, building distribution centers and then surrounding them with stores.

Abraham J. Tannenbaum describes mavericks' calculated risk inclination. "High self-regard has to be actualized through risk-taking behavior; otherwise, it amounts to little more than empty bravado or self-delusion. Sometimes, the gifted who are endowed with strong egos pay social penalties for appearing to be arrogant, but if they did not believe that their abilities were exceptional, they could never prime themselves for maximum effort when they were called upon to confirm their giftedness through yet another extraordinary accomplishment."

"Great geniuses make tons of mistakes," says Dean Simonton, creativity author and psychologist at the University of California at Davis. "They generate lots of ideas and they accept being wrong. They have a kind of internal fortress that allows them to fail and just keep going. Look at Edison. He held over 1,000 patents, but most of them are not only forgotten, they weren't worth much to begin with."

"What distinguishes the genius," says Sternberg at Yale, "is merely the cognitive and motivational capacity to spew forth a profusion of chance permutations pertaining to a particular problem." In other words, successful mavericks play the numbers game with ideas. The more times at bat, the greater the likelihood of a home run or grand slam.

Taking risks exposes one to the powerful winds of chance. "Creators actively court chance," says author John Briggs. "They're always ready to notice and amplify into insight some accident of their environment virtually everybody else thinks is trivial or fails to notice. This capacity is, in a deep sense, what makes creators creative."

An example of such serendipity is an accidental discovery by James Schlatter of G. D. Searle. While studying a chemical mixture he was developing as an ulcer medicine, Schlatter noticed that it was quite sweet. The observation wasn't lost on him, neither was his discovery that the substance had no calories. The chemist shared his unusual findings—which had nothing to do with treating ulcers, the mission of his research—with his employer. The company later introduced the unusual product as an ingredient in diet foods. Today, we know it as Nutra-Sweet®, a billion-dollar sweet success story. Just dumb luck? No. A less observant scientist might have missed the experimental compound's sweetness. And a less imaginative one would have dismissed that characteristic as irrelevant to ministering to ulcers, without a thought to its possible (billion dollar) potential.

They live life on the edge. They "actually create, and even seek to maintain dissonance in their lives as proof to themselves that they are fully engaged in life," Prof. Perrone observes. They don't want a job they're qualified for—boredom burns like hellfire. High-achievers never arrive, they're never satisfied, and never complete all the tasks of which they are capable. And that's just the way they want it.

They have a greater future awareness. Today is good but tomorrow holds more promise, more challenge, more opportunity. Yesterday, what yesterday?

They possess a more worldly view. They want to take it all in; see it all, do it all. Because they're keen observers, quick studies, and adept synthesizers, they gain a sense of "how it all works."

They maintain a sense of social responsibility. The morality of their work matters greatly to potent people. Work and personal values are inseparable. When a maverick believes a certain course of action is undeniably *right* for the organization, it becomes a just *cause* for the individual who is committed to it from hair follicle to toenail. So deep is this commitment that the high-achiever may keep working on a pet project even after his or her boss orders such work stopped.

To a potent person, Life means more than self-gratification. With a great sense of justice, creatives want to contribute their faculties to causes beyond their own temporal interests. As they volunteer their considerable talents to worthy causes, phrases such as "To whom much is given much is expected," and, "No man is an island," sound in the back of their minds.

MAVERICKESE

Mavericks don't wear a sign on their forehead proclaiming themselves, but a trained observer can identify one quickly. An easy way is through their language (window to the psyche). Here is a collection of their favorite phrases:

I think . . . and they do!

What if . . . the first words of all progress.

There's a better way . . . my way.

I've got it! . . . often said after hearing many points of view about a problem discussed in a meeting.

Get to the point/What's the bottom line? . . . utterances of impatient, task-oriented people.

I can't waste my time on that . . . they don't want to trouble a ten billion dollar computer for a ten cent trick.

I'll tell you exactly what's going to happen . . . as good assemblers of experience, observations, and intuition, mavericks project with great accuracy.

I, me, mine . . . high-achievers are the center of their own fascinating universe.

THE PERFECTION INFECTION

Because mavericks are highly capable people, some hold themselves to standards achievable only by super men or women: stronger than all their colleagues, leaping tall problems in a single bound, thinking faster than a speeding bullet. All their lives, high-achievers have heard that they are different, more capable, specially gifted. That reputation must—many believe—be maintained at all costs.

John Markoff, business computing columnist for the *New York Times* reported on the tentative future of NeXt Inc., the computer company Steve Jobs started after losing a major power play at Apple. Noting NeXt's slow progress in the market, Markoff fingered the quest for perfection as an impediment to sales. "Indeed, it seems that Mr. Jobs's eternal search for perfection is often his worst enemy. He has gone out of his way to discourage software developers from just copying their existing programs to his computer—instead holding out for first-time original creations." Software developers, not sharing Jobs's enthusiasm for the new computer, haven't rushed to create new software to help spur machine sales. (But who can blame Jobs? What self-respecting maverick would start a much ballyhooed, high-risk computer venture just to run existing software?)

Some extraordinary individuals develop an intolerance for imperfection in themselves and others. This condition—known as the perfection infection—can be especially pronounced in people who have been "winners" in their school, athletic, or business careers. I am capable of perfection, therefore I must attain it, believes the unusually talented performer. Being wrong, failing, isn't just disappointment, it's *bad*. As in, Bad Boy! or Bad Girl!.

A missed deadline? A failed venture? Better to be hit by a truck. A sick day? What, the invincible man with a malady? Impossible. A professional staffer at a large law firm where young associates push themselves to make partner (worth in excess of $500,000 a year) describes the driven perfectionists with sadness: "It's a dysfunctional ponzi scheme where people without a life compete for a very limited number of slots working 20 hours a day to prove that they are the best. Each of them is sure *they* are going to be the one to win partner. When they don't, they can't believe it—they've always been the best, always won the race."

German poet and philosopher Johann Wolfgang von Goethe defined the perfectionist as someone "whom it is impossible to please because he is never pleased with himself." That pitiful condition is especially troubling when such a person occupies a management post. Then the fanaticism for perfection impacts not only on the perfectionist but on others, inducing stress for all of them.

One who believes herself perfect can't be wrong. Errors, failures, clearly must be the fault of someone else. Who's to blame, surely not I! *They* didn't listen. *They* didn't think it through. *They* didn't countermand me when they should have. (That's my favorite.)

A perfectionist feeling any twinge of uncertainty over a proposed course of action will never admit it. Super Executive unsure? Never! He postpones decisions, demands more information. Or he says, "It's your call," something he almost never says, and buddy, you'd better be right!

Staff proposals to the perfectionist boss are never good enough. They can't be. If they were, SuperManager would lose her status. "What's wrong with it?" you ask timidly. "It's not thought out well enough," comes the intimidating reply. (Translation: my perfect power breakfast is giving me indigestion beneath this perfect power suit; I'm the big brain around here and don't you forget it! Urp.)

This "you're-never-right-no-matter-how-hard-you-try" attitude leads to arbitrary and elusive standards. "You cut costs 5 percent?" Yes, boss, it was tough, but I did it as agreed. "Well, that was just Phase One. I expect at least another . . ."

"Perfect" bosses are unapproachable, especially about the possible error of their own ways. Chris Argyris, who teaches at both Harvard Business School and its Graduate School of Education says, "Accomplished people are the most defensive individuals in the world. They refuse to acknowledge that they may be imperfect and they are therefore unable to learn how to appraise their performance . . . and to learn how to improve it." After all, how does one improve upon perfection?

Someone possessed by the perfection infection can fall prey to paralysis by analysis. One with a perfect self-image must avoid risk because risk tempts fate, which could mean failure, which wouldn't be perfect. *Danger! Danger!* "I think we'd better study this unproven strategy/ product/ process a little further before going ahead [*like until just after I retire*]."

"Perfect" bosses are also known as "control freaks." A manager at the corporate offices of a large bank confides, "Managing a maverick drives me nuts. *As* a maverick, I want to control without being controlled!" The compelling need to run a perfect—not competent, not excellent, *perfect*—operation, leads to a serious case of megalomania, Only I can comprehend all the details, make the perfect decisions. A boss suffering the perfection infection might be mistaken for a workaholic. He is not. A workaholic mistakes compulsive, occasionally aimless, motion for productive work. A perfect boss truly is working on productive matters that he is afraid to delegate to imperfect subordinates. And because he shoulders far more than his fair share, he likely will work himself to a premature death.

Though perfect bosses may engage in counterproductive behavior, organizations tend to reward their dysfunction. Perfectionists *do* appear to do everything right. Because they are so demanding, their operations perform to expectation (come hell or high water), so they collect their bonuses, receive their promotions. If the perfectionist executive's unreasonable expectations drive out a few good junior managers, or if their highly competitive behavior—I'm better than you, see!—drives out a few colleagues, no matter. The perfectionist will bear the burden and work that much longer and harder to cover the talent gap until suitable replacements are found. After all, many highly talented people probably would kill to work with such an extraordinarily bright light as the perfectionist.

In the long run, only the perfectionist, his staff, and his organization suffer.

MAVERICK EMOTIONS IN MOTION

In a scene from the movie *Star Trek V: The Final Frontier*, a charismatic alien rebel offers mental peace to the crew of the starship *Enterprise*. "Each man's pain is unique," says the renegade Vulcan (kin to Mr. Spock). "You can free your mind," he promises, "by facing your pain and drawing strength from it." Some of the ship's senior officers succumb to the siren song, face their deepest inner conflict and find relief. Capt. Kirk, a quintessential rule-rebuking maverick, refuses to exorcise the demons that torment him.

Author's Indulgence

About a decade before I even heard of gifted children, much less read the literature chronicling their journey, I met Harvard law professor Arthur Miller at a cocktail reception. He frequently shows up on television to explain the intricacies and inadequacies of our legal system, or to challenge government/business/ media leaders to think together publicly. As we talked, my attention danced between our conversation and my observations of Professor Miller. Listening to his quick, confident speech elegantly leaping from topic to topic, watching his eyes radiate delight at a twist in the terribly intellectual discussion, I couldn't help but wonder what this fellow was like as a *child*. Did he drive his parents nuts? Did he trade baseball cards? Did he ever play baseball? Would he recognize one? I wondered those things, but never asked him. No matter. He started me thinking about childhood experiences of unusually talented people. Next time fate forces the two of us to drink in the same room again, I'll ask him. I'll probably find out that his experiences are nothing like those you'll read below . . . .

With great passion, the captain scolds the would-be psychic rescuer. Pain and guilt, he declares, "are the things we carry with us; the things that make us who we are. If we lose them, we lose ourselves. I don't want my pain taken away. I *need* my pain!"

Many mavericks draw their drive from the sum of accumulated pains. These high-achievers didn't wake up one morning with their extraordinary abilities.

As they grow up, many extraordinary people walk very much alone down a long, unfriendly road. As successful adults, they're called by such terms of endearment as geniuses, super producers, wizards, and key executives. As children, many of these same people were known as weirdos, geeks, freaks, and nerds. They knew it then, they remember it now.

Most mavericks never were "normal." They were strange kids with strained childhoods. Their perceptive, inquisitive minds, their heightened sensitivities operated at full volume from moment one. They perceived the world on a wavelength different from that of other children. And everybody knew it.

"I'd repressed a lot about my odd childhood," allows a corporate marketing executive. "When I was six, I worked out my own religion. I wrote down tenets, names of ceremonies, everything. I recently came across a booklet I'd made with all these symbols and things, and I couldn't believe I'd done that at such a young age! Back then, my mother—a teacher, no less—couldn't handle my strange interests. She'd just say, 'There goes Bobbie again.' "

When I was in college, a psychology professor of mine fondly repeated this maxim, "Better to be born with two good feet and a strong stomach than a high IQ." What he was talking about is the angst experienced by people with a supercharged sensitivity to the strange world around them.

Linda Kreger Silverman, who runs a center for gifted children in Denver, says,

The intricate thought processes that mark these individuals as gifted are mirrored in the intricacy of their emotional development. Idealism, self-doubt, perceptiveness, excruciating sensitivity, moral imperatives, desperate needs for understanding, acceptance, love—all impinge simultaneously. Their vast emotional range may make them appear contradictory: mature and immature, arrogant and compassionate, aggressive and timid. Imbalances of composure and self-assurance often mask deep feelings of insecurity. The inner experience of the gifted young person is rich, complex, turbulent.

As the mental wheels turn at a frenetic pace, both the gifted child and her little playmates sense the differences between them. Little mavericks make easy targets (they almost seem like magnets) for bullies. As a child growing up in Missouri, Larry Smarr says, "A lot of people thought of me as a nerd." At recess, kids picked on him, even beat him up. After school though, they wanted little Larry's help with their homework—he was a brain. "I got trained in competitiveness fairly early." He survived the playground tussles; grew up to be an astrophysicist. In the early 1980s, when Dr. Smarr was in his early thirties, his competitive nature surfaced in a most positive way. He helped lead the charge for national supercomputing centers in the United States to compete with similar brainy installations in foreign lands.

Larry Smarr's story is a familiar one. Geeky kid grows up to be a success in life. Psychologist and popular business speaker Layne Longfellow says that the skills that make people popular in school are very different from ones that make them successful in life.

While still trapped in that queer period known as childhood, the gifted child realizes—like everyone else—that he or she is the odd one, and is gripped by self-doubt. (What is *wrong* with me?) That doubt evolves into self-criticism and sometimes sours into self-hate.

From childhood on, many creative people seem forever caught in an emotional "mid-life crisis" as they try to resolve a life-long alienation from a world they perceive so vividly. Their keen powers of observation, compounded by lucid insight, bring the absurdities of life into constant, inescapable focus. That 360-degree vision has no off-switch. "I can never get out of my head," complains a chemist. I know how she feels. I started my career as a journalist—the perfect career for one who feels bound to know everything that's happening in the world: A comprehensive world view is a professional obligation. When my career path led me into sales for the Associated Press, I covered two huge states, Michigan and Ohio, logging some 60,000 miles a year, giving me lots of "windshield time," thinking time. There's only so much radio or so many motivation tapes one can listen to while passing time captive in a few square feet of enclosed space. My mind filled the stimulation vacuum on its own. I'd pass a road crew and begin to think. *I wonder how the road maintenance schedule is determined? How much money do those guys riding the jackhammer make, more than the guy raking hot asphalt? How does one qualify to stand and watch the others work? What kind of houses do these people live in? Are they happy? What do they do with their spouses on their anniversaries? How much has the technology of road repair changed in the last 50 years? Do the people holding the sign with Stop on one side and Slow on the other just flip that thing over and over all day? Do they switch positions with the sign-holder at the other end of the work site for a change of scenery? Who buys those big trucks? How do they know if they got a good deal? What company makes those big trucks? How do they estimate market demand? What constitutes a state-of-the-art backhoe? Does a sales representative drive to all these towns cold-calling Department of Public Works bosses to display full-color brochures boasting the latest in asphalt rollers? If so, what moti-*

*vates that sales rep? Is he or she a company employee or a free-lance manu-
facturer's rep? Do they leave calendars with dirty pictures behind with
their prospects? What are the economics of that business? How does one
get started in that line of work? Do companies pay such a person a salary
or retainer or commission only? What about health insurance? Would
such a person ever go to a job site to see their wares in action or is the
equipment just an abstraction save for the catalog shots?* On and on this
stream of consciousness ran without rest until some other line of
thought was prompted by, say, driving past an old-fashioned ice
cream stand. *Where do they get their food products? What's the margin
on a double scoop compared to a single . . .*

The world that superobservant children see does nothing to
relieve their confused feelings. Psychologist and educator Michael
M. Piechowski explains that gifted children "find themselves as
strangers in a strange land where schools do not value learning,
where the ignorant hold power over sages, where the insensitive
denounce feeling as a trouble factor, where victims are blamed for
their misfortune, where authority gains its power from the blind-
ness of the governed, where those who care always seem alone,
and where reality means only the tangible, visible, measurable,
and for sale."

I do not want to overplay the negative aspects of a maverick's
life, that would be unfair. Many gifted children come to terms
with themselves; they use their unusual powers of observation as
a source for humor. (One day, my precocious ten-year-old came
flying down the stairs. "Dad, dad" he yelled. "I'm reading an
autobiography of a founder of *Mad* magazine," he exclaimed. "Uh
huh. That's nice . . . I guess," I say kind of stupidly. "Well," my
enthusiastic offspring continues, "this AUTOBIOGRAPHY
[pause] includes an 'About the Author' section! Unbelievable!"
Indeed, Ben, indeed.)

While all is not gloomy, to understand what makes potent people who they are, you must understand their anxieties, which
have much to do with their motivations (the implications of which
we'll explore later). The net effect of distressing early life experiences is that many highly talented adults carry inside them
unexpungible emotional influencers. Dr. Silverman confirms that,
reporting, "Studies at the University of Denver have confirmed
that gifted adults have high levels of overexcitability in all areas."

Most potent people come to terms with their past, reconciling their unusual fit with the world and celebrating their uniqueness. Others wear this oddity like a scarlet letter. "Some creatives play up that 'tortured artist' routine, but many of the most effective people I've met are quiet and insightful," confides a Madison Avenue advertising executive.

Quiet and conservatively dressed, or flamboyant and emotional, mavericks are compelled to remain true to the integrity of their highly structured personal moral code which permeates everything they do. They refuse to surrender their developed-with-great-pains souls to convention or to acts they can't ethically condone. Forced to do work that runs contrary to their belief system, a maverick will refuse, or perhaps unconsciously sabotage the effort.

If backed into a corner, a maverick would fall onto his own sword before compromising his evolved beliefs. "The *last* boss who's ever going to fire me gave me an article he found on 'managing mavericks' shortly before he gave me the axe. I should have taken the hint, but I couldn't do anything but be me," confides an acquaintance. Now my friend has the last laugh; he makes a good living counseling others on career development.

The childhood experience of being detached from the mainstream never leaves a maverick, though she probably puts it to work for her. M. Scott Peck, in his book *The Road Less Traveled*: "One of the most poignant themes of the Gospels is Christ's continual sense of frustration on finding that there was no one who could really understand him."

Charles Garfield describes the "dual needs of autonomy and affiliation" as "the twin aspects of mission. With them a peak performer lives a dual life, wanting both the rewards of uniqueness and the pride of belonging. . . . " (See Chapter 8 for ideas on how a supportive corporate culture can successfully employ this paradox.)

Not everyone adjusts to this duality positively. Writer Andrew Harvey expresses the tension of his unhappy betwixt and between. "I wanted acceptance from a world I despised, success in a way I disapproved of, approbation from just those people whom I knew to be narrow and corrupt." (The sensitive person's competing feelings about the temporal world send me wondering how many successful entrepreneurs can work so hard just so they can both deny and affirm their instinct to reject materialism. Acquiring possessions in great volume puts one in a comfortable place to say that such things really don't matter to them. . . .)

MELANCHOLY AND THE IMPOSTER SYNDROME

The "temperamental artist" is a stereotype, and like most, it has some basis in fact. Many potent people experience intense emotional reactions to their life experiences; their highs fly, oh, so high, and the lows crash, oh, so low. Moods swing way up when the high-achiever influences her environment—things happen, the universe responds. Moods swing down low for many reasons, not the least of which is plain disappointment in the broken promise of potential. The maverick mind perceiving what could be mourns what is not.

Sometimes this disappointment with failed possibilities becomes chronic; idealism sours into cynicism. Curmudgeonly cynics are mavericks who have lost hope, perhaps only because they feel unsuccessful in making an appreciable dent on the world's problems. These mavericks then challenge the system, not to improve it, but only to punish it. They become chronic complainers and low-achievers. They complain to place the blame for life's imperfections outside their so-lowly regarded selves. They stop trying to improve the world. Inaction by unmotivated mavericks confirms, in their minds, that the world is unworthy of their effort. Thus the inert avoid responsibility for their ineffective influence. The good news, according to James Delisle, president of the Association of the Gifted, is that, "underachievement, first and foremost, is a behavior, and as such it can change over time." (Managers, as we shall see in later chapters, can help effect positive turnarounds.)

Sometimes, creatives' lows stem from twin conditions. The first maverick melancholy relates to guilt. "How can I have so much innate ability and sometimes succeed so easily, while others . . . ." The dark mirror image of this is something called the *imposter syndrome*. This maverick malady stems from a secret fear of not being as good as billed. One of my neighbors is a psychotherapist who sees many patients seated in, or at the right-hand of, power in the capitol of capitalism, New York City. "You would recognize the names of many of my patients," she allows. "At the office they're powerful, successful. Nights and weekends, they're depressed and fearful—terrified that they'll be 'found out.' " Their lament? "I'm not as talented as everybody thinks I am. One of these days, I'm going to be exposed as a fraud—and the whole house of cards will come crashing down. I'll lose everything and be nobody."

Such jaded mavericks and their well-adjusted counterparts, along with armies of others who may have never before even imagined that they could affect the world's course (achievers-in-waiting) can be tremendous assets to an organization. Happy, sad, active, or withdrawn, these are the idea people—the folks who will determine whether, how, and at what speed, your company moves forward. The challenge, obviously, is in managing these people to enhance and gently extract their many talents. The next chapter shows how you, their manager, can make a big difference in their work contributions by your own personal management skills.

Chapter Four

The Maverick Manager: Tearing Down Mental Electric Fences

If you're like a god, people will respect you but they won't come close.

Soichiro Honda

If you are abrasive and aggressive, nobody will ever come and tell you. That's because they're afraid of you.

Albert J. Bernstein, Ph.D. and Sydney Craft Rozen

When we commend, we take away much of the need to command.

George Lumsden

Executives concerned with the management of creative and innovative personnel must maintain awareness of personality. People differ, especially creative types, and the successful manager will be the sensitive manager.

Robert Lawrence Kuhn

How monotonous the sounds of the forest would be if the music came only from the top ten birds.

Author unknown

When I was 12-years old, my family moved from the inner city to the country. As I began to explore the new environment, I was amazed at how the dairy cows knew where one farmer's property ended and another's began. With nothing more restrictive than widely spaced fence posts, the cows seemed happily contained on their owner's land. One day, filled with curiosity and the courage to trespass, I decided to take a closer look. As I went deeper into

"It's pretty! It's exciting! But is it functional?"

"We're waiting to hear if it's okay to use the umbrellas!"

the grazeland, I noticed that there was a kind of fence ringing the field. But it surely wasn't substantial; heck, it was nothing but an itty-bitty filament. Why, a cow that must weigh at least a thousand pounds surely could trample this little line with no effort at all!

I reckoned that a closer look was in order. Filled with that curiosity and courage, I set out to test the strength of that tiny cable. I stepped back a few feet and ran at that puny fence. My charge was abruptly short-circuited by a charge of a different sort. ZAP! My momentum knocked down the nearest fence post and the brief encounter with the wire knocked me on my fanny. The powerful punch of that thin, nearly invisible wire made a lasting impression on me. And it provides us with a metaphor for a serious issue in managing people.

Cows learn to suppress their innate wanderlust after one or two highly charged encounters with the small but powerful line. In the same way, people—highly intelligent entities with judgment and free will—learn to restrain their innate urges to create at the workplace following one or two zaps by a boss, a creature whose small frame belies his awesome power over others. Employees build their own fences around the urge to share their creative ideas with corporate higher-ups, lest they risk a more powerful, even deadly, shock from the boss. Yes, even mavericks learn to restrain themselves (by matter of degree!), causing internal tension for them and lost opportunities for their employers. When you finish this book you may well charge into the office to announce with great and earnest enthusiasm, "Okay, everybody, I want your ideas!" You'll likely be met with dull stares, a few cynical snickers, and some muttering of obscenities. Expect to wait a good long time for the floodgates to open.

THE TRUST BARRIER

A survey by Lou Harris and Associates for Steelcase, the office furniture company, reveals that only 39 percent of employees view their management as trustworthy. Sixty percent don't trust their bosses. Little wonder managers aren't overrun with productive suggestions from their subordinates.

Even in "progressive" companies, intellectual freedom doesn't reign. A poll taken by the **American Productivity and Quality Center** of its own members—arguably among the more enlightened and committed to management excellence—weighed in with some disappointing results. At all levels of management, only slightly more than half (52 percent) of the respondents said that employees were free to express new or controversial ideas to a "great or very great extent." (The remaining choices ranged from "to a very little extent," to "to some extent.") The tint on the rose-colored glasses grew stronger as one progressed in the managerial ranks. About 65 percent of the surveyed vice presidents said they thought the freedom level in their firm was great or very great; while fewer than 40 percent of the first-line managers answered the question that way. We're left to guess at the freedom ratings that might be given by nonmanagement employees; though the managers surveyed did report that most of their organizations didn't do much in the way of including lower-level employees in brainstorming or other group problem-solving activities.

Similar findings were reported in a survey by the Wyatt Company. Two thirds of senior managers said that their companies had a corporate environment with open communication. But in the middle-management and supervisory ranks, it was the exact opposite. Two thirds thought the communication lines were *not* open.

If most people—even large numbers in the management ranks—don't believe the organization allows for free expression of thought, ideas won't just naturally seep into the innovation pipeline and they may not make it there even if management tries to channel them. The walls seem impenetrable.

So how do you effectively release and direct the productive creative energies of system-bucking mavericks and the larger group of achievers-in-waiting? How do you tear down their mental electric fences? Your *personal behavior* as a manager influences the performance of your people more than organizational policies (see Chapter 8), remuneration (see Chapter 6), or the advancement carrots you dangle. In today's organization, management must be more a value-added process than a failure control process.

Brief Aside

At an off-site meeting with my fellow marketing executive colleagues, I was a participant in a small group assigned to make recommendations to the larger assembly on how we could improve
communication among ourselves. Our small group session was
memorable for its candor and productivity. Maybe it was the
sunny, out-of-doors, riverside locale, or something in the local
water, but we began our discussion by trying to identify why we
even needed to discuss ways of improving our communication.

"We don't trust each other," someone bravely observed. "I
think that's true," said another. The revelation was remarkable for
two reasons. First, it was true that we didn't trust each other. Can-
didly and openly saying so represented a leap forward. Second,
there really was no reason why we couldn't trust each other. Everyone at the conference had well-defined areas of responsibility with
little or no threat from the others to their functional or political
standing.

With the real obstacle on the table, we set about to make recommendations for better communication—not the least of which was
more regular and more open information sharing. We took our
admission and recommendations to the larger group where ner-
vous laughter gave way to nods of recognition. A few of us actually
adopted some of the information-sharing suggestions. That commitment has resulted in some successful programs for the company
and more satisfying work relationships for me and maybe some
others.

TO CATCH SOME MONKEYS

When zookeepers need to catch monkeys for their exhibits, they
don't need to chase or lasso them. Monkey hunters place plastic
bottles with nuts inside them on the ground. As they watch from
the bush, hungry monkeys scamper to the bottles with the trea-
sure inside and slip their hands down the bottles' necks. As they
try to retrieve their prize, the monkeys discover they're the
victims of a clever trick—the bottle necks aren't wide enough to
withdraw a clenched fist chock-full of nuts. A monkey's greed

keeps him from releasing his bounty; his bottle-manacles prevent him from scampering away to escape the monkey hunter's net.

Managers with a tight-fisted grip around their organization's (department's) control resemble the self-imprisoned monkey; they are held captive by their fears. They are like children dragging around a worn security blanket—shielding their lack of trust behind a thin and ineffective veil. A boss who does not trust his people cannot expect their trust in return. "When you get to be management something happens to you," notes advertising man Carl Ally, "because when you are down there you want permissiveness and when you're up here you want discipline."

To free our hands from the control bottle, to remove the electric fences from the heads of our employees, we must trust and be trustworthy. We must send our co-workers a clear signal that they have permission to contribute their unique insights and talents to the company's challenges, even if it means questioning time-honored traditions. We're really talking about adopting a new management model.

MANAGEMENT REHABILITATION

How should a manager behave? Most managers don't know—they ascend to positions where they are responsible for the work of others, with little or no training to prepare them. People get a managerial position for four possible reasons, because they are:

- Technical competents.
- Savvy bureaucrats.
- Relatives of the powerful.
- Recipients of good (or bad) luck.

To assume that by possessing any of these qualities one instinctively knows how to affect subordinates' work effectively defies reason. Logic suggests that if managers influence the work performance of their charges, then employees would do better work when their managers are better trained to help them. Put another way, you might be amazed at how much better your staff gets when you are a better manager!

Tragically, formal management training usually teaches little about positively influencing people, and almost never includes content relevant to getting the best thinking or creativity from employees. Most managers don't have an MBA, and those who do belong to an educated elite trained to use techniques with complicated or important-sounding names like management by objectives, business strategy control, PIMS, Gantt charting, SBUs, LBOs, PMTs, environmental analysis, segmentation, growth-share matrices, synergistic niche positioning. . . .

We don't have and don't need an MBA-sounding term for good people-management. And the metaphor for it is not stick, not stopwatch, not carrot. (If we had to have such a metaphor, it might be training wheel—helping people by initially working closely with them, then freeing them to go solo to an agreed-upon destination by whatever reasonable route they choose.)

Managerial effectiveness derives from *influence* instead of power. That scares many managers who intuitively understand theologian Harvey Cox's tenet that "denying the powerful their mystique destroys the fear they must nurture in the souls of the powerless." Managers who found it easy to bark orders to followers may feel quite unequipped to effect change through persuasion. Xerox CEO Paul Allaire allows that "the hardest person to change is the line manager. After he's worked like a dog for five or ten years to get promoted, we have to say to him or her, 'All those reasons you wanted to be a manager? Wrong. You cannot do to your people what was done to you. You have to be a facilitator or a coach and by the way, we're still going to hold you accountable for the bottom line.' "

Managers who want to lead mavericks to achieve their great destinies, to empower achievers-in-waiting to contribute their best thinking to the corporate good, must let go of their fears, free themselves of their distrust. They must undergo *management rehabilitation* and become *Maverick Managers.*

Twenty-five centuries ago in ancient China, philosopher Lao Tzu wrote:

"Evolved individuals lead others by
Opening their minds,
Reinforcing their centers,
Relaxing their desires,
Strengthening their characters."

Is the liberated/liberating Maverick Manager a "touchy-feely" businessperson—a psychologist with a computer? How about a charismatic leader behind whom all others fall in line?

There's nothing "touchy-feely" about simply trusting people and working to develop their competence. One needs no Ph.D. and leather couch to understand that people would rather work— and work harder—for people they respect and like and trust than those they don't.

THE INADEQUACIES OF LEADERSHIP

Popular business literature celebrates the notion of "leadership." Books and magazine articles promise to help you "find your leadership style," as though it were somehow lost. If you're looking to find leadership, better to adopt an ethic. Style will present itself. (Peter M. Senge of MIT says, "It is impossible to reduce natural leadership to a set of skills or competencies.")

Leaders in an organization, the pundits suggest, champion over management. They alone possess a compelling vision that points everyone in the right direction. Leaders decide and act while managers analyze and control, or something to that effect.

Leadership is a perfectly good concept. Organizations certainly need vision, decisions, and action. As a prescriptive ideal for managers in organizations that want to encourage innovation by everyone, the concept falls short. Here's why. By definition, leaders need followers. The head leading the hands. The thinker leading the doers. Sound familiar?

Leadership is a good quality, and just about every organization needs more of it. But it is not an inclusive model for the stewardship of an innovative organization. It is an important part of the supervisory model, but not the whole. E. V. "Rick" Goings, president of Avon, articulates the proper balance between establishing a vision for a firm and enabling everyone in it to pursue that vision. "My job is to (1) set the vision for the company—it's not a committee decision, and then, (2) share that vision with all the people in the corporation so that they are mobilized to fully invest themselves in fulfilling it."

Rick Goings gracefully dances along the tightwire that many executives fear to set foot on. It's strung between two polar management models: controlling employees and process at the one end, and at the other, freeing workers to do what they think needs to be done to fulfill the corporate mission. Goings is saying, "Here's where we're going, you get there by the route and means you think are best." The corporate mission is intact, *and* employees are free to improve the business through their creativity. Goings points people toward a goal, but he doesn't ask them to follow him there while staring at his backside.

One need not be a CEO like Rick Goings to make such an ideal a reality. Every manager faces this tightwire within the arena of his or her own responsibility. And every manager must now master the skills to walk that wire with aplomb or fall fast and hard.

Good management is more a set of principles guiding human relationships and less a system of controls over processes. All business amounts to human relationships involving money. In today's information/ service economy, human contact prevails over less intimate transactions—inside the organization and with customers. Managers must understand human interactions and stand as sterling examples of how to handle them. In this environment, personality is competence.

Good managers help close the gap between current reality and the corporate objective by moving there among their charges—not in front of them, not pushing from behind, not calling the shots from the isolation of a well-appointed office. A good manager lends a helping hand and then lets go.

The Maverick Manager understands the role of manager to be this: taking responsibility for results while enabling others to think and act innovatively to achieve the goals. Management gives one a mantle of responsibility but not control.

METHODS OF THE MAVERICK MANAGER

In the movie *Harvey*, Jimmy Stewart plays Elwood P. Dowd, a character who at one point utters, "In this world you must be, oh, so smart, or, oh, so pleasant." For decades, many managers seemed to buy into that dichotomy. Unlike Elwood P. Dowd, they fell down hard on the smart, tough, shrewd side of the equation. People at work were subordinates in every respect. Nice meant weak, ineffective, on the road to failure. But today, more than ever, bosses depend on positive, humane relationships with their staff to effect results.

Would your staff hire you as a boss? Management is not about winning a popularity contest, but it is about vision, competence, fairness, and equitable evaluation. The model for the Maverick Manager can be expressed in a simple triad that liberates people to think freely about their tasks and to contribute their best ideas. The Maverick Manager embodies three roles: educator, cheerleader and quality assurer. So defining "manager" may break with convention, defy expectation and seem radically nontraditional. But that's the way of the maverick, isn't it?

Educator.   The root of the word *educate* is the Latin *educare* meaning to "draw out." (Ironic, isn't it? To educate means to draw out, not force down.) As people are drawn out, they get better at doing what they do. Father Leo Bartel, Vicar for Social Ministry of the Catholic Archdiocese of Rockford, Illinois, makes a great point about this. "The fact is," he contends, "that if people are properly motivated, developing competence becomes part of their very need."

The Maverick Manager isn't afraid to teach others what he or she knows so that they may know as much and more. Historian Henry Adams said that "teachers affect eternity; they can never tell where their influence stops." As a Maverick Manager/ teacher, you extend your positive influence wide and far, and by doing so enrich others, the corporation, and yourself.

As a good teacher, the Maverick Manager models the kind of decent employee he or she wants to work with, and knows that inconsistency in word and deed—hypocrisy—demoralizes, especially those sensitive people who have the most to give. Allied with deeds not mirroring words is something I call the *compensatory management directive.* Sometimes managers admit their own weaknesses only in their subconscious, while the rest of them apologizes for their true nature. (Alfred Nobel, the fellow who established the Nobel Prize for peace, was the son of a land and naval mine inventor, and he, too, invented explosives, including dynamite.)

A few examples of the compensatory management directive. I knew an executive who had no appreciable people skills: he was short of temper, secretive, mercurial, and frequently offensive in his language. He flip-flopped decisions without telling significant numbers of those affected and . . . often gave to his staff articles and books on communication and people management! Another manager trusted *no one*: he forbade intracompany contact with people not in his department, insisted on reviewing all internal memoranda before distribution, was highly secretive about the most mundane things, pumped people for office gossip. He insisted that his whole staff—except for him, of course—attend lavish "teamwork" workshops. An executive with a trade association told me about a board member who insisted that the professional staff attend creativity workshops to infuse some innovative thinking into the organization. Learning their lessons well, the staff came back to the office bursting with new ideas—none of which were implemented. Seems a certain board member really wasn't too fond of change.

Perhaps these men were well intentioned, professing belief as a substitute for mending their ways. However, the intensity of one's preaching doesn't compensate for the repugnance of one's actions. An old Japanese proverb holds that "sooner or later you act out what you really think."

As a Maverick Manager, you understand that you don't have sufficient time to have all the ideas, or even to control the generation and implementation of ideas from others. J. B. Fuqua, senior chairman of Fuqua Industries, recommends giving people "the authority to act in their areas of expertise. When they do need the input of another knowledgeable person or two, they'll ask for it. But don't waste everyone's time making the decision for them." Maverick Managers encourage their people to reach goals and solve problems using innovative methods of their own design. The Maverick Manager specifies objectives, not methods.

Maverick Managers champion innovation, even if that notion is still somewhat foreign to them. Andrall E. Pearson, who was president of Pepsico for 15 years affirms that "innovative leaders aren't necessarily creative, idea-driven people themselves (though obviously many are). But they welcome change because they're convinced that their competitive survival depends on innovation."

The Maverick Manager need not be a power station of new ideas, just a lightning rod for them.

A great way to get new ideas about how your internal operation is running is to use the fresh eyes of your new hires. Ask them to observe your operations and make notes about what doesn't make sense to them. About four or five weeks into their tenure, ask them to provide you with their observations in writing. Then encourage them to keep making notes for another brief report in about six months.

The Maverick Manager doesn't wait for a crisis to erupt before requesting ideas from the staff. Unfortunately, many other managers practice "rabbit out of the hat" management, where performance pressures build and build, necessitating a little magic. A stressed magician manager—helpless as a person sawed in two—runs to his or her direct reports and demands "some fresh new thinking from you people." Chronic procrastinators and bosses who excelled by cramming for exams in school love to pull rabbits out of the hat. If they like magic so much, they should turn loose the wizards on their staffs. Achievers-in-waiting keep tricks up their sleeves until the boss demands a little sleight of hand. The rest of the time, the boss "sleights" the organization.

One of the ways the educator–manager helps draw out people is to encourage *everyone* to contribute. An analogy: In the dark, a piece of paper with a grocery list written on it looks identical to one inscribed with a cure for cancer. Same applies to people. If we only take them at face value, we don't know what good ideas we're missing from inside their heads. Some of your most potentially productive thinkers and innovators may be in hiding, suppressing constructive contrarian thoughts. These eagles clipped their own wings because they're afraid to fly in the boss's space.

A classic case of where someone successfully felt empowered to contribute concerns a secretary who dared to share her thoughts. Mary Ayres was working at an advertising agency as executive secretary to the partners. Their client, Noxzema, made skin products. The company was looking for expansion ideas to help grow the business. Mary Ayres got the idea that a natural extension for Noxzema would be cosmetics; the Noxzema name should attract women who otherwise found makeup unhealthy for their skin. The ad agency partners liked the idea and so did the client, who created Cover Girl cosmetics. Decades later, the agency boasted about Mary Ayres in a recruiting brochure used to attract new employees, in which it said, "Great ideas don't necessarily come from the top. They percolate from the bottom up, from the middle out." The Mary Ayres story has the potential to be repeated evey day in companies eveywhere, but it's still uncommon.

What is common is for businesspeople to refer to the fear of rejection in salespeople—a group typically bursting with bravado. Interestingly, I've never heard a discussion about the fear of rejection in researchers, secretaries, supervisors, or middle managers. For them, nothing risked is nothing lost. (The common wisdom holds that He who sticks his neck out gets his head handed to him; and, Pioneers are the ones with the arrows in their backs.) Give your people permission and incentive (see next chapter) to contribute and they will. Not all at once, but over time, most will contribute. The rate at which trust grows varies by individual just as it takes all fall and winter for a tulip to germinate while some other flowers seem to do it overnight.

The Maverick Manager as educator also is a learner. Aristotle wrote, "Every wicked man is ignorant of what he ought to do and what he ought to abstain from, and it is by reason of error of this kind that men become unjust and in general bad. . . . "The Maverick Manager fights the ignorance that can make one an unwittingly wicked boss by undertaking a program of constant self-education (see Chapter 10).

John Sculley, Apple Computer CEO, contends that "creativity is a learning process, not a management process." You can't force creativity and innovation, but you'll find it when you create an atmosphere supportive of it. Shaping such an environment means occasionally surrendering your ego. Ask questions to which you don't know the answer (historically a rare and courageous managerial act); you will learn, your people will grow, and everyone's richer for it.

As thinking and learning are individual processes, so is managing today's knowledge workers. The Maverick Manager manages each person as an individual, not as merely a small part of a larger group. Maverick Managers not only monitor and encourage good performance by their people, they help them to discover and fulfill their ever-evolving potential. This emphasis on managing *individuals* is increasingly important as corporate hierarchies flatten.

Companies with fewer managers can't/ won't/ shouldn't create an egalitarian democracy. "Having a say differs from having a vote," says Max DePree. Rather, they must reduce worker–castes to create an organizational society where everyone is a colleague, some with more responsibility than others. "We're seeing the network—not the hierarchy—becoming the metaphor," says John Sculley.

Under the Maverick Manager, directive authoritarianism gives way to relationships based on mutual respect furthered by direct, honest communication. (Even if the whole company hasn't yet evolved to this state, you can create such a culture within your own department.)

The Maverick Manager makes good use of meetings. Rather than a forum for information dissemination, meetings should be used for interactive information exchanges. When several people contribute to a meeting, there's an opportunity for everyone to draw on the cumulative decades of life experience in the room. When the boss does all the talking, there's a limited baseline of information and experience (no matter how impressive).

For the price of a few pizzas and sodas, a lunch meeting can contribute a great deal of insight to the business. I usually avoid food at meetings (they aren't parties) but sometimes a few pizzas on the table make for a better meeting. "Everybody has a vastly greater potential for creative and innovative thinking than the routine workday allows," says Mark Sebell, formerly with Colgate-Palmolive, now a principal with Creative Realities. Pizza seems just enough out of the routine to help people relax and make contributions they might otherwise not.

One way to put people's minds in a receptive mood for exchanging information is to open routine meetings by asking, "What have you read, seen, or heard in the last week that made an impression on you?" The purpose of the question is not to stir up an off-point gabathon (this isn't a discussion). Rather, the intent is to get each attendee to make an initial verbal contribution, and to expand everyone's mental frame of reference, which will make for better thinking in the meeting when you quickly return to the prepared agenda of mundanities.

Close your meetings by always reviewing the decisions so that there are no misunderstandings, and review all pending action items, making clear who will undertake which actions. Then reiterate the deadlines—projects without deadlines amount to nothing more than a wish list.

Communicate frequently with your people but make clear that everyone is responsible for staying abreast of developments in the company and in your area. If you hear, "Nobody told me," respond with, "Whom did you ask?" Grade school teachers write lessons and assignments on the board. In today's fast-paced and ever-changing business environment, adults must take responsibility for keeping up.

Draw out the best of your people by trusting their expertise. Here's an example from my shop. Shortly before we were to go to press with a large color catalog, the art director overseeing the project had a flash of inspiration. He wanted to modify the carefully designed cover with a visual trick to "make the photos pop better." The cover already had several visual elements and I was skeptical.

"What does the design studio think?" I asked, inquiring about the outside contractors who were assisting with the project. "They don't like the idea," Dick admitted. "What about the printer?" I asked. "They don't think it will work either," Dick confessed. "Hmmmmm," I intoned. "You're sure it will work?" "Yes," Dick said quietly. "Let me sleep on it this weekend," I said weakly.

Monday morning, I pulled Dick aside. "Look, Dick, we're printing *hundreds of thousands* of those catalogs. We're not going back to press with this for at least two more years. I know you're fond of this idea of yours, but are you willing to bet my job on it?" Dick blinked, but he didn't hesitate. "Yes." I wish that had been good enough for me, but then I asked, "And your job?" No blink this time. "Yes."

"Do it," I said, praying that he was indeed smarter than all those other experts he consulted. He was. The effect no one but Dick believed would work, worked. It looked great. He was right, I was humbled. And glad I overcame the overwhelming urge to say no.

The Maverick Manager rejects the old prejudice that only some people are creative. "Naturally" creative people, like mavericks and artists, may simply possess an innate ability to freely express their creativity; others may need training in how to find and express it (see Chapters 8 and 10); still others may only need permission to use theirs. (Once I gave a speech in New York City on "Where Do Ideas Come from?" In the speech, I suggested several techniques for generating more ideas. I urged the business audience to think of creativity simply as a set of learned skills and behaviors. Following the speech, an old-line industrialist in the audience rose to compliment my platform skills. Then he took me to task for the *faulty premise* I advanced. "Most people aren't creative. Those who are become the bosses, the artists, but everyone else, well they just don't have it," he scolded.)

The Maverick Manager knows that all people are capable of better ideas.

Maverick Managers affirm their commitment to everyone making an intellectual contribution to the business by *responding* to the ideas they receive from co-workers. An idea has no value if no one does anything with it. Take every staff idea seriously, and consider each one fully. "When managers must pay as much attention to justifying the rejection of promising ideas as to accepting [them], risk taking is likely to be encouraged," says Henry E. Riggs.

Cheerleader.   Anyone who has ever participated in sporting events or witnessed them firsthand knows the power of affirmation. What is the "hometown advantage" but simply the power of lots of positive feedback. Maverick Managers don't carry pom-poms, don't do cartwheels, don't shout, "Good job, good job." Rather, they quietly affirm. "Send this message from management" to all employees, says management consultant Ron Zemke, " 'You are a smart and competent person and we depend on you to do well . . . and we know you will.' "

Cheerleading works not because it's flashy or noisy, but because of its effect on the target of the affirmations. It simply makes people feel better about themselves, and because they do, they perform better. Andrew M. Mecca chaired a special California state task force looking into solutions to many problems that plague young people. The conclusion he wrote in the task force's comprehensive report speaks to the Maverick Manager. Dr. Mecca recommends that we "nurture the four primary ingredients of self-esteem: a sense of belonging, likability, a feeling of significance, and acknowledgment of hard work."

Cheerleading can take many forms: psychic incentives (see next chapter), compensation (see Chapter 6), and affirming organizational policies (see Chapter 8). Among the most effective is treating people like capable adults.

If your employees believe they have your trust and your confidence they'll work hard to keep it. Business consultant and best-selling author Bob Waterman: "When managers believe their staff is competent, employees are not only more effective, they also find their jobs more rewarding. Self-confidence has a proven influence on performance—people do as well as they believe they can." And people's estimates of their abilities are often tied to your estimates of them. One of the most powerful motivational speeches on earth is only six words long: "I believe you can do it."

A big part of positively influencing behavior is direct personal communication. (Issuing memos and distributing company information releases from the human resource department doesn't constitute communicating.) Throw away your "out" basket; get out and interact. Deliver memos to your staff in person; you increase the chance of informal conversation about things they're working on. Those chats can yield good information and insights—ideas spring from informal exchanges as often (or more) as from formal meetings.

When you delegate assignments to people, tell them about the large implications of the problem you're asking them to help solve. That "bigger picture" perspective will help people help you create and execute an action plan to effect a solution. It gives everyone a psychic investment in the remedy.

The Maverick Manager understands that communicating doesn't mean talking. Sending messages is far less than half the communication equation. Messages sent have meaning only in the minds of the receiver. What you meant to mean, means nothing if it isn't the meaning in the minds of those who (mis)receive your message. (Go ahead, read that again.) The real action in communication for the Maverick Manager is in *listening*. We'll never know more than we know now unless we open our minds to the new knowledge.

The Maverick Manager recognizes the importance of language as an influencer in the workplace. Each conversation with a colleague, especially one who reports to you, is similar to a financial transaction. Communication exchanges are nearly never neutral; they register as positive or negative. One of the most overwhelmingly powerful positive communication transactions takes no more than two words. People will walk barefoot on a bed of hot coals for you if they believe you'll appreciate it. Take a second a few times a day to say thank you.

An overlooked but powerful negative communicator is the phrase, *yes, but*. While you may be saying *yes* to show you understand, when you say that little word, *but*, in the mind of the listener you've wiped out everything that preceded it. *I think you're a nice person, BUT . . . .* See?

When you need to bring your experience to bear in directing a project's progress, rather than issuing orders, try asking questions. *What would happen if we approached it this way?* Questions stimulate thinking. They might point one in a certain direction, but they're still open-ended, allowing for the contribution of some additional generative thinking.

While face-to-face communication is nearly always preferable to written, when you need to communicate strongly worded messages, write your thoughts first. That will help you focus clearly on the important issues. Then put the memo in a "24 hour drawer." (Do the same with electronic mail notes. Delay your impulse to write and immediately send a response to an inflammatory or aggravating message.) If what you wrote today has merit, it still will tomorrow. Angry, self-righteous memos have a way of sounding pretty stupid after a night's sleep. If, in the new day's dawn, you feel comfortable with what you wrote yesterday, send it. If not, destroy it and start over. (No one likes to be on the receiving end of a "flamer" but they can really knock mavericks or sensitive employees off kilter for days, weeks, maybe evermore.)

If you want bright, enthused people surrounding you, focus on the positive. There is no immunity from passion.

Celebrate differences in styles, approaches, and ideas that differ from your own. (It's a good habit to get into; by the year 2000,

85 percent of the people entering the labor force will be some demographic *other than* white male.) Great minds may think alike, but equally true, fools seldom differ. If two people in the room approach things in the same way, one is unnecessary.

People who think differently may also look and act different from our own norms. James R. Houghton, Corning chairman, says that as companies reflect more cultural diversity, "they'll become much more tolerant, more willing to use differences, rather than sameness as criteria for individual success within the organization. What a way to spark creativity! What a way to encourage innovation!"

The Maverick Manager isn't threatened by diversity. She or he knows that an idea has no color, no sex, no creed, no credentials, no accent, no ethnic origin—just its own merit.

Being open to diversity means increasing your own tolerance for the variety in humanity—not just ethnic heritage and creeds, but also the realities that accompany human vulnerabilities, frailties, and failings. What I mean by this is that when people trust and are honest with each other, they will reveal the whole of themselves. Removing the steely three-piece-suit facade in an organization opens the channels to better thinking *and* to revealing the fragile human we've all become so adroit at hiding. "Formality tends to be a defense of the insecure," wrote R. Donald Gamache and Robert L. Kuhn in their book *The Creativity Infusion.*

Freeing co-workers to think relates to freeing them to be who they really are: holders of opinions, beliefs, and preferences not previously expressible in the workplace. Not keeping up a "corporate face" frees psychic energy that people have kept suppressed; most of that energy—but likely not all—will get channeled into their jobs, but even that may help performance. Hanley Norins, former Creative Director for the West Coast offices of the renowned ad agency Young & Rubicam, suggests that "the best ideas are often the spontaneous sparks of minds released from tension."

Allowing people to be high-achievers who are free thinkers, to contribute, and to be themselves, is admittedly a greater management challenge than just monitoring arrival and departure times and productivity rates. A parallel can again be drawn with gifted children (see previous chapter). Stephanie S. Tolan, who writes about the gifted, has some advice for parents raising extraordinary children that also applies to people who manage them as grown-ups. She says that the gifted "may be ecstasy, agony, and everything in between. Adults must perform almost impossible feats of balance—supporting a child's gifts without pushing, valuing without overinvesting, championing without taking over. It is costly, physically and emotionally draining, and intellectually demanding."

Quality assurer. The Maverick Manager knows that there is no room for second rate in today's competitive climate. A sign in the office of T. J. Rodgers, CEO of Cypress Semiconductor, reads, "Be realistic—demand the impossible."

You must set high standards and hold people accountable for maintaining them. (But beware the perfection infection—see preceding chapter—which can asphyxiate ambition and severely cripple innovation. You can't nitpick a great performance out of anyone.) Define what *you* mean by high-quality work. If you can't write down a specification, publicly point to it whenever you see it both inside your organization and outside it.

Everyone, in my experience, tends to underestimate the workload, responsibilities, and pressures of their boss. At the same time, they expect everyone else to maintain higher standards than they hold for themselves. A Maverick Manager is keeper of the flame of quality—for himself and his work unit; he helps everyone to understand that maintaining high standards can be a learning event. Evaluation, says creativity author William Miller, "can stimulate rather than stifle creativity by asking the right questions." If things aren't right, ask, why not, what should we be doing differently, what are all the possible consequences of changing a process, supplier, deadline? You'll learn far more about how to improve the business than just fixing the broken expectation.

When it's time for the dreaded annual personal performance review, take turns. First, well in advance of the scheduled review, ask the employee to review her own performance. Then ask to be reviewed—your own performance and that of the department—what improvements could be made, inefficiencies eliminated.

Maverick Managers resist the temptation to rely on a few super-stars. You can push your quality goals ever higher when you involve everyone in meeting and then exceeding them. Create a fighting team-spirit by rallying to defeat the common enemy: mediocrity.

While as a Maverick Manager you are a pleasant, approachable person, that by no measure means you're a pushover. ("You can be too nice, too lenient a boss," says Melissa Lande, owner of M. Lande Promotions. Give people too much room and they'll go wayward," she says.) You must expect, even demand work up to standard; it is your job to deliver that. You have to make tough and unpopular decisions. When you do, you can involve your col-leagues in the process, both before and after you go do what you're paid the big bucks to do.

Before the big decision, seek thoughtful input from people affected (perhaps even indirectly) by the decision. Then after you make the call, thank everyone who contributed to your thought process and then explain your thinking. Some constituency will be disappointed, but in knowing that you made an earnest—not arbitrary—judgment, they won't be demoralized. "The best deci-sion makers are those who are willing to suffer the most over their decisions but still retain their ability to be decisive," wrote M. Scott Peck, M.D. in *The Road Less Traveled*.

If you do a good job creating an atmosphere that invites creative contributions from your staff, you'll actually find yourself saying *no* more often. Chances are you won't have the resources to imple-ment every good idea you receive. Say no with compassion: Deny-ing someone's idea is a little murder; you kill a part of the employee's psychic investment that went into formulating and proposing that concept.

As pointed out above, when you free people to be more crea-tive, you probably unleash a sense of personal freedom that may liberate some personal idiosyncrasies. Just as your employees need not check their humanity at the workplace door, you need not lose decorum or anything else there. Set limits and communi-cate them. If not before the transgressions, which you may not be able to anticipate, a short time later. Before giving in to circulating a memo about the inappropriate nature of wearing cut-off shorts to the office immediately after someone does, first talk to that person in private and explain your preference for other clothing. If the problem is not widespread, there's no need to circulate a formal memo. One of the reasons organizations eventually become overrun with irrelevant and outmoded policies is that fearful managers rush to react to the aberrant behavior of a confused 5 or 10 percent by issuing rules mostly irrelevant but binding to the remaining vast majority.

Mavericks who work for you—those born that way and those you've helped to create—are probably impulsive, so be accessible and responsive. React to their ideas before you forget about them. Or the maverick implements them. Being accessible doesn't mean opening yourself up to constant interruption. Chet Holmes, former associate publisher of *California Lawyer* magazine told me his open-door policy led to a nonstop stream of visits by staff asking, Got a minute? "Instead of being the 'one-minute manager,' " Chet says, "I was turning into the minute-by-minute manager." He solved the problem by blocking out time for frequent staff contact, which allowed him to be accessible while still in control of his own time.

Maverick Managers treat business seriously and people humanely. They love what they do and do it well.

Work is Love made visible.

And if you can't work with love but only with distaste, It is better that you should leave your work and sit at the gate of the temple and take alms of the people who work with joy.

Kahlil Gibran

In the next chapter, we'll look at ways to motivate performance with rewards that make work more lovable for all.

Chapter Five

Maverick Motivation: Psychic Paychecks

My grandfather and father settled for freedom, dignity and pride off the job. My contemporaries and their children want those rewards on the job.

Charles Garfield

People who come into the work force today have a different value system than earlier generations. They weren't raised in a depression or a hierarchical social system.

E. V. "Rick" Goings

In today's work world, few drop dead from exhaustion but many quietly curl up and die from undersatisfaction.

Michael LeBoeuf

People will not sacrifice themselves for the company. They come to work at the company to enjoy themselves.

Soichiro Honda

Whereas instincts provide for biological security in a static world, awareness, knowledge and motivation account for the creativity of human life.

René Dubos

A monk joins a monastery where he must take a vow of silence. He is allowed to say only two words every decade. The monk's daily routine consists of rising from a bed that's no more than a plank at 3:30 A.M., praying while kneeling for hours on a stone floor, eating tasteless gruel, and copying bibles by hand. The monk follows this routine day after day after long day for 10

"Gosh. I didn't think anybody noticed that my new accounting method saved us a billion last year!"

straight years without uttering a word. One day the abbot summons the monk and grants him permission to say his allotted two words. The monk looks up at the abbot with tired eyes and says, "Bed hard." Having said this, the monk returns to his daily grind of rising at 3:30 A.M., praying, eating tasteless gruel, copying bibles by hand, and sleeping on a bed that's no more than a plank. Another year goes by. Then another. Then 5. Then 10. After 20 years of this unvarying routine, the monk is again summoned to appear before the abbot who permits him to speak two words. Without hesitation, the monk snorts, "Food lousy," and returns to his dreary routine. After another silent decade of predawn awakenings, tasteless gruel, arduous copying, painful prayer, and restless sleep on a plank, the monk again reports to the abbot to speak his two words. The bent, tired, and frail monk looks up at the abbot and says, "I quit." The abbot snaps back, "Fine! You've done nothing but complain since the moment you got here."

Let's talk about morale and motivation, vital components to injecting inspired ideas into an organization. When the law firm Grotta, Glassman & Hoffman surveyed corporate managers, 69 percent of them cited the lack of employee motivation as their leading gripe. That's a serious problem because, as you read in the Introduction, we're asking our employees to do more work, to do it to higher standards, in less time with fewer resources. Those are

---

Brief Aside

Corporate managers bellyache about how their workers aren't motivated. "It's why we can't compete," they say. Isn't it ironic that bosses who place such importance on motivation often are the same ones who reject simple programs to enrich worker satisfaction, terming them "soft" and "unbusinesslike"? If workers' enthusiasm for their jobs weren't truly important, no one would ever need to talk about a morale problem.

---

pretty tall orders for people who have no major stake in the incremental success of the business.

To help combat sagging morale, companies collectively spend millions on motivational minstrels who, if they're good enough, help employees find renewed excitement for their jobs—for about an hour or until they go back to work. The Maverick Manager knows that motivation problems aren't fixed by pep rallies. (I've made the mistake of accepting speaking engagements to address employees whose boss described them as suffering from a lack of motivation. Invariably, at the end of the presentation—usually in the parking lot—I'd get questions like "How do we get the boss to stop being such an s.o.b.," or get him to "do what needs to be done to save the business?") Morale problems aren't symptomatic of problems *in* the work force. They do, however, speak volumes about management.

THE RECIPROCAL MOTIVATION DEFICIT

Managers who notice that the motivation level isn't as high as it should be actually perceive workers' frustration. Employees are bewildered by an organization that inhibits them from working to their capacity. Mavericks and achievers-in-waiting alike desperately want to do good work. So many times I've heard employees say, "How we're doing this makes no sense! It's not efficient. We tell management and they don't do anything about it." In circumstances like that, people give up hope, and hold back their best ideas and energy. I call this condition the *reciprocal motivation deficit:* "If you don't care, then I don't care." (Electrify that fence!)

If people believe that what they're doing has meaning—that it makes a contribution, that someone appreciates it, then they're *motivated.* Motivation comes from the same root word as movement—motivated people are people on the move. They're productive. Motivated people accomplish extraordinary feats. Every general knows this truth: people will *kill* for something they believe in. (And, as the Iraqi army proved, people won't kill or even fight for a cause they don't believe in, even when their own lives are at stake. Forced to fight by a dictatorial despot in a cause with no moral appeal, Iraqi soldiers, forced to invade Kuwait, surrendered to Allied troops—with no resistance, with *joy*—by the tens of thousands.)

Compared to generals, corporations ask people to engage in some pretty tame activities—some missed lunch breaks, some long and intense hours, some ingenuity under deadline. How do you get people to give you their all—hard work and best thinking? Emperor Napoleon Bonaparte said, "There are two levers for moving men—interest and fear." Both are powerful motivators. While one such lever can move people only to work long and hard, the other lever can motivate people to both sweat and *think* arduously and inventively. Fear of losing one's job can motivate one to work overtime and deliver improved time-study performance for a while, but it is quite ineffective as a stimulant for innovative enterprise. "I can't do my best work when I'm distracted by a fear of getting whacked for anything that I do," confides a frazzled marketing manager who works for a boss suffering from the perfection infection. In *The Tao of Power*, R. L. Wing writes, "Individuals who do not feel personal power feel fear."

Contrasted with fear, interest—an appealing fascination with work that gives employees a psychic investment in it—propels people to undertake whatever is necessary to achieve greatness. Albert Einstein said that "feeling and desire are the motive forces behind all human endeavor and human creation." Sure, money doesn't hurt either, but like fear, it's not as powerful a motivator as interest and other psychic gratification. We take fiscal paychecks to the bank every two weeks; psychic paychecks we take to heart every day.

Incentive magazine recently stated: "Many employers have long considered that a few more dollars in the paycheck would provide motivation in the workplace. But in sustained practice, experience shows that this occurs only where personnel are underpaid to begin with. When basic compensation is adequate, it takes something extra—and something tangible—to motivate people to greater performance." (For a discussion of monetary compensation, incentive programs, and a modest proposal for change, see the next chapter.)

A Yankelovich survey of American workers found that 90 percent believed it was important to work hard, and 78 percent reported they had an *inner need* to do their very best while on the job. And, notes *Incentive* magazine, "Workers say that work, rather than leisure, can give them what they're looking for: an outlet for self-expression as well as material rewards."

People care deeply about their jobs and the organizations they work for. When employees get together and socialize—even outside work—they talk about their work. Often it may sound like complaining. But listen carefully. What are they complaining about? Not that they must work, not that they're forced to work too hard, but that things could work so much better than what management settles for!

The most effective motivator is *job satisfaction* which derives from far more than the size of the paycheck. Richard Bartlett, president of Mary Kay Cosmetics, says, "What motivates people to go further is not just money, compensation, or status—it's fulfillment and self-esteem." Fulfillment. Self-esteem. Admittedly, those are touchy-feely words. But they're central to what makes every one of us tick. Have you ever seen anyone do better work than when they were feeling good about themselves? Or when they felt part of a worthwhile cause?

Jude Rich, chairman of **Sibson & Co.**, a human resources consulting firm, says, "Employees are likely to be motivated more by a nobler purpose than simply making more money for shareholders or helping top executives earn larger bonuses." Or one might add, an annual increase of 4 to 5 percent, or even substantially more than that.

Brief Aside

Motivated people are *physiologically* different than apathetic or depressed workers. If you've ever attended an inspiring seminar or stimulating meeting, or engaged in personally meaningful work, you know that "fired up" feeling. It's more than a mental state. The pulse quickens, the adrenaline flows, the sparked imagination releases the brain's endorphins and ignites the neural connectors in rapid fire. Your heart is pounding, your mind is racing. You're poised to perform at your peak. Exciting work makes us high.

Look at salespeople. Often they work with no cap on their incremental income. They get paid for the results they produce, usually a result of the effort and creativity they're willing to expend. So sales representatives have a direct monetary incentive: work—produce—receive. Interestingly, salespeople are the ones on whom companies lavish the most motivational awards, from trophies to trips. Why? Don't they have incentive enough with monetary compensation directly proportional to their achievements? People in sales management understand that while money is important, it doesn't drive people to excel the way psychic compensation does. (Pass the plaques, please.)

MOTIVATION IS NOT RATIONAL

Discussing nonmonetary compensation spooks some managers because it is out of the realm of the rational and quantifiable. But humans—even those in business—are not strictly rational creatures. If we were, no one would smoke, overeat, patronize a pet cemetery, drive a sports or luxury car, or purchase from an expensive boutique merchandise available at a discount store; and we wouldn't buy high-priced branded sodas or beers or jeans or analgesics instead of their less heavily advertised counterparts. No, we aren't rational creatures and that fact accounts for a huge chunk of the gross national product.

I'm going to suggest some gestures a Maverick Manager can use to motivate and reinforce good performance. Before I do, a few cautionary notes. When we enter the realm of the psyche—and that's really what we're talking about here—there are neither certainties nor universals. There is much about the psyche we just don't know. The best thinkers in psychology passionately disagree over theories attempting to explain the human mind's many mysteries. (Once, I spoke to a business group holding its meeting at a California resort hotel concurrently hosting a conference of psychologists. Never before or since have I witnessed such heated conversations across a restaurant breakfast table!)

The next caveat concerns anyone who would presume to motivate his or her charges by merely adopting techniques. Shortly after President Bush announced a plan to support innovative approaches to public education, I ran into a friend who is a senior administrator at a large university in New York. We spoke of the president's plan on the Amtrak into the city.

"Sure, some unusual methods will work—but no one will be able to replicate the results in other schools," Ron said. "The people leading the innovations in education make the difference in that school's performance. It's the individuals, not their specific methods that count."

A person's *approach* to methods often matters more than the specific methods. That's why people-management programs that work marvelously well at one firm don't necessarily transfer well to another; the soul is lost in the transplant. Motive and action are inextricable. What follows are techniques intertwined with motivational underpinnings. When deployed with integrity, they help people achieve their best; without earnestness, they are hollow attempts to manipulate.

IN PRAISE OF PRAISE

In the previous chapter, I suggested that to be an effective manager, you needed to be part cheerleader. Innately, people want to do their best, but doing so involves risk and a lot of hard work. Rob Henderson, operations manager for Cormatech, a joint venture between Corning and Mitsubishi, contends that 30 percent of the work force always work hard, 60 percent respond to how they are treated, and 10 percent do a poor job. Applause encourages them all. Roger Milliken, chairman and chief executive of the $2.5 billion textile and chemical company, Milliken & Co., says, "Everybody likes applause. A day doesn't go by in our company when we don't say, 'Hey, that deserves a round of applause.' It tells people we appreciate what they're doing. We think this is an incredibly important part of our whole quality effort." And that quality effort won for the company the coveted Malcolm Baldrige Quality Award.

Paul Cook, chairman of the billion dollar Raychem Corp. concurs and points out the role positive affirmation plays in encouraging innovation. "The most important factor," he says, "is individual recognition—more important than salaries, bonuses, or promotions. Most people, whether they're engineers, business managers, or machine operators, want to be creative."

Recognition of achievement is a powerful elixir. James E. Quinn, group vice president of Tiffany & Co., points out how companies will gear their whole operation for two or three years just to win the Baldrige Award—a trophy that comes with no monetary prize. In pursuit of that recognition, some 400,000 companies have requested Baldrige Award applications. (Might the executives requesting Baldrige applications be seeking the very recognition we're talking about here?)

Quinn believes that the drive to win recognition for a company is the same one that urges sports teams to work painfully hard to win championships. (College, Olympic, and professional sports teams now employ psychologists, "achievement specialists," to help tweak athletes' psyches for that extra oomph in competition that is often won or lost by human performance measured in hundredths of a second.)

Two forces converge in today's corporations to make recognition for performance that much more potent and necessary. First, eliminating middle management jobs by the hundreds of thousands means flatter organizations, which mean fewer opportunities for people to receive promotions. And second, that development comes just when the great swell of baby boomers reaches the age when they expected to move up the ladder. For baby boomers to stand out from their many, many peers they need affirmations outside ascendancy in the ranks.

Recognizing good performance doesn't just mean verbal pats on the back. Shouting "Good job, good job" with abandon cheapens praise just as printing too much money devalues the currency. The point is to pay people something extra, something not compensable by any merit increase. Using the words of Rosabeth Moss Kanter, editor of the *Harvard Business Review*, in her book the *Change Masters*, the point is to "make the people inside feel important—not just well treated, but *important.*" [emphasis in original]

Here are many ways you can say thank you to encourage mavericks and achievers-in-waiting to continue giving their all.

Publicly confer appreciation. Most good work in an organization languishes in obscurity; except to the eye of the one who toiled over it, it is invisible. That's true even in the purportedly glamorous advertising business. Former Young and Rubicam advertising creative director Hanley Norins suggests that "unlike authors and artists, creative people [in advertising] do not have the satisfaction of signing their works." The same could be said of most engineers, financial analysts, warehouse supervisors, scientists, secretaries, computer programmers, production workers, lawyers, trainers, and middle managers. The pride of authorship is mitigated somewhat by anonymity. Recognition by one's bosses or peers offers some consolation. It validates hard work. It says, We care as much about your work as you do.

Probably since man first sat around a campfire, he has engaged in ceremonial rituals paying tribute to the best in the tribe. Extending recognition to deserving and unsung heroes in the modern organization is easy with simple awards such as plaques and certificates (and much less sooty than a campfire). Such pomp effectively bestows acclaim in a public gathering before a person's corporate peers. A variation on the public acclaim theme is to arrange for publicity in a company, industry, or community publication. Ego-intense mavericks eat this validation for breakfast; even shy, modest achievers-in-waiting often get a quiet charge from it too—maybe more than most since they've been in the spotlight so rarely.

Public recognition gives an achiever-in-waiting outward affirmation that he or she is an important member of the company's society. That feeling of belonging is a far greater motivator than the modest pleasure derived from helping to manufacture carbonated sugar water or widgets, or changing money, or any of the other thousands of ways we earn a living. "We've found that innovative people really respond to the admiration of their peers," says Lester C. Krogh, senior vice president for Research and Development at 3M. "We've developed a variety of ways to recognize innovation and excellence—rewards that range from dinner with the boss, to fairly lavish award banquets, to election to the Carlton Society, a select group of the very best 3M scientists. Our recognition programs dramatize over and over again that our company owes its success to the ideas and drive of individual men and women."

At Times Mirror Cable Television, a few outstanding employees from cable systems around the country are selected to join the President's Club. The honor includes a trip to southern California to attend the annual manager's meeting. Following presentations on policy and strategy for the company, the esteemed employees attend an awards dinner with the company president.

Some solemn businesspeople believe that recognition awards are just silliness. "People who win awards don't think that," chuckles Dave Tanner, a soft-spoken, serious man with a Ph.D. in polymer science. As a research manager with DuPont, Tanner used awards to encourage practical and profitable innovations by his technical staff in the industrial fibers division. Fond of Rodin's statue *The Thinker*, in "all different sizes," Tanner gave out replicas of the sculpture for creative thinking, creative leadership, and other categories of successful ideas. Some statues came with checks, some didn't. Tanner believes such awards motivate all their recipients. In one DuPont technical group, scientists exchange awards *among themselves* to recognize peer accomplishments. Because they aren't conferred by management, there's never any cash—just recognition of good work.

"I even gave an award to our chairman," Tanner says proudly. "I understand he keeps it in his office with his other awards." (While in sales, I often noticed senior executives proudly displaying plaques and certificates received for community service. Now my staff gives a plaque of appreciation to senior executives who speak at our "A Team" meetings. Those executives also proudly display the awards in their corner offices.)

Brief Aside

Recognize the conundrum you create when you bolster your employees' ego involvement in their work. By boosting people for jobs well done, you encourage them to assume personal responsibility for what they produce. You also create a condition where it's difficult not to take work-related criticism personally. How do you critique and correct without offending? The Maverick Manager does it with care, objective information, and a solid vote of confidence for superior performance in the future.

In addition to the motivating effect of saying thank you, awards telegraph to the whole staff: *This is what we mean by good work around here.* And there is another value to public recognition. A senior executive friend of mine calls business achievement awards Wizard of Oz motivation. "You have a brain because this piece of paper certifies that you do. Publicly confer on people a high expectation and they will keep rising to fulfill it."

A slightly different twist on prizes for good ideas or work comes from Paul Cook at Raychem who recently started awarding Not Invented Here awards. "We celebrate people who steal ideas from other parts of the company and apply them to their work. We give the person who adapts a new idea a trophy and a certificate that says, 'I stole somebody else's idea, and I'm using it.' The person on the other side, the person who had the idea, also gets an award."

Deliver a letter. Send a "job well-done" letter from you to the achiever (sent to the performer's home for added impact, away from work distractions and closer to familial support). A complimentary letter to the achiever from her boss' boss. A letter from you to your boss about your employee's excellent effort, with a copy to the employee ("Mr. Big, I'd like you to know about the extraordinary accomplishment that Maria Hernandez turned in last month . . . "). Most card stores offer precious little in the way of clever motivational messages, but at least one company specializes in them. They're called *Way to Go Cards* and they are available directly from **InnerTrack, Inc.**

Compliment with your undivided attention. Because managers are busier than ever, your personal attention to someone can be rewarding by itself. As a result of today's streamlined organization, more managers are player/coaches personally performing tasks that in cushier times they would have delegated to others, or they are now supervising more people—affording less time for personal contact, or doing both. Advanced electronic communication also greatly minimizes the need for human contact to exchange information. In my office, the local area network on our personal computers and the voice mail on our phones allows us to communicate instantly with everyone in the company without ever leaving our chairs. I'm not standing over anyone's shoulder while sending E-mail and leaving phone-mail messages.

All this leads to more autonomy for my colleagues, which can give people freedom but just as likely alienates them. They receive information without benefit of the nuances of personal contact. In many cases, it denies workers valuable feedback as to whether they're doing what the company expects. That isolation demotivates.

Maverick Managers make time for the people who report to them. (I think of intentional face-to-face communication with employees as "watering." It's refreshing and sustaining for everyone. While watering won't guarantee that someone will blossom, it's a pretty good hedge against their withering.) Stimulate interaction by asking thought-provoking questions instead of pontificating in your interactions.

Take the time to *listen.* Letting someone blow off steam helps them relieve the mental pressure that can build so quickly in our fast-paced, understaffed organizations. Listening is so powerful a motivator, many people are treated for their psychological needs by professionals who do little more than hear them out.

A complimentary way of spending time with an employee is to call him into your office and ask for his opinion or advice about some challenge you face in your responsibilities. You get a fresh perspective and maybe some new ideas. Sharing confidential information with someone acknowledges their judgment. So does asking "What do you think of the way we're doing things," now and then.

Say thank you with a gesture. A great commercial for American Airlines shows a tired businessman returning to his darkened office to see the answering machine light blinking in the night. The exhausted exec drops into a chair and hits play to hear this message: "Well done, Jack. There's a little something for you in your top drawer." Jack opens the drawer and pulls out some American Airlines tickets. A smile comes to his reinvigorated face. Jack is ready to take on the world once again.

Thank-you gestures need not be that lavish. As the saying goes, it's the thought that counts. Say thank you with flowers, plants (even many macho managers like receiving these), a favorite snack or beverage left with a handwritten note on the desk or in the work area. How about lottery tickets ("While you're on such a hot streak . . ."), perhaps tickets to a play or the movies, a gift certificate for a store or restaurant.

Reward with prizes that help encourage even better performance: books, audiotapes, a magazine subscription. Information in America is mass-marketed at ridiculously low cost (the price of this book for example) and can yield benefits exponential to the negligible investment.

Some companies have policies against such "gifts" to employees (mine does). Managers who recognize the power of recognition often reward employees out of their own pockets. They understand that they are investing in their own success by investing in their people. (Personally, I've always figured that the cost of some plants, cards, lunches, and the like was worth it, although, I admit my preference is for the company to provide money for such things out of the compensation budget. This is discussed in greater detail in the next chapter.)

Arrange for visibility. Allow achievers to personally present to upper management a proposal or report of results for a program with which they're involved. If it is appropriate to your line of work, enter your people's products in a contest for design or quality. This communicates your pride in their achievements,

---

Brief Aside

Training shouldn't be left to the human resources department and we should broaden our perspective on teaching within the organization. Dave Tanner, a DuPont executive, says you train animals but educate people. Educating employees to help them become potent people means focusing on more than their individual job functions. The Maverick Manager, remember, is an educator. That doesn't mean simply expounding your own knowledge, but rather finding educational opportunities for the people who report to you. One of the ways I've done that in my own shop is to make one staff meeting a month in part a learning session. I invite people from other parts of the company to come explain what it is they do—whether or not it has any direct bearing on my group. The more employees know about the *business*, the better they understand the context of their work, and the more of a contribution they can make to it.

---

underscores the value of laboring for merit's sake and not just compensation, and it reinforces the organization's mission to create competition quality output.

Reward with growth.   Turn a good performance into a better one by rewarding with an opportunity to develop even more skills. Send the top performer to a conference or course of her choosing, or a trip to a company operation in or near a desirable destination (by enabling key people to gain more insight into how the company operates everyone benefits; the desirable locale can afford a little mixing of business and pleasure). Then try to provide opportunities for the newly educated to use the new knowledge.

Present a teaching opportunity.   Teaching is an ego-gratifying exercise. The chance to make a presentation to peers, to educate junior team members, to address a company conference, all of these can give a high-achiever a chance to strut his or her stuff.

Arrange for a special project. Everyone has favorite work. Reward top performers with theirs. Create an assignment that makes the most of one's special talents. You might need to shuffle the work load temporarily, but you'll get the benefit of work that wouldn't ordinarily spring from routine channels, and your top performers will get a chance to spread their wings. Unless you're prepared for a more permanent shift of responsibilities, make clear that the special assignment is temporary. This is a perk, not the stuff of false hopes.

A related alternative is to let someone try something new. Everyone you hired is adept at doing more than you hired them to do. By providing your capable people with a diversity of assignments, you'll find them becoming more diversely capable. A good way to do this is to reward an achiever by asking her what she'd like to tackle. (Another way, especially when you have an assignment and don't know who you should give it to, is to ask for volunteers. I've done this many times with great results. Give people a chance to surprise you with out-of-the-ordinary work and they will.)

Provide time to pursue a personal project. As a matter of policy, 3M encourages its scientists to spend 15 percent of their time on projects that interest them, even if totally unrelated to assigned work. That's an hour and twenty minutes out of an eight-hour day. That doesn't sound like much, but if saved for spending in one day a week, it's a good chunk of the day. The key to making this work is to really free the person to enjoy the time you claim to have provided. At 3M, it's an integral part of the corporate culture. If you made such an offer to one of your people without relieving them of regular work expectations, the reward would amount to a cruel hoax. Earning a 15 percent time bonus while still having to meet the same expectations, or doing everything that needed to be done before the award, just means working nearly another hour and a half every day. Some treat! (I admit to falling into this trap. Someone would come to me with an innovative idea. "Great!" I'd declare. "Go do it." But then I see that person struggle to juggle what already was a very full-time job with the pet project.)

Sometimes you just can't relieve a key person of routine responsibilities. Be honest about that. "I can't officially free you up to pursue that great idea, but I'd love to see you develop it if you want to." You might be surprised to see that person burning the midnight oil or working through the weekend on a labor of love with no expectation for additional remuneration, just because she was encouraged to stretch.

Time away from work. A friend of mine who runs a PR agency gives a key staffer time off to pursue her fine-art talents. She knows it motivates more than money and it requires no extra hit to cash flow. Time away from work also helps your hard workers recharge their batteries and exposes them to more experiences which can help stimulate even more achievements in your organization. Fran Tarkenton, management consultant and chairman of Knowledgeware, a successful computer software company, thinks time off is valuable for senior executives too. "Many corporate executives rarely take more than a week off. And during this week they have things faxed to them, they call their lawyers or bankers, and they never disconnect. As a result, they lose their perspective and their capacity to regenerate and rejuvenate will vanish. I think that's very counterproductive." Tarkenton puts his money where his mouth is. "I force my top executives to take one entire month off each year. They've got to take it, no matter what."

Permission to moonlight. Rare is the person whose work meets all their psychic needs. Some modest after-hours professional endeavors—in accord with strict guidelines—can provide a refreshing diversion from the workplace, and stimulating enrichment to bring back there. (My personnel file includes a letter of permission to give speeches; I sign a corporate code-of-conduct agreement every year specifying prohibitions against potential conflicts of interest.)

More independence at work. When people demonstrate that they're good at doing something, let them do it. (But don't take them for granted or ignore them.)

Acknowledge failure. Not all potent people's intense efforts will hit bull's-eyes. If you don't acknowledge the admirable, albeit unsuccessful, effort in a positive way, people soon come to understand that only successes have value. They'll self-censor any risk taking, which just about assures a safely mediocre place to work (until the company is driven out of business by innovative competitors).

At 3M, failures are acknowledged as steppingstones to success. A common saw around St. Paul, Minnesota: You've got to kiss a lot of frogs to find a prince. How can you acknowledge failures without appearing to encourage them? How about a Horseshoe award (close counts!), or a College Try award?

Give an account of how you failed in things you've tried, and how that contributed to your own success. You're not displaying weakness, but rather strength. Let people know that you value and identify with their brave attempt.

Everybody loves a winner, but most winners win by playing the odds—the more attempts, the more likely a success (familiar example: Edison's several thousand failures to find a workable filament). Fewer attempts, less of a chance for success. Pay tribute to the valiant effort and encourage more of the same right away. (If at first you don't succeed . . .; Nothing ventured, nothing . . . ; The best thing to do after falling off a horse . . .; No pain, no . . . ; When the going gets tough. . . .)

Have some fun. Business is serious but it need not be solemn. "If we are not making a lot of money, we won't be having fun. And if we're not having fun, we're probably just not making enough money," quips Richard S. Gurin, president of Binney & Smith, Inc., maker of Crayola Crayons. Gurin takes business seriously (but not too—there's a 25-pound stuffed bear in the head chair at the big conference table); since he moved into the president's chair (alongside the bear) in 1984, sales have leaped 92 percent to $240 million in 1990.

A few good-natured laughs in the workplace can actually help improve performance. Even the best people can't achieve greatness if they're discouraged, bored, or scared. Alice M. Isen, a psychologist at Cornell's management school studies the relationship between problem solving and people's moods. Her conclusion? "People are able to be creative and display responses that people think of as innovative when they feel good." Good humor: good work.

Laughs work best when they're at no one's expense (other than your own as the boss). Besides providing a needed diversion from the routine, humor helps to relax people—you can't be tense and laugh at the same time! Laughter also releases those magic endorphins which may aid ingenuity in the workplace.

Sustaining rewards. When you have the good fortune to have some consistently solid performers, you might feel uncomfortable publicly saluting them frequently or plying them with plaques. A way to say thanks is to mark their birthdays or their company anniversaries with a personal note in a card and some modest ceremonial gift. (I once received an unexpected bottle of bubbly on the anniversary of my start date and it made me feel wonderful.)

The old standards work, too. Promotions, money, and a piece of the business are all worthy rewards. I'll deal with money in the next chapter.

THINK BEFORE YOU TREAT

I know that saying thank you with motivational techniques strikes some business people as frilly and silly. But a word to the hardest-core bottom-liner: This stuff works. It's not childish. (Though these techniques tend to work best when they deal with employees as adults while appealing to the child that lies within.)

Performance rewards aren't "feel good" freebies, and they aren't unbusinesslike. They help keep people focused on organizational goals and achievement. Dispersing these psychic paychecks should be treated as seriously as the fiscal kind. At the same time, these suggested psychic paychecks shouldn't be dangled before workers as a mule's carrot. These motivators are not promised, conditional, or bargained for; they are simply signs of genuine appreciation for accomplishment. The importance of this distinction can't be overstated. Recognizing a job well done lets people know that their *extraordinary* efforts didn't go unnoticed (even if under-recompensed). It's as if you, the Maverick Manager, are sharing in the *joy of creation* experienced in work exceptionally well done. Such recognition is feedback, not payment.

Brief Aside

Philosophical issues notwithstanding, holding out the *promise* of recognition makes no pragmatic sense when encouraging innovation. Many psychological research studies conclude that people do not create for extrinsic rewards, and in fact, they may do less well when told to create to receive a prescribed reward. In a personal testimony to this effect, I remember the stress I felt as a sales representative when I received announcements of special bonus contests for selling certain products in a short amount of time. I often felt that taking time to engineer opportunities to emphasize those products would threaten the larger, long-term objectives the company had previously assigned me—and upon which I would be judged. I also felt that pushing the targeted products instead of selling to my customers' needs undermined them, me, and my company.

A related phenomenon might be called the *Reverse Hawthorne Effect*. As you'll recall, the term *Hawthorne effect* derives from productivity experiments at Western Electric's Hawthorne plant in the late 1920s. No matter what the experimenters tried, productivity went up. It wasn't the tests, but rather the workers' awareness that someone was watching them. With some attention paid to them, they worked harder. For manual piecework, that might be a worthwhile strategy—what gets watched gets done. Not so with more thought-intensive work.

Northwest Airlines stopped monitoring its reservation agents. Productivity slipped, right? It soared and absenteeism plummeted. Surveillance is stressful—did you ever have the feeling that someone was watching you? Was that pleasant or creepy? Studies of young children who know they're under surveillance bear out the same inhibiting effect on their creative output. The message: the boss hunched over a worker's shoulder might inspire some to twist nuts on bolts faster, but it won't stimulate higher-quality or more inspired work.

Simple gestures acknowledge extremely high-quality work and affirm the producer's rightful pride, which in moderation, is a healthy and potent motivator. Pride, after all, simply means that people are happy with themselves for what they've accomplished. Taking pride in work well done encourages employees to make their next iterations even stronger. "It's a self-reinforcing cycle— *performance stimulating pride stimulating performance*—and is especially important for innovation," writes Rosabeth Moss Kanter [emphasis in the original].

The self-perpetuating nature of one's own satisfaction in great work then producing more of the same is important. Recognition by management should be welcomed but not expected; awards are rewards, not entitlements. You would do a disservice to your people to turn them into attention-craving praise junkies. For greatest effect, vary motivational awards, use them sparingly and wisely.

THE SPIRIT OF ACHIEVEMENT

In Roman mythology, a *genius* was a spirit that guided a person. When an individual accomplished something, he often attributed the success to his genius. A Maverick Manager must be like a genius—inspiring (which means to breathe life into) great accomplishments.

The Maverick Manager knows that recognition, pay, and incentives help to spur productivity *and* that the most powerful motivator for ingenious work is *meaningful* work. In fact, the less meaningful and satisfying the work, the greater the demands for payment. Engaging work pays employees with what ad man Hanley Norins calls "the incentive of being educated everyday by the work you do." It give rise to *enthusiasm* which literally means "to be possessed by a god." Motivation is internal.

Chapter Six

Incenting Mavericks: What Price Compensation?

Obviously, what you try to do is to pay just well enough so you don't lose people. You certainly are not influenced primarily by considerations of justice or of equitable distribution. You behave in accordance with the market at the time.

William Shockley

Nine out of ten U.S. workers don't think there is any relationship between doing more and their compensation; it's just the reverse for the Japanese worker.

Pat Choate

Unfortunately, it doesn't take long for an employee to get used to his salary and realize that the quality of his work has little to do with the size of his paycheck. He stops making a connection between salary and performance and even salary and position and accepts the notion that what he's really being paid for is his time—regardless of how he spends it. For the most part, he can either work hard or goof off and the paycheck comes through unchanged.

Buck Rodgers

If you're trying to compress manufacturing cycle time and it involves R&D, design, manufacturing and purchasing, how do you work the financial rewards horizontally across the whole team?

Thomas A. Stewart

Football quarterback Joe Montana makes $4 million a year. Sioux City, Iowa, social programs director Al Johnson makes $13,500 a

year. Roberto C. Goizueta, CEO of The Coca-Cola Company and talk show host Phil Donahue both make $8 million while H. Norman Schwartzkopf and Colin Powell, U.S. Army generals, each make $113,134. The attorney general for the state of Montana makes $48,345. A trial court judge in New York makes an annual salary of $95,000, while a second-year associate at New York law firm Shearman & Sterling brings down $99,000; partners at that firm raked in profits of $860,000 apiece in 1990. Teachers and nurses (and the president of the United States) make less than professional athletes or movie stars.

In our free and capitalist society, everyone chooses his work. And money, in part, influences one's occupational selection and then the degree to which people commit themselves to their work. But compensation seems to have much more to do with what one can get than what one's work contributes.

The subject of money must enter the discussion of managing people to get the most out of them. How should we pay our mavericks to spur—by tangible reward—their best unbridled efforts? How can we use compensation to encourage our achievers-in-waiting to give us all they are capable of? In the previous chapter, we learned that psychic rewards at work were more powerful than fiscal ones. Does that mean high-paying jobs are actually undesirable ones? For example, is running a big corporation so onerous a task—with so few intrinsic rewards—that the bosses in charge of America's largest companies simply must be paid huge sums, about 85 times the average earnings of their rank and file? That's the biggest gap in the industrialized world. If holding the top slot were that vexatious, why would so many bright people sacrifice so much of their personal lives and fight so many bloody political battles trying to secure such a job? Perhaps the awesome income reflects an odd twist on the Golden Rule: He who makes the rules gets the gold.

How does money fit into the motivation equation? Money motivates. Money doesn't motivate. And both statements are true.

MONEY DOESN'T MOTIVATE

Money isn't everything. If money were the prime motivator for most people's work, there would be many more drug dealers, bank robbers, and embezzlers. The people who enter social work, police work, and other low-paying professions—which require skills applicable to higher-paying jobs—wouldn't.

Leave morality and "higher calling" issues aside. If money meant more to people than other aspects of work, wouldn't everyone apply for sales jobs that had no cap on earnings? Even large sums of money won't make someone pursue or stay in a job in which they aren't psychically comfortable.

People rarely believe they are paid what they deserve, so a good compensation plan may be only a neutral, while truly poor compensation demotivates.

An emphasis on money can also tilt the balance of one's work life away from doing great work. Cash, not quality work, becomes paramount. Yale psychologist Robert Sternberg suggests that people can feel controlled by the promise of a reward. Too much preoccupation with monetary rewards, Sternberg cautions, detracts from creative work because people waste time fantasizing about becoming rich and famous, or they worry about the adverse repercussions of not getting the hoped-for money. Executives who devise no-cap sales compensation plans know they must craft them mindful of the potentially aberrant conduct that unlimited incentives might induce. Promising huge commissions or free trips to exotic places can seduce otherwise responsible people into committing counterproductive get-the-prize behavior.

Evidence of big rewards' corrupting effect is easy to find on Wall Street where executive bonuses can amount to many times one's base pay. "You push everything and everybody aside that can't help you achieve the objective," says a well-compensated Wall Street veteran. "When you receive large compensation for good results, you come to expect it. When results fall short, you aren't motivated. Right now, Wall Street has a whole bunch of people who have no motivation to be creative because the monetary rewards won't be as big as they were in the past," he concludes with a sigh. Expecting obscene amounts of money for mere human performance results in inappropriate and even illegal behavior, as the newspapers routinely report, *and* in uninspired work.

Money dangled as a tantalizing prize puts emphasis not on working but on winning.

MONEY DOES MOTIVATE

While the previous chapter championed meaningful work and managerial boosterism as major motivators, neither sweat nor bravos buy bread. Good work may be its own reward, but satisfaction with one's work can't pay the mortgage. Pretty plaques are no substitute for sufficient pay. Money definitely is a powerful factor in attracting potent people to do work that serves the corporation well. If you think of one's motivation as the "fire within," money helps to stoke the embers into a brighter flame. Financial compensation—at some point above the level necessary to provide someone with subsistence—becomes a psychic motivator. We don't just work to survive life, but to improve its quality.

Even people more driven by altruism than avarice appreciate having—and are willing to work harder for—a few extra bucks (even if to allow them to give away more money to favorite causes). "Everyone wants to do their best, they just want to get compensated for it," was the way a friend of mine, an engineering manager for AT&T, put it. In this context, compensation recognizes, not controls, good work.

Monetary compensation provides one with the means to obtain goods and services (or engage in philanthropy) that provide joy. We don't want to work just for some money, we want to earn what we believe ourselves to be worth. Money motivates by providing workers with a social standing, or perception of merit, relative to others. For example, let's say you and I have similar responsibilities or tasks in the same organization. If you make 25 percent more than I do, I assume the organization values you more than it does me. I am either discouraged by that—considering it a breach of fairness, a psychic issue—or I am encouraged to work that much better and harder—more to my capacity, a motivational issue—so that our employer allows me to close and perhaps leap that gap.

Inadequate pay or incentives for extraordinary performance amount to mental electric fences. Reasonable financial rewards communicate that one's contribution is valued. Money paid as a reward for good work encourages more good work.

PAY FOR TIME, PAY FOR BRAINS

Trying to reconcile the tremendous and mind-boggling discrepancies between pay rates for similar work in the public and private sectors, or the relative worth of one job versus another, evokes great discussion about the merits of the free enterprise system, and is beyond the scope of this work. I shall instead focus on issues that present themselves to capitalists who now face new compensation issues in an economic system that increasingly demands that all workers make a thinking contribution to their employing organizations.

Historically, brain power has paid better than muscle work. Mathematician and philosopher Bertrand Russell held that "work is of two kinds: first, altering the position of matter at or near the earth's surface relative to other matter; second, telling other people to do so. The first kind is unpleasant and ill-paid; the second is pleasant and highly paid." By the capitalist law of supply and

Brief Aside

Many companies now employ very sophisticated administrative systems (e.g., Hay) to codify the required skills or experience to perform a given job, and to rate its relative worth. What most such systems lack is a method for specifying requisite skills or experience necessary to develop a job's *potential*. Neither do the systems recognize the contribution such a job can make in the hands of a potent person instead of a market study's statistically average performer with the requisite resume. The systems—designed in theory to scrupulously justify the pay for every position—lock managers into rigid grids for compensating a job *description*.

"The system exists for the convenience of HR—not to serve valid business purposes," fumes a senior executive at a large professional association. He grows angry when describing how pay grades grow at about the same rate as the merit budget. "I can't ever seem to get anybody ahead—especially a young or inexperienced person I hire whose competence grows faster than what the allotted increases allow me to reward [that person]. In some cases, I could fire someone and rehire them for more money than what I can give in merit increases!"

demand, sweatwork didn't have to pay much; there were always able bodies lined up ready to pick up a shovel, hammer, or axe. Bodies were interchangeable because the work required nothing more than willing strength. But what about today's technology-dependent, skill-intensive work environment? Bodies off the street can no longer replace a departed worker simply by picking up an implement and bearing down. (Lest you think Bertrand Russell's comment is greatly outdated, consider this. In late 1990, *Business Week* reported this startling statistic: "White-collar professionals now earn 37 percent more than skilled tradespeople; the gap was only two percent in 1975.)

Work for the masses has changed and pay must too. "Doing business in North America will never be the same again, and the way we reward people will change accordingly," concludes Marc J. Wallace, Jr., who made a study of the way companies pay employees in the new competitive era for the **American Compensation Association.**

What is knowledge worth? What are ideas worth? What is performance worth?

Shouldn't compensation in a highly competitive world reflect both individual contribution to a job function and recognition of resulting corporate success? I will argue for that here because someone needs to make the case. "The majority of employees in North America still receive most of their direct earnings simply for time," reports Wallace.

FIXED PAY, FIXED PERFORMANCE

Show up, stay busy for eight hours and get paid a prescribed amount. That's the uninspiring system most people work under and they recognize it as such. It became standard under the old assembly line puch-in/punch-out model. In exchange for performing standardized duties it provides a fixed income for employees who show up on time and don't leave before an appointed hour. Such a system provides little incentive for achievement.

Most people want their employer to make a profit because everyone knows that unprofitable companies pare their payrolls. But here is a significant question: Do most of your employees care how *much* profit your company makes?

If employees have no stake in the company's relative success—their pay remains essentially constant however the company performs—why should they invest themselves beyond a minimum level of exertion, or perform duties other than those precisely prescribed? With no opportunity to improve one's fixed lot, work becomes little more than abstraction save for the fixed income, socializing, and any intrinsic reward it provides. (This is probably even more true for people toiling for large conglomerates. Employee benefits dependent on the performance of the whole conglomerate, for example, company stock accumulation, seem negligibly influenced—if at all—by actions of even very senior employees.) When a worker's pay isn't tied in some way to the performance of the company, the success of the company becomes incidental to filling the day with minimal keep-from-getting-fired work, or self-gratifying activity (which may center more on the joy of coffee break chitchat, or for those with greater autonomy, work that is personally interesting but not necessarily the most productive for meeting corporate goals or maximizing profit potential). With no incentive for outstanding performance, the company loses out on the psychic investment of the work force in striving to help the company fulfill its potential.

At the same time, a company that gives no stake in its success to the workers who help create it communicates a very negative message to them: we consider you incidental to the organization's success; you are but a necessary tool to executives acquiring bonuses.

Fixed pay may provide some people with a sense of security, though as hundreds of thousands of workers in all classes discovered, it provides no guarantee of employment. It doesn't even assure that one can maintain a modest standard of living: workers operating under the flat-pay system lost actual purchasing power in recent years. *Fortune* magazine reported in 1991 this saddening statistic: the average weekly paycheck is 5 percent smaller than it was 10 years ago. The only gain in household income came from more dual income earners under one roof. (At the same time, household debt, including home mortgages, was up to 84 percent of annual after-tax income, a leap from 65 percent in 1980. Workers chase the elusive American dream increasingly on borrowed money—just like their debt-ridden government.)

Workers ask themselves, "Why should I bust my buns with little possibility of any real reward? I can't get promoted—the company recently eliminated several supervisory layers. And I can't make more money than a 5.5 percent increase no matter how hard I work." At the same time, companies—increasingly under financial and competitive pressure—must ask its workers, "Just because you're here another year, are you worth more to us?"

INCENTIVE INCREASES?

Why do companies reward workers with about 5 percent increases across the board? "Managers have a hard time making a distinction between the better performer and the poorer performer, or they don't like to make that distinction," contends

Victor Rodriguez who has made a career of setting up compensation systems for major companies including Citibank, Equitable Insurance, Pfizer Pharmaceuticals, and now Continental Insurance.

When all compensation augmentation comes out of a fixed merit budget, workers in the same group essentially compete against each other for their piece of the merit increase pie. Most managers instinctively dislike that idea and tend to reward everyone with pretty much the same increase. "The better performer gets 6 percent and the poorer performer gets 4 percent," says Rodriguez. "Very few get zero, very few get double digits—which delivers the wrong message to the better performer, who says, 'Why should I go out of my way to do additional work or *very* good work when I'm going to get six percent and Joe Blow, who sits next to me and does average or less than average, still got four percent?' "

The mostly set-increase ompensation system impedes our nation's competitiveness. "The entire U.S. economy can't continue to increase salaries 5 percent each year," warns Rodriguez, "because that goes right to our prices. And that's what's killing [American business]." Management expert Henry Riggs concurs, saying that, "Paying above average for average employees is a road to disaster." And, so is paying average for above-average performers.

The "move everyone along at about the same pace" compensation practice finds root in the American myth of "created equal." We don't really believe that everyone is created equal or we'd live equally under socialism rather than divergently under capitalism. Yet we don't want to overtly recognize differences between how we compensate people in the work force. Compensation is considered a highly confidential matter. Why?

Our national psyche is torn by competing ethics: equality and meritocracy. When we are very young, we're placed in classrooms with other children with whom age may be the only thing we have in common. While individual performance may vary greatly, typically all the children advance to the next grade level. By passing students along with little regard for performance, students who might have fallen short of their potential learn that they aren't really expected to meet it, instilling an ethic of Just enough to get by.

Brief Aside

The American discomfort with status difference penetrates other areas of society. I attend a mainstream church where the congregation sings a hymn that longs for the valleys to be raised and the mountains made low. That's not my idea of heaven. Whenever the choir breaks into the catchy little tune, I poke my wife in the ribs and whisper, "The communism song."

Americans struggle with their dissonance over this question of equality versus meritocracy. We know that some people drive big, expensive cars and live in big, expensive suburban homes, while others can't even imagine aspiring to that. But we act as though that's not the case. Perhaps, if compensation systems were more oriented toward achievement—without dependence on arbitrary judgment of supervisors who might harbor their own agenda or prejudices—some who now feel excluded from the good life might have a shot at it.

MAVERICK COMPENSATION: RISK, PERFORMANCE, AND PAY

Earlier, I suggested that most employees had no interest in the degree of their employer's profitability. Why should they? So that they can estimate the size of their boss's boss's bonus? For all the preaching about teamwork in many corporations, the number of potential winners among the participants constitutes a small fraction—those eligible for executive bonuses.

Variable pay (read variable enrichment) for the *selected few* is a throwback to the mentality that gave birth to the I-I syndrome: thinkers at the top, doers at the bottom. Not so in today's organization. Intelligence and decision-making responsibility are diffused throughout the organization. And thus, so are the keys to success. In fact, the ideas—as pointed out several times in other chapters—that will propel an organization forward in the competitive arena are spread throughout the organization. Rewards for individual and collective effort will help tear down the mental electric fences that stand between mediocrity and greatness for a corporation.

If everyone had a stake in profits, everyone would be conscious of how they spent the company money directly and indirectly, and how their work might maximize those profits. Teamwork (and peer pressure) would be encouraged. Good work—which can be rewarding in itself—is now put in the context of monetary objective, not intellectual exercise.

If companies are to stimulate better performance without raising their compensation costs, they must do more than hold out modest and mostly set increases to salarly as incentive. For people riding herd on company expenses, base pay is like a hungry lion in a feeding frenzy. Someone needs to get control over it before its consumption reaches dangerous proportions. Companies should quit playing the escalating entitlements game by making worker income gains relative to individual, team, and company performance. For everyone.

Gains in compensation should reflect company success and risk assumed by workers. Risk is a four-letter word; but rather than offensive, most people find it foreign. The business risk idea may be unfamiliar to people who never took a business or economics course (the majority of the work force?). I recall vividly when I came to understand the concept. Early in my career, I was the news director at a radio station in Milwaukee that promoted my newscasts. The campaign was a success. I felt entitled to some additional compensation based on the increasing number of listeners to the news I gathered. I brought my righteous case to the station's general manager, who calmly replied, "Don, the radio station took the risk and spent the money on the promotion, not you. If the ad campaign were not a success, we wouldn't have cut your salary. Because it is a success, we're not going to raise it."

Stockholders must see themselves as risk takers, but people inside companies generally do not. "The major problem for those of us . . . who would like to implement [variable] compensation programs—is that of our managers and their employees not being risk takers," says compensation specialist Victor Rodriguez. "You have to culturally have them accept that, and that's not easy to do

---

Brief Aside

Executives are supposed to understand risk, and their compensation is supposed to reflect a component at risk and tied to achieving certain objectives. Critics say those bonuses have become as much an entitlement as the 5.5 percent increase at the lower ranks. "The problem is that management tends to introduce a new incentive plan the moment it appears that disappointing operating results are going to produce disappointing executive bonuses," claims Kenneth Mason, former president of the Quaker Oats Company. He says that the pay-for-performance school seems to have evolved in the keep-compensation-rising school. With executive compensation rising faster than that of the work force at large, and often irrespective of corporate performance, "Many corporate executives are receiving entrepreneurs' rewards for doing bureaucrats' jobs."

---

overnight. What you see most companies do is start with the top of the house." Rodriguez implemented a variable compensation program at Equitable Mutual Life in 1980 starting with the top 20 people. In 1985, when he left for another company, more than 6,000 Equitable employees were in the variable compensation plan.

While the idea of trading a modest albeit secure raise for compensation at risk may strike some as a wild departure, in fact, even fully salaried employees assume risk in their compensation. Their variable is 100 percent or 0 percent: employed, unemployed. Recall that fixed compensation implies no security. Still most people never think of their compensation as at risk, but it is. A variable pay program acknowledges risk and provides motivation for better than mediocre performance with the promise of better than mediocre reward.

Risk is relative and should vary by position and, like personal investments, one's capacity to assume risk. Rodriguez says a chairman might have 50 to 100 percent of compensation at risk, while someone at the lowest levels might have only 5 percent at risk. "The key to variable compensation," Rodriguez says, is that "it's got to be something that I know that I can control as an employee. That, yes, if I do [my job] very well, there should be some kind of reward." A concept familiar to every waiter.

Some companies already use incentive compensation to encourage better performance; in fact, a poll by human resource consultants **Sibson & Company** found that just over half of the surveyed companies offer variable pay programs to employees below the executive level and others are planning to add them. The largest growth of variable pay plans is at the nonexempt level, where 64 percent of companies with plans include salaried nonexempt employees and 50 percent include hourly nonexempt employees.

At Raychem, chairman Paul Cook says, "Of course, people do use financial yardsticks to measure how they're doing. So you have to pay well. We pay our people above average, but only slightly above average—60th percentile or so. Bonuses give them an opportunity to move up a fair amount based on overall corporate results and individual performance."

General Mills—which values its employees and invests in their continued training and development, and encourages teamwork with less management oversight—is testing incentive-based compensation programs and has a stated goal of putting *every* employee on a performance-based incentive program. John L. Frost, senior vice president, says that General Mills is "considerably different than most companies in that we believe that [employee] awards should parallel rewards that go to our shareholders."

Motorola ties merit raises and performance bonuses to quality goals. At Motorola's Cellular Infrastructure Group, merit pay is as much as a third of base pay. "All skill-based pay and merit pay are evaluated—and at risk—at each [employee] review," says Rick Chandler, vice president and director of manufacturing, of his manufacturing operators. The company is hoping that the incentive pay helps to reduce the need for management. Right now, the operator to supervisor ratio is 48:1. His goal is to get to 75:1, with a total ratio of all working levels to management of 30:1. To accomplish that goal of worker self-sufficiency, the Cellular Group is educating its employees and clearly communicating expectations.

At Victor Kiam's Remington, he pays a third below market compensation and encourages his workers in the factory and marketing organization to make up the difference and exceed it based on incentives. "If you produce, you'll make more," Kiam promises his people. (But he doesn't reward his accountants on an incentive program. "We don't need more paper!" he jokes.)

SOME MAVERICK PROPOSALS

Here are some ideas for your consideration. They are only starting points and represent significant challenges—with accompanying headaches and potential for greatness. These general concepts can be expanded into many possible permutations to fit particular situations.

"Time is easy to measure. Productivity, quality, and customer responsiveness are not readily assessed—especially when money is involved," warns Marc J. Wallace, the compensation expert. Poorly conceived and implemented incentive plans can do more harm than defaulting to the current flat merit increase. "Incentives cannot mask other problems," cautions Bruce Bolger, editor and publisher of *Incentive* magazine. One reason variable pay plans fail is that some employers initiate them as a "knee jerk reaction to what the competition is doing," says Charles Cumming, national director of compensation management consulting for Sibson & Company. "These programs can actually cause more harm than good if the wrong type of plan is installed." He says companies should have a clear strategy for implementing an incentive compensation plan.

Before you throw your entire organization into a state of panic and disarray over any radical change in how you pay your people, I suggest that you get professional help from consulting outfits like Sibson, Towers Perrin Forster & Crosby, or **Hewitt Associates.** You also might want to request a copy of the very helpful 32 page guide, "How to Run an Incentive Program," from *Incentive* magazine, 633 Third Ave., New York 10017. Meantime, here's some food for thought.

Devise a plan to reward workers (probably a microcosm of the whole when you start, test before you leap) by which you reward people for obtaining *explicit and specific* goals that are measurable and attainable. If you have no particular goals in mind, there is no

good reason to initiate an incentive program. Assuming you identify the mission, the program could reward individual contributions in the job function as well as work in task teams, attaining or
beating well-defined company goals, and overall company performance in a given year and over a rolling five-year period.

You may want to give people options for the level of risk they
wish to assume under the new incentive plan by reducing base
pay and/or forfeiting or reducing the amount of regular merit pay
they can receive. Increased risk could yield increased rewards
(and the converse, so you might want to be paternalistic and
restrict risk for jobs at lower pay levels).

Devise a multicomponent rating system for any increase over
current base pay:

Personal performance variable. This is most like the current, standard merit reviews. Except that you now give greater
emphasis to criteria such as initiative, creativity, and problem *identi-
fication* as well as problem-solving skills, new knowledge acquisi-
tion—company sponsored and other. Ideally, this performance
rating is tied to specific objectives determined with the employee's
input. This might constitute 50 percent of merit rewards.

Team performance variable. This underscores to mavericks that they need to function not just as Lone Rangers, but as
members of a group. At the same time, this component can
reward the unsung "Steady Eddies" who competently execute the
high achievers' big ideas. Have members of a team rate the relative contribution of their own members. If someone serves on several teams, several report cards. Administrative nightmare?
Perhaps. But that may be a small price to pay for getting the best
out of people who may not have been giving it. This might constitute 25 percent of individual merit reward.

Company performance variable. You reward for achieving whatever criteria seems appropriate, for the company as a
whole or by job function. Such criteria might include quality measures, market share, return on investment (ROI), return on equity
(ROE), customer satisfaction, profit levels, and the like. When cer-

tain sales or profit goals are a major component, you can reward greater percentages of results over target to workers. For example, if the company hits better than 105 percent of goal, some percentage of the "excess"—say 25 percent—is distributed to employees proportionately based on annual income.

Long-term variable. This encourages long-term thinking rather than "gunning and running" to obtain rewards for positive short-term results that may be counter productive in the long term. (Merck & Co. recently offered its 37,000 employees an option to buy 100 shares of company stock during a five-year period between September 1996 and September 2001. General Mills has for the past few years asked its executives to voluntarily accept company stock options in lieu of pay increases; 90 percent have. Biomet, which makes orthopedic devices, gives stock options to all employees after five years' service.) The long-term incentive could increase in value the longer a person is with the company, recognizing cumulative experience as more valuable. The long-term achievement bonus provides partial payment every year for achieving incremental progress on long-term objectives; this is a "rolling" plan with objectives and payments redefined annually.

The value of these components vary from year to year, so compensation becomes a more variable rather than fixed expense. The net effect: employees own a stake of the business they serve and are incented to perform as well as possible; at the same time, the swelling entitlements budget holds to a very modest level while other compensation components are more achievement-based and funded from incremental revenue.

How does one pay for incentives not tied to incremental revenue growth? Try taking your company's merit increase budget and setting some of it aside to use as alternative incentive pay (for example, if you budgeted a total merit increase of six percent, set three percent aside). Remember to allocate some of that new incentive budget to cover new administrative and communication costs (which certainly will be high in the first year of the new plan). Use the now-reduced merit budget as the component to pay the standard individual merit increase for the average performers,

---

Brief Aside

Benefit costs now amount to 37.6 percent of payroll expense. This includes days off, medical benefits, unemployment insurance, pensions, etc. All these goodies come from the same pot of money as payroll, yet they are invisible to—or at least taken for granted by—most employees. Companies make a tragic mistake by not communicating the true dollar value of the benefits they provide to their workers.

If someone enrolled in a group plan quits work to strike out on his or her own, they'd be in for a severe shock when trying to replace all the benefits they receive at good old Paternal, Inc. Every paycheck should carry a statement as to the value of benefits received during the pay period and year to date. And companies should do a better job of communicating how those costs have escalated almost exponentially in recent years.

Corporations spend real dollars for services of great value that they can't use to pay dividends or increase salaries. Those points need to be made.

Millions of full-time workers have no health insurance while millions of others take it for granted.

---

and the remaining pool to motivate the higher fliers with heavier rewards.

Reducing the rate of increase to base pay by shrinking merit increases limits the company's fixed-expense obligation. It also keeps top performance constantly in the mind of workers who expect an ever-expanding salary (because they equate it with an assessment of their self-worth). Variable pay minimizes the *I can relax a little now because I've made it* attitude in people who've reached a comfortable salary level. Additionally, the smaller merit component to overall compensation relieves a company from forever paying a large and continually higher base that may have resulted from one good year's performance five or ten years ago. Under the current system in most companies, the merit pay received for today's performance constitutes an ever-growing obligation until retirement.

BONUS ON THE SPOT

Let's say the foregoing suggestions are too radical (or complex) for what your organization can reasonably implement right now. Here's an alternative: take a much smaller percent of the compensation budget and set it aside for spot bonus and special recognition awards. You might make it one percent of the regularly budgeted compensation budget (reducing the merit increase allowance accordingly). Take that special allowance and distribute it among managers who are given a quarterly allotment, based on the number of people they supervise, for use as special achievement bonuses for their people. Here's how it works: You see someone knock themselves out solving a customer problem, or creating a solution to fix a vexing process, or working night and day to meet a deadline, and presto!, you hand him or her $100 or $500, maybe $1,000 or more. Or alternatively, a gift certificate redeemable for entertainment, travel, or merchandise (these kinds of awards have a special panache, "trophy value"—you can't spend them paying for junior's braces).

"You want to tap the individual performer on the shoulder as soon as possible after that event that made them a winner," advises Victor Rodriguez. "You don't want to have to go all the way up the chain of command. That's where a lot of companies run into a problem," Rodriguez says. "They're afraid to let it go down to first-level management." (It's now a familiar refrain, but if there were more trust in the workplace, work would be so much better!)

Unlike annual bonuses that become entitlements charged with great expectations, spot bonuses employ the element of pleasant surprise, and help to immediately associate the reward with the action it rewards. And it says, loud and clear, we see what you're doing, and it's appreciated. A psychic paycheck one can take to the bank!

Federal Express managers can give employees spot awards they call Bravo Zulu (Navy jargon for well-done). The BZ awards of cash, dinner, or gift certificates are worth about $50. When customers compliment employee service, the FedEx heroes are eligible for a coveted Golden Falcon award that comes with ten shares of company stock and personal recognition by Federal Express's chief operating officer.

The Veterans Administration's Philadelphia regional office uses spot bonuses. Managers receive a stack of On-the-Spot awards—worth $25 each—they can give to employees who go beyond the call of duty. This VA office also puts an interesting twist on the spot bonus idea and uses it to reinforce teamwork among its employees. Every worker, during the month of his or her birthday, receives the right to hand out a spot bonus to a fellow worker who admirably serves internal customers. The Extra Step award is worth $30 cash.

You can also use spot bonus money to pay for programs that reinforce desired behavior without assigning a precise monetary value to it. That puts the spotlight on appreciation, not compensation. At Fran Tarkenton's Knowledgeware, it's not just salespeople who go to Hawaii for outstanding performance. In a recent trip where 51 people—out of 800—qualified for the company's Sterling Club, the group included a receptionist, computer room operator, and a shipping and receiving employee.

Business Incentives markets a program that features lottery-type cards that managers can hand to their star performers. The cards reveal randomly selected combinations that represent prizes of varying amounts. By using this system, the thrill of winning an unexpected bonus is compounded by the excitement of chance. A similar tack was taken by an enterprising telemarketing manager for Citibank who stuffed balloons with $500 worth of cash in amounts ranging from $10 to $100. He put helium in the balloons. At the end of a shift, all the telemarketers who had made their dialing quotas were handed a long stick with a pin at the end and told to take their best shot, keeping whatever they found inside their balloon. Performance and chance married to yield some fun in what can be a repetitive and very discouraging job.

Finally, if you can't bear to change the time-honored flat annual salary merit increase method of rewarding performance, here's a helpful suggestion from Victor Rodriguez at Continental Insurance. Point out to the achiever receiving more than the average increase that it represents proportionately more recognition; stress the ratio. "So, if I give the average performer 4 percent and I'm giving the better performer the 8 percent increase, that's 200% and that sounds like a bigger number."

Chapter Seven

Stuffing the Suggestion Box: A Systems Approach

If we're going to be competitive in the world market, we have to do things better each year. One way to do that is to formalize the process of people contributing ideas.

Syd Kershaw, Parker Hannifin Corp.

We're talking about a baby boom generation that grew up asking 'why, why, why.' Asking them to come up with new ideas could be a way to satisfy their questioning minds.

James Canada, American Airlines

Helpful suggestions do not have to be either high-tech or a major departure. It can be something like: 'We now make two copies of this document, but we really only need one.'

Cynthia McCabe, Ohio Bell

Money is the incentive that gets people interested in these programs, but it is the excitement of seeing changes adopted that keeps people interested. People seem to be much more interested in the company when they think they've contributed new ideas to it.

Howard Schimerling, San Diego Gas & Electric Co.

While the Maverick Manager encourages and welcomes ideas, some proposals that mavericks and achievers-in-waiting want to offer their organization can't be evaluated or acted on by their own managers—their scope exceeds the manager's influence. Someone in shipping with a great idea for marketing probably won't get very far lobbying the shipping manager. What organizations need is an ingenuity pipeline that gets bright ideas from anywhere in the organization to anywhere in the organization.

FROM BOX TO BIG-TIME

Enter the suggestion box. It's a tradition that goes back nearly a hundred years. To April 8, 1898, to be exact. That's when William M. Connor, an Eastman Kodak worker scrawled on a suggestion blank the following historic words: "I suggest that the windows in Black Paper Slitting room be washed." For taking the time to improve the environment at Kodak, Connor received $2.

The timeworn suggestion box is an easy target for funmaking. A reporter for the *Cleveland Plain Dealer* wrote, "Years ago, many employee suggestion programs amounted to dusty, rarely opened boxes with scrap paper and pencil stubs, often used by workers to write nasty notes to the company or their bosses." In many companies, today's suggestion box is still unassuming, but now it's venerable, backed by a computerized tracking system, a committee of workers who evaluate suggestions made by their peers, and often, glitzy awards or significant cash payouts. The well-designed and well-run suggestion system is a powerful management tool that publicly invites innovative thinking and communicates to employees, Your ideas count around here.

In Kodak's case, from the humble $2 payout nearly a century ago, its suggestion system now pays out millions in award money annually for the multiple millions more it realizes in savings generated by employee ideas. The company receives about 9 suggestions for every 10 employees. (Only about 40 percent of the work force actually submits suggestions in a given year; the average is raised by prolific suggestors. Still, the percent participating in Kodak's suggestion program is many times the national average.)

In 1942, about a half century after Kodak first bolted its suggestion box to a wall, officials from 35 companies got together and formed an organization that today is known as the **National Association of Suggestion Systems (NASS)**. Now its members number more than 900 organizations—public as well as private, including the U.S. Army—with nearly 13 million employees. Members exchange information and serve as a resource to one another for improving their suggestion programs. NASS members reported saving $2.3 billion from worker suggestions in 1990 alone, an increase of 15 percent over the previous year. Award payments to enterprising employees whose suggestions were adopted totaled $161 million.

NASS-member employees suggest new products, devise ways to cut manufacturing costs, and propose better ways to serve customers. Here are just a few examples. A nurse and a physician suggested that Kaiser Permanente's San Francisco Medical Center set up a high-risk perinatal center to reduce the backlog of high-risk patients in the labor and delivery unit; the resulting savings amounted to over three-quarters of a million dollars in one year alone.

An employee of U S West Communications devised a better way of connecting fiber optic cables between customer switching equipment and a central office. That innovation saved U S West $142,000 and earned the enterprising employee $19,000.

Joseph Grisbach labored for Baltimore Gas & Electric for almost 38 years. He had an idea he thought management should consider, and submitted a suggestion to the company's Work Smarter program. The proposal: install in the city the same less-expensive vaults the company used for electrical hookups in rural areas. Management studied the concept for a year and determined the savings would amount to more than $115,000 in the coming three years. Joseph Grisbach received nearly $12,000 for his creative proposal that the company make better use of its technology.

Stephen Schroeder, a civilian electronics technician at a navy air station in California with 29 years of government service, became frustrated with trying to buy some electronic replacement parts. To special order the few he needed would make the per unit cost astronomical. He was sure other military agencies must use a comparable part. He discovered that they did—but each purchasing unit in the Department of Defense issued its own purchasing specifications and cataloged parts under unique identifiers. No catalog of interchangeable parts existed for the various military units. Schroeder suggested a computerized system for Defense Department agencies to exchange technical information on components with multiple application possibilities, thereby reducing procurement expenses. That computer system now cross-indexes 137 government databases and saves taxpayers an estimated $700 million. For his initiative, Schroeder was awarded $35,000, the most a civilian can earn in a government suggestion program.

SUGGESTIONS FOR SUCCESSFUL SUGGESTIONS

A suggestion system can open up a channel for everyone in an organization to share their good thinking and have it formally considered by the company. NASS offers the following 10 tips (shown here in bold) for running a suggestion program. I've added a few thoughts following each NASS recommendation.

1. **Enlist the support of top management; this support is essential to the success of the program.** Human Resources can initiate a suggestion program, but if senior management doesn't talk it up and sanction it with enthusiasm, the potential impact is far diminished. Successful suggestion programs require an investment in administrative and promotional support on an ongoing basis. If throwing a spotlight on the old suggestion box amounts to this month's hot program, results surely will disappoint.

2. **Determine the objectives top management hopes to achieve through the program.** Some company programs focus almost exclu-

sively on cost cutting; some on quality or customer satisfaction improvement. Some programs welcome suggestions on improving worker benefits, others specifically exclude it. Whatever is fair game in your shop should be communicated clearly to all eligible participants so no one invests time and energy making suggestions the organization isn't prepared to implement or even consider.

3. **Provide an environment in which managers and supervisors are receptive to ideas from others.** Ideas out of the suggestion box aren't approved in a vacuum or implemented by fiat. To evaluate employee proposals adequately, front-line managers must be willing to question current procedures and recognize, even embrace, a better way of doing things. A suggestion program in a prevailing atmosphere of, We've never done it *that* way (or, We've always done it *this* way), will do little to improve the business, and may actually demoralize workers whose expectations for greater work involvement were raised falsely.

4. **Designate an individual to administer the program; this person does not accept or reject suggestions but acts as a liaison between employees and management. (Suggestions should be forwarded to the manager whose area the suggestion would affect.)** Some organizations assemble a committee of employees representing various functional areas and levels of position to monitor suggestions. This employee involvement keeps the program on the up and up in the minds of the work force and, because of the collective experience in the group, often can spare functional managers from responding to suggestions that propose unrealistic, redundant, or extraneous solutions.

5. **Determine an awards schedule and be prepared to follow through with it.** Cash is still the predominate form of award, although some companies use savings bonds, merchandise, and other noncash awards such as tickets to theater performances and ball games. Commonly, companies award suggesters with somewhere between 7 and 10 percent of the estimated first-year savings realized by their ideas, and give nominal awards for ideas that improve the organization but are unquantifiable. Furniture maker Modern of Marshfield, in Marshfield, Wisconsin, awards employees 10 percent of the first-year savings. Plus, to sweeten the pot and encourage more participation, Modern sets aside an additional 10 percent that it splits between all

employees who had an idea adopted in that calendar year. (A discussion on the merits of cash versus other awards appears below.)

6. **Inform employees about the plan with a written announcement explaining how the system works, how they can turn in suggestions, and how they will benefit from the program.** Effectively setting expectations is the key to success. If employees might not receive an answer on the disposition of their suggestion for several months, they should know that. If cash awards are capped at some amount, they should know that. If two people make the same suggestion, and it's first-come-only rewarded, they should know that, too.

7. **Publicize the program on a regular basis, through an employee newsletter, bulletin board, or other means.** Every great idea loses impact when it becomes commonplace. The suggestion program competes for employee attention along with a million other distractions in and out of work. Keep the program fresh and "top of mind" by merchandising it. A catchy name and logo lend themselves to promotions that attract attention.

At my company, we put up colorful posters proclaiming, You don't have to be a genius to have a bright idea. Even eye-catching posters lose effectiveness as they become familiar fixtures on the landscape; when we notice suggestions dwindling in number, we move the posters and responses increase! To focus attention on the potential rewards the system offers, our monthly newsletter carries a regular column on the suggestion committee meetings, and prominently displays photos of award winners receiving their checks. Another way to promote the program more fully is to recognize everyone who participates in evaluating and implementing a suggestion with a certificate of appreciation.

8. **Respond promptly to each suggestion, whether or not it is adopted, with a letter explaining the company's decision and the reason for it.** The suggestion should be acknowledged immediately upon receipt, thanking the employee for participating and indicating the likely time frame for judgment on the employee's recommendation. A common response might be, Interesting idea, tell us more about what you had in mind. The information-gathering responsibility can be shared between the system administrator and members of the committee. Some programs, such as at Ohio

---

Brief Aside

Giving a suggestion program a cute name may or may not encourage useful submissions, but cute names abound. Here is a sampling: I CARE (Ideas Can Assist in Reducing Expenses), Genesee Brewing Co.; The 10% Solution (employees receive 10 percent of estimated first-year savings), San Diego Gas & Electric; *GENIUS* (Generating New Ideas Uncovers Savings), Matthew Bender & Co.; *IdeAAs in Action*, American Airlines; I-POWER (for the power of concepts like imagination, ideas, innovation, industriousness, all starting with letter *i*), Boardroom, Inc.; IdeaClub, Philip Morris; Enter-Prize, Ohio Bell; and *CARE* (Creative And Resourceful Employees), Kaiser Permanente.

Bell, require the suggestor to fully investigate a suggestion to determine its merits.

When an idea is rejected, the suggestor shouldn't receive a form letter saying thanks but no thanks. The suggestor is entitled to a personalized and thoughtful explanation of the investigation his or her proposal received, and the rationale for rejection of the idea. Anything less invalidates the program.

9. **Keep complete and accurate records of all transactions relating to the suggestion system; this helps to ensure proper allocation of awards and prevents duplication of payments.** NASS reports that over 80 percent of its members have computerized their systems. The more successful a program, the more a computer is necessary. The collective memory of the administrator and committee members isn't reliable as time passes and suggestions grow in number.

Another reason to computerize: an idea suggested three years ago may have seemed ahead of its time; today, when it's suggested by someone else, it catches the imagination of those who can implement it. Should the original suggestor be paid? Rules should make that clear in advance; and the computer database program should produce the name of the person who submitted the original version, the date the suggestion was received, the reason the suggestion was not accepted, and the names of the people who made that decision. Because of its importance, the computer database should be maintained by professional staff on a constant basis. This function is too important to be left to volunteers with many other responsibilities tugging at them. 10. **Whenever possible, have an officer of the company make the presentation of major awards for suggestions which have been accepted.** High-level recognition (along with a little pomp and pizzazz) provide as much motivation as the tangible award, and perhaps more. While the company president may not make the presentation, he or she can telegraph support by sending letters of congratulations to winners, mentioning support for the program in employee communications and encouraging other managers to talk up the program.

Here are a few other thoughts garnered from my experience on a suggestion committee.

Fully investigate submitted ideas and overcome the urge to "blow-off" ideas that may seem frivolous. Shortly after helping to set up my company's suggestion program, our committee received a suggestion to remove the fresh flowers in the reception area as an austerity move. Some around the table snickered. We discussed the relative merits of greeting our guests with fresh rather than faux flowers. Then our young committee decided to consider the suggestion in earnest, and assigned a member to quantify the flower expenditure. At the next meeting, several jaws dropped when the flower investigation revealed that the company was spending several thousand dollars for fresh flowers, not only for the reception area, but also for hallways and offices in the executive wing. Let them have silk flowers! was the consensus of the group comprised of both nonexempt and exempt representatives from each major functional area.

The committee voted to retain fresh flowers in the lobby as a quality greeting to visitors, but to excise excess foliage from the executive quarters. Senior management agreed, and the company pared more than $5,000 in operating expenses. The suggestor received a check for more than $500 for a suggestion that wasn't implemented precisely as prescribed, but which led to a cost savings nonetheless.

Involve the suggestor in testing the suggestion's merit. The employee involvement helps to ensure the proposal is fully evaluated, and participants derive a greater sense of company cooperation out of the experience.

Empower the suggestion committee to take apparently valid suggestions to levels above a yeah-butting manager suffering from the Idea-Inertia syndrome. Change scares some people so much that they reject even valid, beneficial ideas with little or no consideration. No one manager should have the power to kill an idea with prima facie potential.

Assure swift resolution of pending suggestions. Many companies wrestle with suggestion system backlogs, some going back *years.* Interminable delays on deciding the fate of one's suggestion does nothing to endear the program to the work force. Receipt of a suggestion should be acknowledged immediately, with a projected date for when a decision can be expected. If anyone must wait more than 90 days, they should receive an interim status report assuring them that their suggestion is still under review and outlining action to date. (Possible solution for overwhelmed systems: special review committees for suggestions concerning specific functional areas.)

Offer wide eligibility to participate. Many suggestion programs exist in manufacturing environments where incremental improvements in process can be quantified as specific dollar savings, and where tradition implied that workers weren't paid to think. Off the factory floor, savings often are harder to specify, and managers are presumed to be compensated for contributing all their ideas. Many companies' programs specifically prohibit managers from participating in the company suggestion program—a tragic foreclosure on original thinking.

Because an idea's potential value may not be quantified easily is no reason not to consider it. Managers already may be paid to think, but that doesn't assure the company that their innovative ideas receive an adequate reception and careful consideration. Not every Maverick Manager works yet for a boss who welcomes new ideas with enthusiasm. The company suggestion system offers an independent conduit for consideration of ideas, especially those ideas not within one's boss's functional area of expertise.

Customize the program to your culture. My company has three major offices and three different suggestion programs, each developed mindful of local conditions and preferences.

VARIATIONS ON THE THEME

Some companies evolve different kinds of suggestions systems. Instead of an appointed committee ruling on centrally deposited suggestions, management routinely invites worker ideas and dutifully acts on them. At Ritz-Carlton Hotels, managers respect their carefully recruited and trained workers. The corporate culture supporting the elegant inns calls for managers to foster employees' pride in their work. The hostelers pledge to make an employee's work as efficient and enjoyable as possible by recognizing that the person doing the work understands it intimately. Employees are encouraged to make suggestions on improving service and workflow, and managers are obligated to implement any reasonable suggestion at least on a trial basis. "Participating in the design of their work gives workers more pride in their work so they do better work," is the way one Ritz-Carlton banquet manager explained the system.

If it's not broken, you haven't looked closely enough, is the guiding principle behind Ritz-Carlton's Quality Network program designed to tap employee initiative. For example, a major recycling system was driven by a room-service waiter. After the waiter proposed the idea, management asked him to research the program. Armed with impressive findings, the young man appeared before the hotel's executive committee which authorized the purchase of some expensive machinery. "Our resulting environmental waste-management program is a success," declares Horst Schulze, president of Ritz-Carlton. That recycling system is now paying for itself with fees for recycled materials, and reduced trash pickups.

Employees at Baldrige Award-winning Milliken & Co. can post quality improvement suggestions on their department bulletin boards. They can expect that within 24 hours, their managers will respond to a suggestion, and within three days explain what action they plan to take.

Gargantuan General Electric (nearly $60 billion in sales of everything from clock radios to locomotives) pioneered an innovative system for soliciting no-holds-barred suggestions. It uses an open meeting, called a Work-Out, where managers literally face their staffs' complaints and recommendations. Here's how the

Work-Out works. Employees at all levels go offsite for three days of head-knocking on productivity issues. Divided into small teams facilitated by an outside consultant, employees spend two days cooking up a menu of ways to make their work better. On the third day, the boss—who hasn't been in on the meetings—stands before the assembled workers to hear their rapid-fire proposals. By the Work-Out rules, the boss must respond to a suggestion in one of three ways: approve it, deny it, or ask for more information. Invoking the last option requires the manager to assign a team to get the necessary information by a declared deadline.

GE's Work-Outs have trimmed millions of unnecessary forms and dollars wasted on inefficient expenditures and procedures. Support for the process is a criterion in a manager's annual review. The process has caught on with workers who occasionally get together for their own impromptu Work-Out sessions. Since GE debuted the Work-Out system in 1989, both productivity and ROI headed upwards.

Boardroom, Inc. which publishes *Boardroom Reports* (a fortnightly newsletter jammed with useful management insights) developed a simple system that an individual Maverick Manager could adopt in his or her own department without a formal, companywide system in place. Boardroom requires its staff members to come to meetings with ideas to save money, make money, or improve work. When staffers reveal their thinking, they are rewarded with candy, dollar bills given out singly or in pairs, and, alternatively, bangs on a gong or honks from a hunter's horn. (In contrast, an executive I know excuses from a meeting anyone who comes up with three good ideas during its course. Is that negative or positive reinforcement?)

Martin Edelston, Boardroom president, swears his modest rewards and noisemaking have encouraged plenty of ideas to improve company performance. "The flow of ideas has *increased*, rather than decreased, as the program has gained momentum." He attributes hundred of thousands of dollars in savings and better business operations to the merriment. Edelston reports that his staff see themselves as agents for change, with better attendance records and more team spirit than before. Edelston commits himself to following up on every idea and reporting its disposition to the suggestor. Monthly, Edelston circulates a report listing the recently submitted ideas with a ranking of each idea (those in the top rank receive $10; the contributor with the most top-ranked ideas in a month receives an additional $50). Managers meet to pick the idea of the month for an award of two tickets to a show or concert. When an idea results in big-money savings, the company makes a special cash award.

REWARDING INNOVATION

All suggestion systems benefit from rewarding eligible suggestions (those meeting the criteria for possible reward) with a visible sign of appreciation. The first step is to show gratitude for simply participating in the program. In our company, we distribute mugs imprinted with the suggestion program's logo featuring Albert Einstein, and the words, "Genius at Work." Some companies distribute lapel pins, hats, sweatshirts, or plaques.

When it's time to give an award for winning ideas, the great debate is evoked: Cash versus Merchandise. Experts disagree on which makes a better incentive. As someone who has designed incentive programs for hundreds of salespeople, I can attest that each kind of incentive works for some people some of the time. Here for your enlightenment and confusion are the leading arguments for each reward type.

Merchandise. Noncash awards can satisfy emotional "wants" (stereos, trips, and the like are more rewarding because they're purely indulgent). If cash goes to pay normal household obligations like groceries or the electric bill, it's quickly forgotten. Merchandise, which has a life of a few years, serves as a sustaining reminder of the reward for achievement, which may help build loyalty. Cash, once it's spent, quickly is out of mind forever. Merchandise has "trophy" or showoff value ("See my new TV? My company gave me that as a special award."). Bragging about the money one earns, even as a special award, is considered boorish.

Cash, unless it's offered in huge amounts, doesn't promote as easily. Prizes, on the other hand, can tie to a theme (Fun in the Sun, Let's Get Cookin', From Here to There). As prizes change, you can stir up new interest in the suggestion program. Dollar for dollar invested, merchandise can offer more sizzle than money. For example, giving a winner a choice between a nice totebag, umbrella, or clock radio might be more enticing than $20 (which turns out to be a check for less than that after mandatory tax deductions take their pinch). Cash awards may also be misconstrued as raising a worker's basic compensation rather than a one-time special award.

A caution on offering noncash awards. To be effective, motivational awards must appeal to those you want to reward. If someone gave me an all-expense-paid trip to the world's best golf resort, it would mean little to me because I don't golf (a trip to a ski resort, that's a different story!). At Briggs & Stratton in Milwaukee, hourly workers who make suggestions receive gift certificates to J. C. Penney. Chuck Loose, a manufacturing administrator, says those certificates "get the whole family involved . . . [allowing] them all to enjoy something special instead of just buying groceries with prize money."

Cash. Money is universally appealing, especially to low-wage earners who can use a few extra dollars a lot more than a new toaster. While trinkets and trips promote well, no one doesn't want more money. Cash allows winners to buy precisely the reward they want; I might want $50 to put toward a new car stereo more than any of the prizes the company offers me.

Cash leaves no doubt as to the value the company put on the suggestion. Merchandise bought at wholesale might lead the employee to believe that he or she received less than full value from the company. A related objection to merchandise arises at tax time when the 1099 income statement shows the value of a prize to be more than what an individual believes she can purchase the product herself. Cash awards are much easier to distribute than other prizes that can involve many administrative chores before they reach the winners. And cash—when it really is cash—presents well publicly when crisp bills are snapped and then handed to the fortunate recipients.

The most powerful incentive may well be *recognition*. While the case for publicly conferring credit for worker contributions is made in Chapter 5, here's a powerful testimonial to its effect on the suggestion program at Corning, Inc. "Last year, we received more than 18,000 suggestions from employees," says James R. Houghton, Corning chairman. Significantly, that number was "about 11 times as many as we got in the best year under our old system where we offered money for useful ideas. (As did—or do—

many companies.) Now there's no money, simply some form of recognition—the employee's name on a board, a coffee mug, a bouquet of flowers, a free meal. There's no more eloquent testimony to the power of Quality than this. Clearly, people *want* to be productive, they *want* to contribute, they *want* to be involved." [emphasis in original]

KAIZEN AND OTHER CONSIDERATIONS

A suggestion system is no substitute for the ingenuity-enhancing practices of the Maverick Manager. Bosses cannot defer their idea-fostering responsibilities to the company suggestion program. Many of the continuous improvements that ratchet up an enterprise from competence to greatness will never find their way into the company's formal suggestion system. Small incremental adjustments to one's work environment often don't find their way into the elaborate suggestion systems found in many companies. NASS statistics indicate that the average suggestion results in savings of more than $7,000, resulting in an award of about $500. Those statistics impress both company officials and workers. But promoting large savings and awards may actually discourage employees from submitting the hundred small improvement ideas that will influence day-to-day work quality more than the larger award winners.

In Japan, suggestion systems work just the opposite. There, an ethic known as *kaizen* (constant improvement) encourages workers to continually think about bettering their work (and to fill out suggestion cards in their off-hours, outside work). This expectation by Japanese management yields far, far more suggestions per capita: about 2,500 suggestions annually per 100 employees. In contrast, only a dozen suggestions per 100 American workers are submitted. The actual number of people making suggestions also contrasts sharply; in Japan, two thirds of the work force drop cards into the suggestion box, while only 9 percent of American workers do. Surely there are cultural issues that explain some of the differences; the Japanese historically have emphasized individual contribution for the betterment of the society. Perhaps, too, management attitudes have much to do with the stark differences in participation. Japanese managers not only expect worker proposals, many companies educate workers on how to *think* about improving their jobs.

While Americans adopt fewer than one in three suggestions submitted, Japanese managers implement four out of five. The Japanese workers make suggestions that individually have a smaller monetary value than employee ideas implemented in the United States (resulting in much smaller award payments to Japanese suggestors, about $3 on average). All those small improvements add up to cut costs and improve productivity significantly— the average savings per employee in Japanese companies is *10 times* that for their American counterparts.

Formal suggestion programs lend themselves to improving existing operations only in quantifiable ways (Modify this part to eliminate wear; Change that process to speed it up). More qualitative improvements (Wouldn't our customers prefer us to give them a choice in shipping/ billing/ model colors?) stem from a more inventive attitude prevailing throughout the organization. That results from a maverick culture, and that is the subject of the next chapter.

Chapter 8

Encouraging Innovation: Evolving a Maverick Culture

The key is to see the dynamic within the static.

Robert M. Pirsig

The IQ of the team can potentially be much greater than the IQ of the individuals.

Peter M. Senge

Peak-performing teams inspire peak-performing individuals, and . . . peak-performing individuals build peak-performing teams.

Charles Garfield

We're all smarter than we realize. We're all more educable than we realize. Better thinking in an organization is not a matter of smart hiring, it is a matter of setting up the processes and systems to allow information and technology to flow, to encourage people to think, and allowing that thinking to be used.

Thomas A. Stewart

American managers need to get off their asses and implement innovation in their organizations—not think about it, not talk about it, do it! Think, implement. Think, implement. Think, implement. They need an on-going system to implement innovation, not just go to seminars about it.

Raymond A. Slesinski

To be an innovative company, you have to ask for innovation. You assemble a group of talented people who are eager to do new things and put them in an environment where innovation is expected. It's that simple—and that hard.

Paul Cook

"It translates — 'but we've always done it this way - why change?'."

THE GAMES LAB JUST BEFORE
THE BIG BREAKTHROUGH

In the introduction to this book, I suggested that American businesses need to innovate to compete with many other economic powerhouses from around the world (some emerging almost daily, it seems). The word *compete* comes from the Latin *competere* which means to strive together. The very essence of competing is working toward a goal as a team. With that in mind, the real competitive challenge may be less from other companies selling similar goods and services, and more in overcoming shortcomings within our own organizations.

Popular business literature dwells on the competitive threat from companies based in Japan. A cooperative, duty-bound, society-before-the-individual culture, apparently prepares them to fare well in the competitive world economy. In American culture, businesses draw on a rich heritage of entrepreneuring and Yankee ingenuity—backed by abundant natural resources—to blaze economic trails. Is the rugged, imaginative and will-driven spirit that gave the world incandescent lighting, global communications, and miracle medicines in danger of losing its utility?

One might argue that the creative American spirit isn't so prevalent anyway. Edward L. Hennessy, Jr., chairman and CEO of Allied-Signal, Inc., believes that U.S. industrialists became complacent in the face of their success. "America's real strength *is* its culture. We produced a nation of free-thinking individuals, then unleashed the forces of creativity and enterprise on the road to building the mightiest manufacturing machine in the world. It's no accident that the Japanese learned many of their manufacturing techniques from Americans. But then something happened. Somewhere along the way, we stopped *challenging* ourselves. We stopped asking the hard questions . . . and demanding thorough answers. This created a vacuum which the Japanese and other foreign competitors were only too eager to fill."

Many companies abandoned the innovating entrepreneur's ethic some time ago in favor of safe, error-preventing bureaucracy. "Most companies are designed for the steady state rather than the always threatening uncertainty of the truly new," concludes R. Donald Gamache, chairman of business creativity firm **INNOTECH**. Competing through ingenuity isn't necessarily about the battle of the breakthroughs. (Many companies don't capitalize on their breakthroughs anyway. Classic examples:

Ampex developed videotape technology; Sony introduced it to consumers. Xerox pioneered mouse-based and icon-based computing, Apple brought it successfully to market.)

Competing through creativity is about constant, incremental innovation by everyone in the organization who in turn cooperates, in a systematic way, with everyone else in it. That means attention to process improvement as well as product development. Economist Marie-Louise Caravatti studied more than 1,100 large American manufacturing companies for the Federal Trade Commission. She found that a "disproportionate 81 percent of American corporate money went to product innovation and only 19 percent to process innovation." Of Japanese companies she surveyed, only 17 percent engaged in new product development while 26 percent were improving their manufacturing processes and 46 percent were adopting technology developed by others.

The question is not which nation's cultural orientation should prevail. The model for successfully competing in the new world economy melds both the traditional Japanese and American orientations. That new paradigm blends initiative and creativity with cooperation and efficiency. It is neither radical nor experimental.

SUCCESSFUL CULTURES OF INNOVATION

In several preceding chapters, I tried to make good on my promise to speak to the actions that individual maverick managers can take to influence directly the people who report to them. In this chapter, I'll take a broader look at corporate policies that encourage innovation. As renowned Chinese military strategist Sun Tzu observed in *The Art of War*, "Generally, management of many is the same as management of few. It is a matter of organization."

Throughout this book, I've suggested that everyone is a potential font of innovation and that management's task is to tap the organization's bottomless reservoir of creativity. Managers must also channel those ideas and see to it that they are put to work; gee-whiz invention is not a reason for being in business. Christopher Columbus's landing on America 500 years ago would have held little significance if he had not been followed by settlers who worked to develop the opportunity. And we'd all still be living in

drafty log cabins without indoor lighting or plumbing if those settlers hadn't innovated ways to improve the methods of everyday
life.

A corporate culture of innovation isn't necessarily one that's
identified simply by the size of the R&D budget or the frequency
with which executives participate in brainstorming meetings. A
corporation that's truly innovative approaches novel ideas with
rigorous discipline. Idea generating sessions aren't games for
relief, they're drills for results on specifically defined problems or
opportunities. Promising proposals emanating from R&D laboratories, market research, or staff meetings are subjected to defined
criteria (see Chapters 7 and 9). And then, the concept becomes
reality only after sufficient sweat investment. As Paul Cook, chairman of the Raychem Corporation, says, "What separates the winners and losers in innovation is who masters the drudgery . . . the
real work—reducing the idea to practice."

Some highly successful companies have mastered that drudgery.
While the examples that follow are mostly from huge public companies (because they've had to grapple with these issues sooner rather
than later to protect their large interests, and because information on
them is readily available), the lessons they offer us can apply to most
any enterprise. (After all, the big boys didn't get to be big boys by
accident; and each has large competitors that aren't so successful,
despite their size. We can profit from the winners' significant investment in developing their successful methods.)

Wal-Mart, the discount-store chain based in Bentonville,
Arkansas, with sales over $25 billion beats larger competitors
Sears and K mart on profits as a percent of sales. It ranks as one of
the 10-most-admired corporations in *Fortune* magazine's annual
poll of U.S. executives. CEO David Glass says, "We have no
superstars at Wal-Mart. We have average people operating in an
environment that encourages everyone to perform above average." The firm encourages its store department managers to run
their corner of the shop as though it were their own business.
"Instead of having one entrepreneur who founded the business,
we have got 250,000 entrepreneurs out there running their part of
the business," Glass explains.

For five straight years, that *Fortune* magazine poll ranking
America's most-admired corporations ranked pharmaceutical-

maker Merck number one. Grabbing the top honors for five straight years is a feat no other company has matched. Between 1985 and 1990, Merck sales doubled while the number of employees rose by only 10 percent. The company ranks 63rd on *Fortune* magazine's list of 500 top industrial companies, but ranks 10th in profits, and 5th in profits behind such larger firms as IBM, Exxon, GE, and Philip Morris. Merck wasn't simply riding the wave of rising health care costs to its profitable success. CEO P. Roy Vagelos, M.D., points out, "The lion's share of this growth has come from increased volume, not price increases. In 1990, for example, sales were up 17 percent; of that, 12 percent came from increases in volume, only 2 percent came from price increases."

What makes Merck so successful? It has a culture of innovation. The world's largest maker of prescription drugs, Merck has invented more new medicines than any other U.S. pharmaceutical company. Since the beginning of the 1980s, the company increased its R&D spending by 14 percent per year. CEO Vagelos says, "The competition in our field is enormous, and the more original thinkers we have, the better I like it." He recruits some of the best minds in medicine to work at Merck, and the innovative spirit carries right through to the factory floor. For example, a team of packaging line workers at Merck Chemical Manufacturing Division suggested that the company switch from square bottles to round ones, and saved the firm nearly $250,000 in downtime.

Merck pays its people well, treats them with respect, and works their tails off. In a periodic employee survey, nearly 10,000 employees (better than half the work force) responded to questions about their satisfaction with the company. In 1990, 84 percent of Merck's employees rated the firm as a better place to work than other companies they knew. Merck management compares its survey results with 30 other large companies (which belong to an organization known as the Mayflower Group) such as AT&T, IBM, Du Pont, and Johnson & Johnson. Merck's 84 percent satisfaction rate compares to a 54 percent average rating for the other companies. Interestingly, in one category Merck employees scored significantly less favorably than the norm: workload—workers feel overworked. Still, a solid majority, 68 percent, are pleased with their pay. At those other firms where people don't feel so burdened, only 43 percent were satisfied with their pay.

A legendary leader in innovation is Minnesota Mining and Manufacturing (which also makes the top-ten list of most-admired companies). 3M makes and sells some 60,000 different products, including 900 varieties of pressure-sensitive tapes (for everything from disposable diapers to tapes so strong they compete with bolts, rivets, and other metal fasteners). One of the reasons 3M makes everything from fire-fighting foams to photographic films and medical imaging systems (as well as Scotch™ Tape and Post-it™ Notes) is that innovation is the leading tenet in the corporate creed. No matter how many winners it has, 3M is never satisfied with its product line. Divisions are expected to generate 25 percent of their sales each year from products that were introduced in the last five years. Researchers are encouraged to spend up to 15 percent of their time thinking about or tinkering with new ideas that might (or might not) lead to some new innovation. Products developed from employees' ideas account for some 70 percent of 3M's sales.

To make sure that 3M's diverse units share technologies, the company sponsors tradeshows for the exchange of information between employees from different divisions. They might well find profitable new applications for technologies developed on the other side of the house. Former CEO Lewis W. Lehr once observed, "The real mother of invention may not be necessity. It is opportunity."

With its commitment to innovation, 3M keeps finding and exploiting opportunity. In 1990, more than 30 percent of the company's sales came from products introduced in the previous five years. Despite a soft U.S. economy that grew 1 percent, 3M achieved record sales and earnings with net sales up 8.6 percent, and earnings per share up 5.5 percent. 3M invests in its continuing success; also in 1990, research and development expenditures rose 10.4 percent to $865 million. Those R&D expenses equalled 6.6 percent of sales.

While its renowned laboratories were cranking out new inventions, 3M put its innovative thinking to work on the productivity of its processes. On a worldwide basis, the company cut the amount of labor necessary to produce its products by 35 percent.

At the same time, it cut its manufacturing cycle time by 21 percent. Plant layouts were altered to speed production and reduce waste.

3M people love the company, and word gets around. In one recent year, 3M received upwards of 30,000 applications for a mere 300 technical job openings. A. F. Jacobson, CEO and chairman of 3M, says organizing a company for innovation requires more than intention. "It certainly means making it clear to our people that we expect innovation. We expect them to break the mold, to try things a new way. We have to provide resources and we have to live with the results of innovation. In other words, we have to put our money where our mouth is."

Corning Inc. puts its money where its mouth is. The company makes 60,000 products as diverse as Pyrex® dishes, optical fibers for telecommunications, ink-jet printing components, armored piping and Steuben crystal. And it's a partner in a number of joint ventures. Corning's history of innovation includes production of the first incandescent lamp-bulb enclosures for Thomas Edison. Like 3M, it invests significantly in R&D and has a goal of deriving 25 percent of its revenues from new products. Corning, too, seems to be heading down the right path. Its 1990 sales were 21 percent higher than the year before. It also believes in empowering workers to do the job right. At its Specialty Cellular Ceramics plant, workers helped design the facility. Forty-seven different job classifications were rolled into one. Employees rotate jobs weekly, receiving higher pay for each skill they acquire. Defects dropped from 10,000 parts per million to 3.

IBM, a mammoth and historically successful technological enterprise, is trying to redefine its culture. Often perceived as a company long on service but short on innovation, IBM technologists did invent, among other things, magnetic disk storage, and the current high-tech RISC (reduced instruction-set computing) technology. Controller Mike Van Vraken says that since 1987, IBM's "investments in research and development and capital equipment have increased at rates substantially higher than our revenue growth rate."

Big Blue's 1990 annual report gave a glimpse at the awesome contractions it's suffering in the transition to a more innovative culture. It said the company "consolidated numerous headquarters and manufacturing sites, and trimmed support operations, eliminating more than 63,000 staff positions since 1986. The company reduced layers of management, decreasing managerial positions worldwide by 7,800. Another 65,000 employees were retrained. . . ."

In the face of that upheaval, John Akers, IBM's chairman, reported to his senior managers that the company improved its productivity by 12 percent, shipped more products with fewer people and improved the bottom line with a 10 percent increase in revenue—unfortunately, half the revenue growth came from fluctuations in world currencies. IBM in the U.S. grew by 5 percent.

In other important measures of productivity, revenue per employee is up some 30 percent over 1985. Product cycle time has dropped by a third; the goal is to cut it in half. IBM has committed itself to manufacturing products to a standard of virtually no defects known as *Six Sigma*. That engineer jargon for an acceptable defect level of only 3.4 defects per million parts, or 99.99966 percent of perfection. It expects to reach that goal in 1994. It's an ambitious target—that level of quality would improve the company's 1990 standard by 20,000 times.

To make its ambitious goals, IBM is committing itself to reinvesting in its work force. The annual report states, "We are a 'learning company' because, increasingly, our ability to create value for customers will depend on specific knowledge and problem-solving skills. That is why we are both educating the men and women of IBM and encouraging them to take risks by advancing new ideas and innovations. Investing in our people is essential because, in the long run, success will accrue to the quickest, smartest, and toughest-minded."

One of the things IBM management wants everyone in the "learning company" to understand is that it's engaged in a severe competitive challenge. The business press eagerly reported Chairman Akers's castigation of his managers in 1991 for their apparent complacency in the face of lackluster results. IBM's employee magazine, *Think*, underscored the competitive situation by running a multipage-spread featuring the color pictures of, and quotes from, top executives of competing companies (including Hewlett-Packard, Apple, Intel, Siemens AG, Microsoft, Cypress Semiconductor, Digital Equipment Corp., and others).

John Armstrong, IBM's vice president for science and technology, articulates the challenge for the corporate giant. "Management isn't the main source of answers here. Our programmers, engineers and manufacturing workers will have to come up with some very good ideas. This is a cultural revolution that is beginning to permeate IBM, and it's an absolute prerequisite for us to continue to have technology leadership, and to regain it in areas where we may not have it."

INNOVATION AS GROUP EXERCISE

The word innovation leads easily to the familiar image of Edison, Marconi, and other inventors toiling away in virtual solitary confinement to make the big breakthrough. But in our technologically advanced world innovation is not restricted to the inventor's bench or lab, and it's not a solo sport. "An individual's achievement has limits. Big achievements need the support of organizations," says Isamu Kuru, executive vice president of Nippon Motorola in Japan. "Even Nobel prize winners accomplish their research with good support."

Innovation frequently comes from teamwork and in large companies. Creativity authors Yuji Ijiri and Robert Lawrence Kuhn write that "Successful ideas are rarely connected to solitary individuals. They are not connected with small groups. New ideas that work are ideas in which the organization takes a great deal of pride."

Robert M. White, of the National Academy of Engineering of the United States, points out that the support of a large organization frees researchers and inventors to pursue their interests with a modicum of distraction. "A structured environment offers great advantages—to relieve the day-to-day pressures of business. . . . It concentrates expertise from dozens of disciplines at the inventor's fingertips." The organization, then, can incubate creativity rather than stifle it. Not only does it provide physical and technical resources, it also provides social and psychic support which can help spur innovators to greatness.

Teamwork can be enhanced by creating a sense of belonging to an exclusive club. *This* is the place to be. You're okay, and I'm okay because we're all okay. The ad agency for the Marines knew the powerful attraction of belonging when it created the recruiting slogan, The few. The proud. The Marines. In my shop, people in my group proudly call themselves the A-Team. I didn't assign the label to our group, but I observe that it gives our team an identity as one that produces more work, better and faster than any other department in the company or industry. The implied boasting is a great motivator and it's tied to pride in our work, pride in our company, and faith in the capabilities of our co-workers. We receive our share of accolades from the people we serve, awards from our peers, and joy from work well done.

EDUCATING FOR INNOVATION

No one is ever trained or educated. Skill development and enhancement isn't a scheduled event, but a continual process. It works best when it doesn't happen by accident, but it doesn't happen intentionally often enough. The American management Association's *Management Review* recently reported, "Today, corporate America spends an average 1.5 percent of payroll on training. In comparison, training in Europe weighs in at 5 percent of payroll." Marsh Fisher, president of **Fisher Idea Systems,** reminds us that when a company wants people to dig ditches, it furnishes them with shovels and instructs them on how to handle them safely; when it wants people to innovate and employ creative problem solving, it should provide the tools and instruction to do the job right. Some companies do just that.

Corning, profiled above, is committed to all employees spending five percent of their time in job-related training.

When Ritz-Carlton Hotels hires chambermaids and kitchen help, it doesn't just hand them dust mops and cleavers. Before new hires head to their work areas, they spend three days learning the exclusive hotel chain's *philosophy*. Once assigned to their work area, they carry cards detailing 20 service principles that truly sets Ritz-Carlton service apart. (Among those guiding principles: We are ladies and gentlemen serving ladies and gentlemen; Create an atmosphere of teamwork, with employees both within your department and outside; Respond to guests' wishes within 10 minutes of the request. Follow up with a phone call within 20 minutes to ensure their satisfaction.)

Honda broadens the perspective of its research and development engineering recruits by introducing them to the company with a one-year education. The new hires spend three-month assignments on manufacturing cars and then selling them at dealerships. That's followed by another six months working at a variety of jobs in R&D.

Motorola, a global electronics producer and a winner of the first Malcolm Baldrige National Quality Award in 1988, competes head-on with many Japanese manufacturers. Like IBM, it is striving for the quality level known as *Six Sigma*. To get to that ambitious quality goal, the company is training its workers to think and perform at higher levels. (Much of that training must begin with remedial teaching of basic skills. About half of the company's 250,000 manufacturing and support people in the United States couldn't pass a seventh-grade English or math test.) The company set up what it terms Motorola University to offer a diversity of educational courses to employees at all levels. The company views its educational expenses as an investment which, for some programs, pays back a return of $33 for each dollar spent. William Wiggenhorn, president of Motorola University and the company's corporate vice president for training and education, says this of Motorola's education investment: "Our commitment is not to buildings or a bureaucracy but to creating an environment for learning, a continuing openness to new ideas. . . . We not only teach skills, we try to breathe the very spirit of creativity and flexibility into manufacturing and management." Successful companies in today's business climate, he says, "must not only train workers but build educational systems."

Accounting firm Arthur Andersen spends more than 7 percent of its revenue on professional education, employing 200 people to develop instructional materials, and maintaining a large training center that can house more than 1,700 people. Its many classrooms sport nearly 1,000 computer workstations.

Frito-Lay, Inc. (a Pepsico subsidiary) a giant in the highly competitive snack-food business turned to creative problem-solving training when sales plateaued. "Every function in a company is going to have to be more creative to stay competitive," says Dave Morrison, Frito-Lay group manager. So far, more than 7,000 employees, from vice presidents to hourly

---

Brief Aside

A wonderfully useful thinking skill that's both easy and inexpensive to teach people is Edward DeBono's *six hat thinking method*. In a short, provocative book called *Six Thinking Hats*, DeBono illustrates six different ways to think about things. He assigns colors to the hats (hats as in thinking cap) and the functions they represent. The white hat is for gathering facts. The red hat represents emotions and feelings. The black hat is (as you'd expect) for negative or Devil's advocate thinking. The yellow hat connotes positive, constructive thinking. The green hat evokes creative thinking. The blue hat represents control over thinking and the selection of other hats. (Mary Gentle, a colleague, suggests there should be a seventh hat—a grey one for confused thinking!)

This simple system, clearly explained in the 200-page book available from Little, Brown, gives a work team a frame of reference for discussing challenges and opportunities. My staff uses the hat language in meetings and in regular conversation. The hat terms even pop up around the dinner table in our house; my wife discovered the book, urged me to read it, and we've introduced our children to its methods as well.

---

workers have taken a three-day course on creative problem solving. Morrison attributes more than $500 million in savings to ideas inspired by the process. (The Frito-Lay problem-solving model, based on the Osborn-Parnes method, uses an eight-step process: Problem finding; Fact finding; Problem definition; Idea finding; Evaluation and selection; Action planning; Gaining acceptance; Taking action.)

Du Pont, an industrial giant with 140,000 employees around the world, values creativity skills of its people. It recently set up a Center for Creativity and Innovation at its corporate headquarters in Delaware to function as an information clearinghouse and training resource for Du Ponters who want to become more creative. The center has a professional staff and about 100 volunteer facilitators, some of whom are line managers in Du Pont operating units. Dave Tanner, former head of Research and

Development of Du Pont's Industrial Fibers Division, directs the center. Du Pont people from all over the world come to the center to learn more about creative thinking. But the center doesn't train people. "You *educate* people, you *train* animals," explains Tanner.

Tanner says employees at all levels and from all functional areas (even legal) have sought improved creativity skills. And the education pays off. Tanner points to a technology that worked in the lab but failed in practical application. "When we tried to scale it up, we ran into a stone wall. We had our best engineers on the job and they threw their hands up." The frustrated engineers "somewhat reluctantly asked for ideas" from a Du Pont group trained in various creative thinking techniques. "They came out with many ideas," Tanner says, and the program is well underway toward commercialization. "That technology—that looked hopeless outside the lab—will materialize into a $30 million stake to Du Pont."

In another example of how the creativity skills helped solve real-world problems, Tanner relates the story of engineers who were frustrated by having to shut down production of a fibers plant because vacuum hoses collapsed after process chemicals softened them. One of the manufacturing team members wrestled with the problem for weeks to the point where he couldn't sleep. One night as he was finally drowsing, his mind filled with images of popping springs. Eureka! Put springs inside the hoses and they won't collapse. Two days after some scribbled notes in the middle of the night, the costly problem was fixed.

Recently, Du Pont started offering its creative problem-solving capabilities to *customers* to help them tackle problems and opportunities of mutual interest, making creativity a marketing tool for Du Pont.

Tanner and his creative associates at Du Pont assembled short essays and cartoons on creativity to publish an entertaining and enlightening book, *Are We Creative Yet?* (For ordering information, see the Resources section.)

Some companies reimburse employees for taking courses on any subject to encourage them to expand their minds continually. "We pay for any course—even hot-air ballooning—that our sales people want to take," says the senior vice president of a large financial services firm. "We want our people to be interested and interesting. They don't always get that result from taking just another business course."

One way to educate your own employees is to tap the knowledge resources in your own company. Invite people from other functional areas to educate your people in staff meetings. Other good guests include vendors, customers, and business acquaintances. (Du Pont's creativity center, profiled above, started when Director Dave Tanner was a research manager in the fibers division. Instead of technical reviews at some staff meetings, Tanner brought in outside speakers to give lectures on creativity.) Encourage your employees to read the company sales literature, advertisements, instruction manuals, anything your customers see.

In the maverick organization, the learning concept expands to include informing and teaching by everyone. Information flow evolves from a boss saying to someone, "I'll tell you," to, "Tell me what I want to know," to, "Please, tell me what you know."

Encourage a culture of discovery, one that has everyone asking:

- What do we know?

- What do we need to know?

- What do we know we don't know?

- What else is there to know?

Set expectations of creative enterprise for your employees. While all ideas are welcome, not all can be implemented. In fact, in an environment that successfully encourages ingenuity, the number of ideas almost always will exceed the resources requisite to act on them. Maverick Managers welcome ideas as well as set and communicate priorities for their implementation. When he was CEO of 3M, Lewis W. Lehr said, in his view "The real stumbling block to innovation in large organizations is not lack of creativity. It is unsureness about priorities."

Clarifying priorities may actually lead to reduced numbers of innovation programs. As part of a restructuring in a tough economic climate, Kodak closed down its intrapreneur programs which funded ventures based on innovative technologies

---

Brief Aside

It is quite fashionable to describe organizational priorities as rooted in a vision or mission. At an extreme, visions and missions take on a dimension outside what is usually thought of as businesslike. Some have likened employees' emotional connection to a corporate mission as having religious overtones. "A corporation can't save your soul, but it can stand in for the age-old idea of people collectively pursuing a path that has real meaning to them," says Peter Senge of MIT's Sloan School of Management.

If you think about it, some management systems might easily be confused with a religion. Corporations decree a system of Beliefs and issue a creed to be recited (or at least adhered to) by high priests in the executive suite who behold the Vision. With missionary zeal, these true believers bear witness to others in the organization seeking converts to the holy corporate creed. These prophets of profits proselytize the company flock so they might find salvation on the true path of productivity. The anointed ones perform sacraments in the hallowed corporate temple, bless good deeds, extend indulgences to the chosen few, offer absolution for minor sins against the corporate mission, and even pronounce penance for more serious transgressions.

Business creativity writer Robert Lawrence Kuhn believes that contemplating the purpose of business enterprise naturally raises questions of spirituality and the purpose of human life. He asks, "What are organizations and their members trying to achieve? What is the ultimate nature of organizations, economic and other? What is human fulfillment? What is human potential? What are human beings? Why are we here?"

---

developed by Kodak employees. Some of the nascent ventures were sold, some were incorporated into the parent organization, and some were shut down. Kodak wanted to devote its attention to what a spokesman described as businesses "strategic to Kodak's core strengths."

Clear priorities also designate the course of action the Maverick Manager should take with those by whom the invitation to contribute ideas is too well received. When a prolific suggestor means well but is off-target—recommending that management install a hot tub in the restroom, or that the company buy all its competitors, and such—explain why the proposals aren't appropriate. Try to steer all that creative energy in the right direction by showing the suggestor some examples of recommendations that help the business. You may soon be inundated with valid proposals.

BUREAUCRACY BUSTING

The first chapter decried the debilitating corporate malaise I termed *Idea Inertia*. In this chapter, we're discussing means to convert idea inertia into idea implementation. Here are several suggestions for doing that in a maverick organization.

Question corporate rules and procedures. Constantly evaluate policies and methods by asking:

- What are we doing?
- Why are we doing it?
- Does it need to be done?
- What are better ways to do it?

When outmoded or useless policies or procedures are uncovered, hold a public execution. With some celebration and ceremony, tear up or burn useless forms or pages from policy manuals that no longer govern make-work activity. Invite everyone in attendance to nominate other restrictive or useless policies for destruction. Post signs advising: Assume nothing. Challenge everything. Or how about, Why?

Don't overevaluate suggestions. In trying to assess the merits of proposed improvements to procedures, you can get bogged down in trying to justify an intuitively good improvement. One senior publishing executive overseeing the quality improvement process at his company confides, "We burdened our program with too many evaluation requirements. My directors groan when we bring up the subject. Overdocumenting the process puts a big damper on the enthusiasm for it."

Evaluate managers. Not just by their quarterly numbers, but by how well they serve the people serving the company. Federal Express does this routinely with its Survey-Feedback-Action (SFA) program. This annual, anonymous survey of employee opinion on how well the corporation functions in general—and one's immediate bosses in particular—draws the participation of 99 percent of the FedEx work force. The survey is no idle statistics-gathering exercise. Action is a key component to the SFA plan. Managers and employees each receive copies of the survey results; they are required to meet six weeks after the results are distributed to identify areas needing improvement. Managers must then prepare written plans for resolving problems. The first 10 questions on the Federal Express survey (reproduced on page 170) all relate to rating the performance of one's own boss, indicating whether one strongly agrees or strongly disagrees with such statements as: I feel free to tell my manager what I think; My manager lets me know what's expected of me; My manager asks for my ideas about things affecting our work; My manager treats me with respect and dignity. The 10 questions constitute what Federal Express calls a Leadership Index, and it has teeth: a manager's rating on this index is a criterion for two annual bonuses.

Other evaluation criteria might center on rating managers' innovation contribution. Consultant Ray Slesinski, president of **Genesis Training Solutions,** suggests measuring a middle manager's improvements of procedures. "You might have assigned targets for cutting costs or improving productivity but you'd need to demonstrate that you made these goals using innovations." William Miller, a creativity consultant, says that while it "might seem impossible to set goals for creativity and innovation," he suggests two ways. The first is directly, such as, "Develop two new product concepts that meet the following criteria, or produce a new information-management system to meet these requirements." The second kind of creativity goal is indirect, where a realistic outcome is specified, but the individual must stretch for the means. Miller says these might be goals such as achieving an increase in sales revenues with current staff or maintaining productivity while taking a decrease in budget.

SURVEY FEEDBACK ACTION PROGRAM

FEDERAL EXPRESS CORPORATION

HOW TO ANSWER: Read each statement carefully. Then to the right of each statement mark the bubble which best expresses your agreement or disagreement with the item. Mark only one answer for each item, and remember to respond to all items. Remember that "workgroup" means all persons who report to the same manager as you do regardless of job title.

UNDECIDED/DON'T KNOW
STRONGLY DISAGREE
DISAGREE
SOMETIMES AGREE/DISAGREE
AGREE
STRONGLY AGREE

1. I feel free to tell my manager what I think.

2. My manager lets me know what's expected of me.

3. Favoritism is not a problem in my workgroup.

4. My manager helps us find ways to do our jobs better.

5. My manager is willing to listen to my concerns.

6. My manager asks for my ideas about things affecting our work.

7. My manager lets me know when I've done a good job.

8. My manager treats me with respect and dignity.

9. My manager keeps me informed about things I need to know.

10. My manager lets me do my job without interfering.

11. My manager's boss gives us the support we need.

12. Upper management (directors and above) lets us know what the company is trying to accomplish.

13. Upper management (directors and above) pays attention to ideas and suggestions from people at my level.

14. I have confidence in the fairness of management.

15. I can be sure of a job as long as I do good work.

16. I am proud to work for Federal Express.

17. Working for Federal Express will probably lead to the kind of future I want.

18. I think Federal Express does a good job for our customers.

19. All things considered, working for Federal Express is a good deal for me.

20. I am paid fairly for the kind of work I do.

21. Our benefit programs seem to meet most of my needs.

22. Most people in my workgroup cooperate with each other to get the job done.

23. There is cooperation between my workgroup and other groups in Federal Express.

24. In my work environment we generally use safe work practices.

25. Rules and procedures do not interfere with how well I am able to do my job.

26. I am able to get the supplies or other resources I need to do my job.

27. I have enough freedom to do my job well.

28. My workgroup is involved in activities to improve service to our group's customers.

29. The concerns identified by my workgroup during last year's SFA feedback session have been satisfactorily addressed.

Lease perspective. While everyone inside the company should be encouraged to lend their thinking to the enterprise, the corporate perspective shouldn't be limited to those who draw their income from the payroll. Prudent use of outsiders can add unique experience, vision, and most importantly, candor to the thinking process. Consultant need not be a dirty word so long as management defines a specific and terminal assignment for the hired-gun.

Ban the term *department*. Its literal meaning is *to divide*—not a useful function when we're trying to compete (strive together). The word sounds too much like compartment, and people have for far too long treated their departments as self-contained compartments. Edward Hennessy, chairman of Allied-Signal, likens the barriers between departments to "the many 'Berlin Walls' that have been built up over time in our corporations." He calls for a change in how people in companies act toward their colleagues in other departments, overcoming "organization boundaries that restrain knowledge and expertise."

My suggestion: Eliminate *department* and substitute the term *work team*—it implies a task-focused unit of cooperative individuals rather than a fiefdom unto itself. The other advantage to the work-team concept is that the individuals in them can change with the tasks. Departments are rigid, prescribed, and insular; work teams are flexible, adaptive, and open. Members of work teams have a primary assignment in identifiable functional areas (research, accounting, promotion) but might serve on several task-oriented work teams. The work-team concept functions best when its members are drawn from across the organization, so members of a given team might represent functional areas such as marketing, management information systems (MIS), finance, manufacturing, and so on.

Harvard business school professor Rosabeth Moss Kanter concludes that "ideas for innovations begin to take shape in companies in which the first essential power tool—information—is available, and exchange of ideas is encouraged."

Provide a stimulating environment. Winston Churchill said, "We shape our buildings, and afterwards our buildings shape us." A workplace well suited to facilitating the tasks assigned to it will aid productivity. Physical surroundings and furnishings need not be fancy, but they should be sufficiently functional to do good work, and pleasant enough to encourage doing more of it.

Push the standards. "The organization performs up to the level it thinks management expects," says Derwyn Phillips, vice chairman of the Gillette Company. If you raise those standards, not unreasonably so, people will aspire to meet them. Expecting better work from people prevents the work atmosphere from becoming stale with predictability, and more importantly, it encourages continually better work that yields a reinforcing sense of accomplishment.

A little intramural competition can also raise standards and productivity. Ad agencies typically pit internal teams against one another to provoke more and better creativity. Motorola sponsors intracompany competition between teams as an exercise to build esprit de corps among corporate staff teams around the world. The participants work on three-to-six-month projects related to the company's key goals. They are judged on their competence using analytic tools, use of teamwork in arriving at solutions, and effectiveness of results. The company sponsors the competition to emphasize employee participation in solving problems, to recognize outstanding performance, encourage continuous improvement, demonstrate the power of teamwork, and recognize top team achievements.

Push your vendors to raise their standards. It's hard to be better than your weakest component. Motorola, a Malcolm Baldrige Quality Award winner, insists that its suppliers apply for the prize.

Changing a corporate culture doesn't happen overnight. As systems thinking expert Peter Senge observes, "Cause and effect are not closely related in time and space." Incremental improvements at the right places, like increasing the number of Maverick Managers in an operation, eventually can yield big payoffs. Some people feel compelled to resist change and will fight it vigorously. Avon, the world's largest fragrance company and maker of fashion jewelry, underwent traumatic change in the 1970s when its traditional homebody customers joined the ranks of the employed. The century-old company had fewer in-home customers to sell, and fewer women at home from whom to draw its sales representatives. On top of that, the product line didn't offer much for the diversity of tastes in an increasingly affluent market. Sales dropped. Profits dropped. The company stock price plummeted. Change—or death—was inevitable.

I asked Rick Goings, president of Avon's U.S. operations, about the change process in the corporate headquarters. "Did heads roll, or did you teach the old dogs new tricks?" Goings says it amounted to a little bit of both. "We sent out symbols and signals that we needed dramatic change. Resisters to the new ways were gone shortly. But management exercised patience with the people who were trying; they eventually came to understand what we were trying to do and made it happen." And make it happen they did. Today, Avon boasts some 450,000 U.S. sales representatives, with more than a million others abroad, including some in places as unlikely as Eastern Europe and China. It introduces as many as 500 new products a year, from cosmetics, fragrances, and toiletries to gifts, jewelry, and videos. More than 100,000 consumers order from Avon every day, pushing net sales to about $3.5 billion a year. During the past five years, direct sales revenues grew at a compound rate of more than 10 percent, while pretax earnings grew at a rate of more than 15 percent.

Working together to achieve common goals through cooperation and teamwork doesn't mean seldom is heard a discouraging word. In the next chapter, we'll explore how too much harmony can strike a sour note.

Chapter Nine

Conflict, Confrontation, and Maverick Creativity

Division is the same as creation; creation is the same as destruction.

Chuang-tzu

Politeness is organized indifference.

Paul Valéry

The only available method for changing ideas is conflict . . .

Edward DeBono

Apathy is worse than resistance—better to have bosses argue about ideas than ignore them.

Raymond A. Slesinski

Managers who are good at their jobs—who are competent, who are strong—are much more likely to encourage suggestions, arguments, blood-on-the-wall fist fights!

Thomas A. Stewart

At a recent meeting, a fascinating proposal for change was put on the table. After advancing the concept, its author—a competent, secure manager—concluded by announcing in a small voice, "It's just a thought." That hedge, that implied declaration of an apology for an idea that might disturb the status quo, bothered me greatly.

Too many of us suffer from the nice-ification of the workplace. Most of us now toil in a sterile, play-to-the-boss, phony "have a nice day" environment. Constant agreement lacks energy, creativity, life. English poet Lord Byron wrote that "adversity is the first path to truth."

Homogeneity of thought yields neither passion nor progress. After IBM suffered a revenue decline of some 48 percent and a stock price plunge of nearly $13 a share, Chairman John Akers was reported to have chastised his managers saying, "The tension level is not high enough in the business—everyone is too damn comfortable at a time when the business is in crisis."

Friction can generate the spark of a new idea (in fact the word *conflict* derives from a Latin term meaning to "strike together") creating an energy that well-intentioned colleagues can positively direct to problem solving. Creativity author John Briggs points out that perfume is often made of contrary-smelling substances such as skunk oil and flowers. In the same way, opposing ideas bumping against one another can give rise to totally new ideas better for the conflict than their undisturbed progenitors.

Emotion, conviction, intensity—all show that one *cares* about the business, not that one lacks team spirit. Teamwork doesn't mean compliant submission to harmonious, bureaucratic mediocrity. Some of the most creatively productive meetings I've ever participated in gave birth to new ideas amidst raised voices, table pounding, and displays of naked emotion. We need not fight to progress, but we must avoid avoidance.

Disagreements in the work place need not be win or lose contests between people. Conflict is only energy. Energy comes from polarity: what good is a battery with only a positive terminal? Isn't it interesting that our most familiar symbols for creativity are the lightning bolt and the light bulb? The lightning bolt is created by the clash of opposite electrical charges, and the energy for the light bulb is produced in the same fashion.

Most bosses, according to a survey by the **American Productivity & Quality Center**, don't handle conflict very well. Fewer than half of the respondents to the poll—employees of companies that subscribe to the Center—agreed with the statement, "My boss handles conflict in my work unit constructively." An oddity: in service sector companies, where one would think the interpersonal skills run high, almost two thirds of those surveyed felt their bosses didn't handle conflict well.

In this chapter, you'll find some techniques Maverick Managers can use for engendering creative dispute without risking insult. But first, a few words about positive disagreement.

REAL MANAGERS AREN'T AFRAID OF CONFLICT

Federal Express convened a task force to identify characteristics of effective managers. The employees on that task force identified six leadership qualities. At the top of the list: *Courage.* Here's what their report said about good managers who embody the number one leadership requirement: "Stands up for unpopular ideas, does not avoid confrontations, gives negative feedback to subordinates and superiors, has confidence in his or her own capability, desires to act independently, and does the right thing for the company or subordinates in spite of personal hardship or sacrifice." A perfect prescription for qualities that Maverick Managers should embody in themselves, and encourage in their people.

Earlier in this book, I suggested that managers should welcome the ideas of everyone in the organization. Doing so invites conflict. New ideas imply a challenge to what is, and managers manage what is; a new idea, therefore, conflicts with the status quo and challenges a manager. The Maverick Manager solicits unvarnished provocations.

"Being honest and candid about problems in time to do something about them should be as much a condition of employment as not cheating on your expense account," proclaims Dick Garwin, IBM Fellow at the Thomas J. Watson Research Center. Unfortunately, Garwin's exhortation is foreign to many managers who so value stability in the workplace that they unwittingly incubate self-destructive, blind-to-reality *groupthink*. Famed journalist and lexicographer H. L. Mencken argued that "it is only doubt that creates."

By no means am I suggesting that you should foster a combative attitude in your shop. To the contrary, Maverick Managers work hard to preserve the dignity and emotional security of those who work for them. They provide a secure environment where people feel free to disagree without fear of repercussions from managerial thought-police. Fear never produces a creative idea, but questioning does. Alfred North Whitehead, mathematician and philosopher, wrote that "wherever ideas are effective, there is freedom." And vice versa, I might add.

The Maverick Manager knows that people can express unconventional ideas, question policies, and differ with the boss without threatening management's authority. Disagreements and even arguments with colleagues don't represent a breakdown in organizational integrity. To the contrary, earnest dissent is a sign of trust and respect. The most compliant environments often are the most disharmonious and dysfunctional.

COMPLIANCE COSTS

People who acquiesce to policies or procedures that they honestly believe are harmful to their employer experience stress. What happens when we make nicey-nice at the office even when tensions rise? We outwardly display calm while internalizing that conflict; so we go home and do what? Blow up at our spouse and children, directing pent-up emotion at those who will accept us even when we're being total jerks.

Often that tension arises out of the dissonance we suffer when acting in conflict with what we truly believe is the right course. The energy we expend to hold our tongues clashes with the energy we want to disburse finding better solutions to our employer's problems. All the emotion that could be directed positively at effecting innovation stays negatively suppressed. The organization forfeits vitality; individuals internalize stress.

Imagine what would happen if that honest emotion and passion were directed at their real source—the issues at the office that evoked them. Ulcer and headache medicine sales would plummet, and managers would come to grips with problems before they grew into crises.

ORGANIZED CONFLICT

Injecting constructive conflict into the work environment doesn't necessarily mean arguing about everything all the time. It means airing differences and considering a multitude of viewpoints, always an enriching experience. As Justice Oliver Wendell Holmes suggested, a "mind stretched by a new idea can never go back to its original dimensions."

Here are some techniques for orchestrating dissent.

Spirited group discussions. Occasionally, especially when trying to solve a troubling problem, creative confrontation can raise the adrenaline level and get the creative juices flowing. Sometimes, heat generates light. A spirited discussion can act as a "neural booster", stimulating synapse-firing better than all the positive affirmations in the world. Ideas exchanged in dialogue grow and evolve, expanding with each constructive exchange. Open discussion also validates the process by which an idea develops (or doesn't).

One of the easiest ways to get a group to discuss controversial matters is simply to put the taboo subject on a meeting agenda. That removes any latent fear of reprisal for raising unpopular issues. Rather than leaping into the sensitive issue, work up to it by first dealing with more mundane matters.

Considerations for constructive conflict:

1. No-holds-barred discussions should be encouraged only between a small number of people with equivalent organizational status where no one holds the power of retribution over another. (What is more inhibiting to the free exchange of ideas than for a boss to call together all his or her direct reports for an idea session

only to announce, "Here's what I think. . . . Now what do you think? ")

2. Passionate discussions should always focus on issues and *never* on people. A business associate of mine laments "think tank" meetings with other executives in his company. "The real problem is when two of the super achievers get into a room together and start talking about important issues. In no time, they're at each other's throats, battling for position. By the end of the meeting, there's blood on the floor." A properly run meeting should never allow that to happen. Advertising executive John M. Kiel, author of *The Creative Mystique*, advises that in intense discussion the "leader has got to be able to step back and know when emotion is furthering the cause or when it's furthering more emotion."

3. Open discussions probably work best when chaired by an outsider with no allegiance to any position or faction. In fact, it may work best when the moderator has an entirely fresh perspective outside the shared assumptions of people in the company or even its industry. If the facilitator isn't an outsider, he or she should be someone who can function with no fear of political consequences, and someone whose unique personal experience brings a dimension to the questions before the group that it wouldn't otherwise have.

The mediator should keep the focus on exploring possibilities, not defending positions. Personal rivalries or animosities that arise during the discussion should be directed away from participants and toward the problem at hand.

4. The group might contain a few "thought provokers" otherwise unaffiliated with the participants. R. Donald Gamache, chairman of business creativity consulting firm, INNOTECH, suggests that a company's knowledge base is like an erector set where the finite combination of parts gives one a limited number of structural possibilities. For more possibilities, you need more parts. INNOTECH, a firm that specializes in a very formalized approach to creative problem solving, often seeds a discussion group with some wildcard participants (such as an expert on insects). Their frames of reference are totally foreign to others present, and their spontaneous contributions to the discussion might help it to springboard to some wonderful unanticipated places.

5. Everyone at the session should participate. The moderator should draw out more reticent participants; the discussion is not an exercise solely for the brave or vocal. One technique some group leaders use is known as the Talking Stick or the Conversation Ball. An object such as a stick or a ball is handed to whoever is talking. This visible sign of dominance makes each speaker aware of just how much time they are in control of the dialogue. It also assists control over the discussion's decorum, reminding all participants that all benefit most from listening to one speaker at a time.

6. The discussion should be allowed to stray into sensitive areas and even wander off course. To fully exploit the creative possibilities in the session, all avenues of thought should be explored without caveat. As creativity expert Roger von Oech advises, "The answers you get depend on the questions you ask."

Thinking expert Edward DeBono points out that "to look only for things that are relevant means perpetuating the current pattern." Irrelevant, even bizarre ideas, stimulate fresh thinking, and often provoke laughter. Levity and frivolity help to catalyze more connections and combinations, which can lead to striking insights.

Even-handed debate. Factions at odds over a controversial proposal debate the proposition before their colleagues. Here's the twist: Each side must come prepared not only to present their case, but also that of the other school(s) of thought. Thus, everyone must thoroughly think through all the positions, advancing their best thinking on all possibilities. A postdebate discussion, led by an independent moderator may yield an improved, or entirely new approach to the question on the table.

Silent ballot. A venerable method for raising unpopular notions involves collecting anonymous contributions from interested participants. Specific methods vary but practitioners of this process generally write their controversial suggestions (or reactions to such a proposal) on cards or slips of papers. A moderator collects the tickets, sorts them (perhaps posting them if not handwritten) and frames additional discussion to which the participants again react.

Advantage to the ballot technique: reflection. Writing reactions to a proposed concept gives everyone the benefit of the thinking that's a requisite precursor to putting words on paper. The time between when someone advances the idea and everyone else reacts tends to minimize emotionally laden responses. And the permanence of written responses tends to minimize reactions directed to people rather than the merits of the idea under consideration.

Disadvantage to the ballot technique: delay. There's less dynamic interplay between—and spontaneous springboarding off—other participants' ideas given the lag that the mechanics of using the written word entails.

A high-tech version of the ballot method was developed at the University of Arizona and put to work by IBM. In its Decision Support Centers, meeting participants react to the questions at hand while keying thoughts into a central computer database simultaneously. Meeting-goers can see what their colleagues have entered into the meeting database and critique it under the cover of anonymity. The system can also be used to tally votes on proposals before the group.

THE CONFLICT IN JUDGMENT

What is a good idea? All ideas are equivalent without a standard against which to measure them.

Creativity books always warn that creative idea sessions shouldn't be punctured by judgment of an idea. (I prefer *ideafest* to the term *brainstorm*, which sounds like an epileptic seizure to me. If the idea-generation meeting is accompanied by food, it's an *ideafeast*.) Judging an idea is considered negative, confrontational, and therefore inhibiting to idea-session participants. Withholding judgment while engaging in a free-flowing discussion is good advice for producing more ideas. But it shouldn't be construed to mean that ideas shouldn't ever be judged! Aristotle wrote that "thinking is . . . in part imagination, in part judgment: We must therefore first mark off the sphere of imagination and then speak of judgment."

Ideas not subjected to scrutiny can't be assessed for their potential utility. "Use judgment and intuition to choose the best ideas . . . the selection is also a creative process," says ad man Hanley Norins. And judgment, by definition, involves conflict (for, not for, against).

Business creativity consultant Mark Sebell of **Creative Realities** says, "We actually nurture conflict in something that we call 'war games.' After we help create the ideas, we help people attack them and try to kill them from a number of competitive and internal perspectives to test their mettle." Testing the mettle of an idea is a time-honored tradition; scientists, for example, are notoriously confrontational when testing new ideas.

Just how does one assess the mettle of an idea? So often the critique of a creative concept is expressed no more succinctly than, I don't like it. *Right, boss, back to the drawing board.* To a creator, a response worse than "I don't like it," is, "Ehh--," accompanied by a shrug of the shoulders. (Equally damning is, "That's . . . uh, interesting.") A nonresponse condemns worse than a vituperative reaction to a creative work. The Maverick Manager doesn't reject ideas without reason.

Let's return to the central question. What is a good idea? To the Maverick Manager, it is a concept that fulfills the criteria. Productive idea-generating sessions should yield many more ideas than one could possibly employ. Sorting through those ideas to find those most suitable for solving problems or seizing opportunities should be more than guesswork. The folks at INNOTECH suggest establishing criteria for good (meaning effective) ideas in three groups: *musts, desirables, bonuses.*

Good ideas are those that have qualities on the *must* list (e.g., must not require additional personnel or investment), and possibly also have desirable characteristics (appeals to most current customers, saves money while not impacting production). An attractive idea that has many desirables and a few bonuses may not be a good idea. For example, building a new production facility in Naples, Florida, to make a new product appealing to current customers meets one of our desirable characteristics. The proposed plant site's proximity to great recreational facilities is a bonus. But the idea is not a good one. It fails our "must" test in that it requires additional investment and personnel.

R. Donald Gamache, INNOTECH's chairman warns that "the biggest downfall of most lists of criteria are the 'phantoms.' A phantom criterion is one that is lurking somewhere in the organization—in the back of a senior manager's head—but is never expressed. Worse yet, the individual does not even realize its existence."

The Maverick Manager evaluates ideas not on whim but on criteria that can be spoken aloud and shared with everyone, and *that* is in everyone's interest. Management expert Henry E. Riggs suggests that, "When managers must pay as much attention to justifying the rejection of promising ideas as to accepting projects, risk taking is likely to be encouraged." Establishing the criteria by which ideas are assessed may be a confrontational exercise itself, but that's just part of the creative process.

And the creative process, particularly the one in your own head, is the subject of the next chapter.

Chapter Ten

Brain Gain: How to Think More like a Maverick

Human beings have been and remain uniquely creative because they are able to integrate the pessimism of intelligence with the optimism of will.

René Dubos

The love people feel for their work has a great deal to do with the creativity of their performances.

Robert J. Sternberg

Everything has been thought of before, but the problem is to think of it again.

Johann W. von Goethe

Be content with a little light, so it be your own. Explore, and explore . . . Make yourself necessary to the world, and mankind will give you bread.

Ralph Waldo Emerson

Creativity is an exhilarating expression of one's humanity. Yet the word *creativity* puts off (and even scares) many people in business. "It's perceived as fuzzy-wuzzy soft edges," says Marsh Fisher, cofounder of Century 21 Real Estate and president of **Fisher Idea Systems**, which makes a great creativity software program (described later in this chapter). "For years, creative people have been associated with fine arts," Fisher says, "so if you wear an earring or your hair long, you're assumed to be more creative than somebody who wears a suit. That [mythology] has been perpetuated by creatives—they don't mind being different." Fisher says the mistaken notion that creativity is art has long been

"Nope! NEXT!

perpetuated by schools. "A teacher compliments a child who paints a beautiful sunset or tree, tapes the picture up on the wall and pretty soon other kids who just can't do that as well say, 'Well, I'm just not a creative person.' "

The irony is that creativity—rather than being foreign to business—always has contributed to success in business. Ingenuity, invention, improvement of process; what is more basic to business success than those creative elements?

Some business people who believe themselves to be *serious* shy away from so-called soft skills like creativity. The disciplined mind, the misinformed apparently conclude, seeks solutions to problems using analytic reasoning skills, which restricts creativity. "The majority of businessmen are incapable of original thinking, because they are unable to escape from the tyranny of reason. Their imaginations are blocked," claims advertising great David Ogilvy.

Logic confines because its possibilities are finite. Intuitive thinking is boundless and full of infinite potential. Logic excludes, while free thinking includes. "It is characteristic of insight solutions and new ideas," says Edward DeBono, "that they should be obvious after they have been found. In itself this shows how insufficient logic is in practice, otherwise such simple solutions must have occurred much earlier."

Logic can lead one to a satisfactory solution but not necessarily the best or most inspired. Creativity expert Roger von Oech cautions that "if you think there is only one right answer, then you will stop looking as soon as you find one."

Logical reasoning skills are learned in institutions of higher learning (perhaps), but they are handicaps. Business success requires skills far different from those contributing to achievement in academe. Schools prepare one to recite and perhaps analyze the past. Prosperity in business necessitates that one invent the future. If there were one right answer to winning in business (as there usually is for school test questions), everyone would employ it. And that, of course, would render the answer wrong; success in business comes not from conformity but from differentiation. "Nothing is more dangerous than an idea when it is the only one we have," suggests Emile Chartier. If all our products, service policies, manufacturing methods, advertisements and distribution channels were identical, most enterprises would be unnecessary redundancies; their managers would be extraneous and among the unemployed.

Society's collective prosperity depends on constant innovation by the many. Our individual financial health depends on our own creative contribution to those who pay us for our time and effort. (When it comes time for another round of "downsizing," who is the corporation more likely to retain—someone who can merely analyze why the company is troubled, or someone who can innovate success from the mess?)

BORN OR MADE?

You probably know someone you'd call creative. Most likely that person seems endowed with a natural ability to fit your definition. Genetics conspire to predispose all of us to doing certain things extremely well. In his book *Fire in the Crucible*, John Briggs asks the question, "Are geniuses born or made?" He answers, "It would be easy to think they're born. If so, we could excuse our own failures of creativity."

Genetic diversity makes our world the wonderfully interesting place that it is. But natural talent's apparent dispersal doesn't preclude each of us from learning to do what appears to come more naturally to others. René Dubos, a Pulitzer prize-winning scientist, suggests, "We become only one of the many persons we are capable of becoming. All of us are born with a wide range of potentialities that enable us in theory to develop an immense diversity of attributes. . . ." The innate characteristics that we develop may well determine whether we are creative.

Before we become adept we must become initiated. Genes may determine where one starts, but they exert virtually no influence on where one goes. Marsh Fisher contends that creativity is nothing more than a learned skill. "We've got to get creativity out of the realm of mystics; we need to do away with the notion that the muses court you but they don't court me." The Maverick Manager understands that developing creativity depends on applying the force of will to acquire and then master skills.

Leonardo da Vinci posited that there were three classes of people: "Those who see. Those who see when they are shown. Those who do not see." By improving your creative skills you'll see farther, wider, and with greater clarity.

CATEGORIZING CREATIVITY

When considering creativity skills, recognize that being creative doesn't mean possessing artistic ability. (Though there seems to be little shortage of it. Ever go to a flea market? There's plenty of artistic creativity on display: quilts, carvings, rag dolls, candles, photos, paint splotches on canvas, tantalizing treats, hand-fashioned toys, on and on.) Chemical engineer Thomas P. Carney eloquently described the joy of creating that transcends artistic expression:

> There is a grandeur in any act of creativity. There is mystery in the formation of a new idea. A new idea is one of the most precious things in the world. It comes along all too seldom. But when it does, revolutions are caused, industries are born, and, in some cases, other industries die as a result of the same idea. It is a marvelous thing to know you have thought something no one else has ever thought, and done something no one else has ever done.

Just as creativity isn't only artistic expression, it also isn't restricted to inventing what no one else has, or thinking what no one else has thought, or even pulling together disparate ideas to form *the* big idea. Creativity encompasses a wide range of manifestation.

The Latin *creatus* and the Sanskrit *kar* mean "to make something," while the Greek *krainein* means to" accomplish something." Making and accomplishing—concepts perfectly suited for business people. Here are some unconventional creative business skills employed by the maverick thinker:

Anticipating. Some business people have an uncanny knack for identifying trends or seminal events in their industry. These people are keen observers, assemblers of diverse bits of information, and responsive to the intuition they've developed based on experience.

Surfacing. Uncovering new applications for a product, a process, a facility, even individuals' skills, is a creative talent.

Inspiring. Remember, Maverick Managers need not generate all the good ideas themselves. Creating an atmosphere that fosters innovation and ingenuity is in itself a creative act.

Seeking. Dissatisfaction with the status quo and questing for alternatives is a creative act. When personal computer rivals IBM and Apple decided to join forces to share technology, the Associated Press wrote: "The arrangement also signaled a profound shift in thinking at International Business Machines Corp. and Apple Computer Inc., which together control nearly half the market for personal computers. Historically they have detested and poked fun at each other." Ironically, that brave stroke of independent thinking by those companies was reported on Independence Day, 1991.

Discovering. Stumbling onto a fortunate find requires a grasp of the possibilities, and thus qualifies as creative. Hanley Norins, the former Young & Rubicam advertising creative director, says the best way to "take advantage of serendipity is to cultivate an attitude—the attitude of openness, which enables us to recognize the lucky incident when it happens."

Many organizations (e.g., Bell Labs, 3M, IBM, and others) fund basic research without chasing a specific application. Creative evaluation and chance observations of the results often yield fortuitous new products. 3M had 100 people experimenting with certain fluorochemical compounds for seven years with no practical application in sight. Then one day some accidently spilled on a researcher's sneaker. She noted that the chemically-stained area of her white shoe stayed cleaner than the rest. Scotchgard® brand fabric protector and a line of related products was thus born.

Sifting. Surveying all the possible innovative opportunities that come to mind, or across one's desk, and being sensitive to the nuances that whisper, "Great possibilities here."

Embellishing. *Creative* doesn't mean totally new and unprecedented ideas that spring from nowhere. Improving or refining what exists qualifies as creative. Japanese companies have demonstrated facility for this in their miniaturization of electronics. Often this adaptive form of creativity involves combining existing concepts to form a new one. Someone, whose name history has failed to record, combined the juice of the bitter lemon with water to dilute it and sugar to sweeten it to make a most refreshing drink. Johnson's Wax changed the pesticide market by combining poison (old idea) with the aerosol can (old idea) to create a phenomenal success known as Raid bug spray.

Focusing. Setting priorities for an organization, or eliminating distractions so people can concentrate on productive work is creative.

Wondering. Asking Why? and What if . . . opens one up to possibilities, paving the way for additional creative work. Creativity springs from inquiries; it is a child of questions.

Sharing. Innovation results from ideas in play. One idea leads to another. Collaborating with others exponentially increases the interplay of potential ideas and permutations of thought.

So creativity is more than cleverness with words, or aptitude for music or art. In business, innovation has both purpose and many manifestations.

CREATIVE BEHAVIOR

Humorist and businessman John Cleese maintains that creativity is less a talent and more "a way of operating, a mode of behaving." Behaviors can be learned and improved by developing appropriate skills. Enhancing your creative skills doesn't mean engaging in mystic rituals or adhering to a prescribed regimen. There is no one true way to expanding your creativity. Joseph Campbell, the literature professor who made mythology his life's work, warned against following a guru's path suggesting that "maturity consists in outgrowing [dependency on others] and becoming your own authority for your life."

Entire books have been written about developing one's creative abilities. For example, Roger von Oech's *A Whack on the Side of the Head* (Warner Books), Michael LeBoeuf's *Imagineering* (Berkley Books), or *Creativity in Business* by Michael Ray and Rochelle Myers (Doubleday). That said, I'll now describe a series of behaviors that constitute what you might think of as The Way of the Maverick. This collection includes both the Zen-like and the screwdriver-like, appearing in no particular order.

Perceiving.   Heightened perception can be a learned skill. In my youth, I was never a quick athlete with lightning-like eye-body coordination. I perform poorly on videogames—the dancing images move too fast for me. I did, however, learn as an adult, to see and react in *one thirtieth* of a second. That ability surfaced when my professional duties involved editing videotape.

Like film, videotape images convey movement by a succession of still-frame pictures. One second of videotape contains 30 still frames. When editing videotape, one electronically joins images from different scenes, just as you record one show after another on a VCR.

Let's say you set your VCR to record a show at seven o'clock on one channel, and another show at eight o'clock on another channel. When playing back that tape, one single frame of a commercial—one thirtieth of a second in duration—was sandwiched between the end of the one show and the beginning of the next. Would you see it? Most days I wouldn't either. But when I'm concentrating on a video production, my visual acuity is so finely tuned that I can detect such split-second clutter. (Professional video editors call that slice of unwanted video a flash-frame and they find them easily.) Interestingly, research done by SRI/Gallup found that top professional hockey players perceive the movement of a puck on ice to a 30th of a second!

We can perceive our world in extraordinary ways by attuning our senses to function in extraordinary ways.

Discover the world with eyes that have not seen before by focusing your attention outside yourself. Listen with ears not accustomed to sound. Detecting the world free of assumptions opens you to stimulations and information that have always existed around you but which you have denied yourself. To truly see what is there, close your eyes to what you think is there. Only then can you perceive what is and what might be.

Imagine you *know* nothing to observe everything. Renewed perceptions lead to new thinking about old problems.

Absorbing. Empty yourself to take in the world. Absorb everything by containing nothing. As you watch and listen to the world around you, try to turn off the voice inside your head that narrates to you. Experience purely what is there, saving reactions for later reflections.

Marveling. We are surrounded by miraculous creations that easily escape our attention because their familiarity renders their wondrousness invisible. Here is a short list of things I'd encourage you to see with fresh, amazed eyes.

- Stacked interstate highways carrying tons of cars and trucks.
- A rose.
- A microwave oven.
- The U.S. telephone system.
- A sketchbook of the human anatomy.
- A loaded jumbo jet in flight.
- A laptop computer with a built-in CD-ROM drive containing 250,000 pages of printed material.
- A friend's face.
- Live color television broadcasts from anywhere on the planet.
- A metropolitan subway system (for the neatest picture, contemplate the Metro in Washington, D.C.).
- A honey bee.

- Automatic Teller Machines that allow you to withdraw money from your California bank savings account while you're traveling in New York City.
- One blade of grass.
- Plumbing in a skyscraper.
- Express elevators in a skyscraper (they work quickly in *some* tall buildings).
- A forest.
- Made-to-order automobiles.
- Delivery from door-to-door, coast-to-coast *overnight*.
- A square-inch of beach.
- Televisions as tall as a building and as small as a watch.
- The array of products in a supermarket.
- Cameras that focus for you.
- An octopus.
- Satellites that can photograph an object on earth from 23,000 miles away.
- A human organ transplant.

This list of literally wonderful and fantastic creations is as endless as the human imagination. What wonderful things can you contemplate?

Adventuring.   No progress is made by the comfortable. Do something thrilling; release some adrenaline!

Relaxing.   Too much excitement blocks the insights one gains in quiet moments.

Balancing.   Aristotle spoke of the golden mean in life. One of the most thrilling *and* relaxing experiences of my life was a trip down the Colorado River in the Grand Canyon on a raft. Hours of quiet, peaceful, even boring drifting were punctuated by quick moments of sheer terror! Experience at both ends of the scale makes most of our time in the middle more meaningful.

Inquiring. Ask why. Ask why again. Ask why five times. Then twice more. This is a popular Japanese problem-solving method. To wit, the car abruptly stopped. Why? It ran out of oil. Why? It hadn't been serviced. Why? I didn't get to it. Why? I've been too busy lately. Why? I've had to work much longer hours than normal. Why? We're short-handed at work. Why? I've been reluctant to delegate. Aha!

Thinking. One of the best ways to have great ideas is to have many ideas. Assign yourself a quota; starting with just two ideas a day, you'll accumulate more than 700 per year. In a decade, that's over 7,000 ideas. The ideas you write down need not come from trying to think of ideas. In fact, trying to call forth ideas seems to scare them away. Ideas come from things you hear or overhear, or see in the paper, along the roadside, on television, or in your dreams.

In addition to generating ideas, try to think multidimensionally about your ideas. Ask yourself, what are the possible immediate consequences of these ideas for me, for others? What are the possible longer-term consequences for me, for others? Where else might these ideas lead?

The more adept you get at thinking skills, the more adept your thinking becomes. You may find yourself developing simultaneity of thought where you handle major thinking tasks in tandem while enjoying greater clarity and less exertion.

Recording. A thought unwritten is an idea lost. Always carry a device for capturing your fleeting thoughts (pencil and notebook, a tape recorder; 3 × 5 note cards make a great traveling database). The proverbial pen and pad of paper on the bedstand truly is a good idea. (Waterproof pad for the shower, anyone?)

Breaking habits. Habits put you into a rut (which someone once described as a grave with a tunnel at each end). Habits, even good ones, confine us. Doing things differently may actually affect a physical change in your brain. While research on the brain reveals new information all the time, it appears that our actions relate to connections between certain cells in our brains. When you act out of the ordinary, you may create new neural patterns. Just as you can change the performance of a bicep by exercising it, you may physically alter your brain patterns. New actions influence new thinking. Think of breaking habits as exercise for your brain.

Here are some habit breakers: Try going up steps with your right foot first instead of your left. Change the route you take to work. Change the hours you work. Eat lunch with someone you haven't before. Eat lunch alone. Put your jacket on left arm first instead of right first. If you don't exercise, do so; if you do, change the routine. Read a section of the paper you never read. Listen to a radio station you never tune in (and may not even like). Visit a restaurant you never tried before, order something you've never heard of before. Call an acquaintance you haven't spoken to in years. Break (politely) an obligation. Commit yourself to something you've been avoiding. Read a novel. Read a joke book. Buy a book for a friend. Go away with your significant other for a weekend. Give up drinking alcohol or eating dessert for a week. Volunteer for a charity. Play a sport you've never tried. Take a long, slow walk around your neighborhood, trying to see it for the first time. Find some fresh flowers to smell; close your eyes and savor the aroma. If you can't remember jokes, commit two to memory. Throw a party. Stay home and do nothing one weekend. Seek and spend time with someone significantly older than you, then someone significantly younger. Buy a crossword puzzle book and do at least half the puzzles. Send a romantic card to your spouse (read as many cards as you can before selecting one, especially the funny ones). Watch something on public television for which the listing sounds as dull as flat paint. Watch a raucous game show. Switch brands of toothpaste. Observe a stranger and try to imagine his or her life story. Take a class unrelated to work or your hobbies (how about cultural anthropology or physics?). Reserve time to spend with your children (or someone else's children—they'll appreciate that more than you can know, and you'll get back in touch with your childlike self).

Throw open new windows to your mind. Clear out the mental cobwebs. Surprise yourself.

Speaking originally. When was the last time you actually wanted to kill two birds (or even one) with a stone? Is the expression relevant? How about *axe to grind*? or *blue blood*?

Eliminate cliches from your conversations and writing. The next time you're tempted to shout, Now that's a horse of a different color! stop. Think about the phrase. You know what you mean when you use it, but what does it really mean? When was the last time you actually needed to speak of horses? (When was the last time you saw a horse?) While you can buy dictionaries of cliches and idioms in the reference section of most bookstores, any phrase you have to look up to decipher probably miscommunicates. And it certainly draws on (and shows) no originality on your part.

Cliches are verbal habits. They trap us in the rut of repeating others' expressions (some go back centuries and have no relevance in the modern world). Try creating your own metaphors. You'll draw on (and improve) your creative powers by forcing more of those important neural connections in your cranium, plus you'll add interest and impact to your communication. To paraphrase jazz great Thelonius Monk, sometimes you'll say things you never heard before.

Learning. You can never know all there is, or too much. The personal motto of Michelangelo is one we should all adopt: "I am still learning." The greatest aid to learning is curiosity. Look for revelations and insight in all your activities and interactions.

Invest in your brain. Tim Connor, president of TR Training Associates in Ann Arbor, MI, points out that most people spend hundreds of dollars every year on the outside of their heads (for hairstyling, makeup, fragrances, clothing) and thousands more on an automobile to transport themselves to work in high style. He asks, "What did you invest last year on the inside of your head so you would know what to say when you got there?"

Use idle time to learn more. Read while waiting in line. Caught without reading material? Strike up a conversation; everyone can teach you something (even if it's an appreciation for solitude). Read while you're vacationing. Read before falling asleep. Listen to informative tapes or broadcasts while commuting. Take 15 minutes out of every lunch hour to read, and you'll gain more than an hour's worth of knowledge every week.

End every day with a question: What did I learn today? That reflection often will present you with new insights.

Impulsing. "False conclusions which have been reasoned out are infinitely worse than blind impulse," postulated Horace Mann. Logic only limits possibilities, and even logicians recognize that. "Even in the most purely logical realms," mathematician Bertrand Russell contended, "it is insight that first arrives at what is new."

To open yourself up to insight, release yourself from the restrictions of reason. Some people escape from reason's confines with great difficulty (unless they're lost on a dark, stormy night and happen by a cemetery). Intuition is cultivated by use; it correlates to self-trust. Give in to your gut instincts. Experience, true feelings, and hopes all speak quietly through the intuitive voice within. When that voice is a trusted friend, it can be a most powerful counselor.

Reflecting. Often that quiet inner voice can come forward only when one blocks out the din of other stimuli. Our busy, plugged in, megawatt/gigabyte world seduces our attention ever so easily. Learn to shut it off. If you don't reflect on what you've experienced you can take no meaning from it. In the midst of your hectic life, find time to listen to silence. Your mind will fill the sensory void with productive and sometimes amusing or even startling thoughts.

Many people use commuting time as meditating time. Video producer Steve Eiffert refers to his car as a "self-contained meditation unit." When you drive with the radio off, your mind can wander. When it wanders into some productive thinking, pick up the tape recorder. Talk to yourself in the car. Out loud. Dialogue with yourself is a great idea starter, tension reliever, and is much cheaper than a therapist.

Don't drive? Not a problem. Many people reflect while commuting to work via bus or train. When my colleague Mary Gentle gets ideas while riding the rails, she describes the experience as a "trainstorm."

Most businesses don't yet provide quiet places for people to reflect, but you might scout an empty office, unused cubicle, a quiet corner in the cafeteria, or other refuge for stealing a few moments of quiet during the work day. This can help you clear your head of the many interruptions and distractions around your normal work area.

Try to find solace every day. Your creativity productivity will increase as you grow accustomed to listening to your own thoughts. In fact, the more you're in touch with your innermost thoughts, the more you'll find them breaking through the noise of the daily routine with solutions to the challenges that confront you.

Pondering. The Latin root of the word *ponder* means "weight." An unresolved challenge, a postponed decision on an opportunity, weighs heavy upon the mind. The burden can make one tense, grumpy. One of the reasons many people seize the first possible solution to a problem is to relieve themselves of the anxiety that comes from dragging around a problem in the subconscious all day. Inspired solutions often bubble up after the difficult problem has stewed in the mind's juices a long time. Creative people may be those who can endure the strain of living with a problem until it's fully decomposed by the brain's digestive juices.

Carry your problems around longer than you'd like; you'll reward yourself with brilliance born of considerable contemplation.

Ignoring. We live in the age of *OmniMedia*, a time where news events are reported instantaneously and ubiquitously. We are awash in information about trivial events. When the president has a cold we know about it. Is that of value to you? What other matters of no consequence distract you? To open up deeper channels of thinking, avoid the backwash of minor events. Turn off the steady flow of bits and pieces. Edward DeBono points out that, "There is unfortunately no switch in the mind which can be flicked one way for dealing with all important matters and the other way for dealing with minor matters." We must be vigilant protectors of our precious consciousness, looking for sources of insight on patterns and causes rather than reports of events and trivia.

As a former journalist, I'm not suggesting you become an uninformed citizen. I am saying that you should be a discriminating consumer of information, choosing wisely the words and ideas you spend your precious time examining.

Knowing. To stimulate better thinking about your professional field, expose yourself to everything in it. Consistent with the advice above, don't savor the insignificant. Survey not by studying but skimming every trade journal, looking (with an open mind) at many competitive products, seeing as much of the landscape as possible. Then choose the items you wish to invest time in absorbing. You'll know a little about a lot—so nothing should surprise you—and more about what's important. "Chance favors only the mind that is prepared," advised Louis Pasteur (who was an artist as well as scientist). You'll be prepared to come up with better ideas and make better decisions. Career growth in our new economy is not title inflation, it's expansion of the self through self-directed improvement and renewal.

Borrowing. No one has a lock on original ideas. No one requires that a workable idea be original (unless, of course, it's patented or copyrighted). Thomas Edison admitted, "Most of my ideas belonged to other people who didn't bother to develop them." Many (most, all?) creative people are idea borrowers who add value to a good idea by making it better. Borrowing and improving is different than outright thievery. "Better to fail in originality than to succeed in imitation," wrote novelist Herman Melville.

Giving. Man does not walk the earth only to produce and sell widgets. Volunteering your substantial talents to worthy causes puts you in touch with people, experiences, and a part of yourself you might otherwise not encounter. Try to do charitable work where you aren't in a leadership role—not holding an office, not assuming responsibility—but just lending a hand. This humbler giving will fill a different part of you.

Questioning.   Doubt everything. Most of all, your truths. Beliefs, like logic, limit more than free. Maria Mitchell, 19th-century American astronomer, wrote: "Besides learning to see, there is another art to be learned—*not to see* what is not."

The root meaning of the word *ingenuity* means "free thinker." To be ingenious, you must be free to see what is and is not true.

Risking.   Following the rules rarely gets one in trouble, or forges any progress. The tried and true amounts to the tired and stale. "Keep doing what you've been doing, and you're going to keep getting what you've been getting," says motivational speaker Les Brown. All progress comes from trying something that hasn't been done before.

Throughout history, reputedly creative people often were those willing to risk being wrong. When you try something that doesn't work, that's not failure—it's feedback. When Edison went through some 1,000 different filaments trying to find one that worked, he said he hadn't failed, but rather "succeeded in identifying a thousand filaments that don't work"—useful feedback that led to the one filament that did work.

Walking.   Ample literature documents the body/mind connection. Exercising the physical benefits the mental. I am partial to walking. It puts me in motion but not so fast as to miss the opportunity to observe what I pass.

Hoping.   The glass is not half full. And it isn't half empty. It's full of potential.

When you run smack into a cold, hard, immovable object in your path, ask: Is this a brick wall or a steppingstone?

Accepting.   The world is not perfect, guaranteeing even the most ambitious among us sufficient challenge. Imperfection yields creative energy. In his book *The Fifth Discipline*, Peter M. Senge wrote that "for painters, composers, or sculptors, creating involves working within constraints—for example, the constraints imposed by their media. If one had but to snap one's fingers and the vision became reality, there would be no creative process."

Fretting and regretting won't change things beyond your control. Use your energies to find solutions for, and effect change in, challenges you can influence.

Take comfort in Joseph Brodsky's observation that "there is no embrace in this world that won't finally unclasp."

Laughing. Every day do some chuckling, grinning, guffawing, smiling, cheering, winking, and giggling. Clip and post cartoons. Put four boxes on your desk, mark them: *in, out, too hard, beats the hell out of me.* Seek levity in gravity.

Singing. I can't carry a tune, but I find they carry me. Music expresses and induces emotion. Most of our waking hours are spent hiding or keeping our emotions in check; music frees them. Broaden yourself by sampling music of the world; experience the rhythms that move people around the globe.

Imagining. Let your mind wander to unfamiliar places—insight resides there. Fantasize. All progressive actions begin as visions of possibilities.

Acting. *Wait and see* is a motto fit only for bird-watchers. A maverick makes things happen. "The life of wisdom," wrote M. Scott Peck, "must be a life of contemplation combined with action."

GENERATING IDEAS

Where do ideas come from? They spring from an active, aware mind. Creativity, as pointed out earlier in this chapter, is not just producing novel ideas. But sometimes new ideas are exactly what you need. How do you summon them forth? One of the great, frequently perpetuated myths about creativity is that it strikes unpredictably like lightning with an "Aha! Eureka!" jolt of recognition. New ideas often come calling much more subtly than that.

I categorize idea generation into three basic states which are neither distinct nor exclusive, but which describe different aspects of the creative problem-solving process:

1. Epiphanic. The familiar Eureka! in the shower.

2. Associative. One thing leads to another; for example, insights that bubble up in your mind during an otherwise routine meeting. Humor, with its juxtapositions and tension-relieving laughter, often can lead to unexpected and meaningful associations.

3. Intentional. Entering into exercises to summon insight, such as participating in an ideafest.

Viewing creativity as an epiphany is to see it as passive—wait for the lightning bolt to strike, for the lightbulb to click on. Ideas do pop into our heads when we least expect them, and people regarded as creative may simply pay attention to the cognitive surprises we recognize as the epiphanic creative state. Often, though, the enlightening thought that sneaks into our consciousness while taking a walk or drifting off to sleep is like a sprout growing from a seed planted in our subconscious. Many creativity methods advise walking away from, or sleeping on, a problem for a few days to allow our minds to work on it behind the scenes of routine distractions. After sufficient time, voila!, up pops this mental seedling.

Sometimes we don't know we've planted those seeds—they enter our mind's garden pollinated by observing life. The seeds then yield a harvest of ideas.

The associative creative state may come while you're sitting at your desk reading a memo or journal, while in a laboratory or meeting discussing routine business but not specifically looking for a solution to a problem. It's that moment when your insides burst forth with, Hey, that gives me an idea! Sometimes this association of ideas results in something not necessarily new but an unusual parting with tradition.

For example, one might try associating customary banking with good retail merchandising (aha!). At a Banc One branch in a suburb of Columbus, Ohio, the bank doesn't look or act like a bank. A receptionist seated behind a curved counter in the peaked glass atrium greets guests. She points them past color pictures of local people and events, past the glass-topped table and low, contemporary couches to the glass-enclosed financial boutiques headlined by blue neon script signs proclaiming their specialty.

Alongside Home Equity, New Accounts, and the like, there's a travel agency, and realty service. The branch bank (which Bank One marketers prefer to call a "financial marketplace," thank you) holds deposits of about $50 million and processes an enviable 50,000 transactions a month. To rack up all that money changing, the little suburban branch bank that could is open seven days a week, until 7 P.M. weeknights when customers who finished working at their own jobs can come by and do business (Eureka!). Once a year, the bank holds a "sidewalk sale" complete with hot dogs, zoo animals, balloons, and bargains on certificates of deposit. When interviewed by a reporter for the *New York Times*, Michael Bradley, manager of this unusual bank asks himself, "Is that innovative?" And he answers, "No. Hell, retailers have been holding sidewalk sales and midnight madness sales for decades. It's just unusual for the banking industry." And a good example of associative creativity.

Creativity-inducing exercises and instruments that conjure the intentional creative state are receiving renewed enthusiasm in many quarters as organizations grope for ingenious answers to their perplexing problems. A new twist on the intentional creative state is the advent of computer software to help business people generate ideas. I use a tremendously helpful program called *IdeaFisher* published by **Fisher Idea Systems**, founded by Marsh Fisher. He's a man who opened himself up to absorb life: Cofounding Century 21 Real Estate in California after growing up in Davenport, Iowa, and teaching high school and working for the *Denver Post* and working as a travel manager for American Express in Hong Kong and living in New York, recording for RCA Records.

Using the *IdeaFisher* program is like assembling a bright group of colleagues to help you generate ideas to solve the challenges before you. Because in reality, it's just you and the computer; using the responsive software is like playing ping-pong with your own subconscious.

The mammoth *IdeaFisher* program (loaded on about 20 floppy disks, requiring seven megabytes of hard disk storage and one megabyte of RAM) includes some 3,000 questions to provoke one's thinking about clarifying a problem, defining a business strategy, or evaluating potential courses of action. It also boasts a database of more than 60,000 idea words that are brilliantly organized and thoroughly cross-referenced into more than 705,000 direct idea associations from which one can freely springboard to an infinite number of other word associations. You can make notes on the screen as your subconscious kicks up related ideas, and you can add your own words and associations to the database for use in future sessions. The company says everyone from R&D engineers to ad copywriters to song writers to ministers is using the program.

The powerful tool is predicated on the premise that you can't remember everything you know. "We have a high capacity for recognition, but a low capacity for recall," explains the booklet accompanying the software. It suggests that creativity is based on "the new Three Rs."

1. Recording information.

2. Retrieving information (recalling or reconstructing it).

3. Recombining information (pulling various pieces together in a different way).

Marsh Fisher explains that our minds don't categorize information alphabetically. For example, "car" isn't filed under C in your brain. You associate the word car with many possibilities: the first car you rode in as a child, the car you own now (or want), the act of getting from here to there; it's associated with driving, roads, tires, chrome, Sunday drives, status, freedom, and so on. The software program, by listing many possible associations—gathered in hundreds of man years of development with people from many walks of life—jogs one's memory, evoking personal associations that then lead to new ideas or frames of reference. The software lists not only words but names of famous people, phrases from popular songs, movie titles, and expressions.

Another, more portable and far simpler, intentional creativity device is the Pocket Innovator from **Creative Learning International**. It's a hand-held paper-based tool that combines hundreds of words on color-coded slips of paper mounted on a post that one can flip through in a seven-step creative development process. Those steps are Preparation; Investigation; Transformation; Incubation; Illumination; Verification; and Implementation.

With a pen, a blank piece of paper, and the little four-inch Pocket Innovator, you can walk yourself through a thorough creative thinking session, anywhere, anytime. The cards—each with a one word trigger—suggest a variety of ways to look at the problem and possible solutions. On the flip side of the cards are suggestions for having an ideafest by yourself, for leading a more creative life; and there's even a collection of quotations related to creativity.

Less systemized idea-provokers also are available commercially. Creativity author **Roger von Oech** markets something called a Creative Whack Pack. It's a stack of cards offering amusing anecdotes under various thought-stimulating headlines (e.g., Think like a kid; Avoid arrogance; Put a lion in your heart; Make your own rules). When a problem has you stymied, reach into your drawer to draw a card or two to jump-start your thinking into a higher gear. Creative Learning International markets a large inflatable vinyl lightbulb to throw around at meetings to alter attendees' normal business mindset.

Creativity tools don't replace human ingenuity, they augment it. "The hoe doesn't replace the farmer," says Marsh Fisher who adds that "the world doesn't give any credit to Michelangelo's scaffold or brush for the ceiling in the Sistine Chapel."

Before there were such commercial aids to generating ideas, there were plainer, brain-powered drills in which one could engage to summon the creative muses. Some of those concerning groups have been described elsewhere in this book. A classic technique worth repeating here is known as SCAMPER. This seven-step process gives you several ways to look at a challenge or opportunity. The acronym *SCAMPER* spells out the process.

S What can you substitute?

C What can you combine?

A What can you adapt?

M What can you magnify, miniaturize or multiply?

P What can you put to other uses?

E What else, who else, where else?

R What can you rearrange or reverse?

Why spend the time (or money) to use involved techniques to call forth new ideas? As Elliott Jaques wrote, "There are always better alternatives that have not been thought of."

COSTS OF CREATIVITY

Your enhanced thinking skills—born of intentionally practiced behaviors—can influence your life in dramatically positive ways. Still, like all good things, improved creative capacity comes at a cost. The price is extracted in a few ways.

With greater awareness of the world, your sensitivity to its problems usually increases. You can perceive complexities to which others are oblivious. With your heightened awareness of self, you recognize that you are empowered to effect positive change but incapable of solving all the world's problems. At the same time, you likely become more aware of opportunities that you haven't the time, energy, or resources to exploit. It's emotionally taxing to uncover wonderful endeavors that make sense for your enterprise that you simply must neglect. Two suggestions:

1. As recommended in Chapter 9, adopt criteria for evaluating your ideas.

2. File those ideas for future use!

Creative output may improve your productivity, but it also creates more work. When you open the floodgates to ideas, they rush fast and hard. Channeling them, implementing them is hard work. Seizing the opportunities that you discover often requires more labor, on top of everything you're already doing.

When you're a creative problem solver, word gets out. Your boss may compliment you with the curse of doing good work: Here, do more. That vote of confidence probably boosts output and performance quality initially. However, when resources don't increase proportionately to the workload, quality inevitably suffers. Good people can get crushed under the weight of "just one more."

Just as your boss recognizes your improving talents, colleagues who haven't invested in themselves the way you have will seek your creative counsel. When the ego gratification wears thin, you're left with more demands than time. Other colleagues may resent your creative facility—the "smart alec" syndrome. You may feel peer pressure to self-censor your insights. Resist the temptation to hold back unless you are just showing off. You invested in your skills to put them to work, not to hold them in abeyance.

While your creativity may be enhanced by edifying intellectual pursuits, contemplation, and reflection, your creative output can make you crazy. Every untested or controversial concept carries risk as well as potential reward. While your ideas prove themselves, there's inevitable anxiety attached to the testing. Even great new ideas imply change which is always stressful during the transition.

Bertolt Brecht, who wrote the lyrics to the "Ballad of Mack the Knife," wrote this line in a play: "You know what the trouble with peace is? No organization." I believe a parallel can be drawn to creativity. Know what the trouble with creativity is? No peace.

COMMUNICATING CREATIVITY

I had the same idea; I just didn't say anything. Have those words ever tripped across your tongue? Or how about, *I suggested that last year, but do I get the credit?*

Psychologist Robert J. Sternberg says that, "We can view creativity as an act of persuasion; that is, individuals become 'creative' only insofar as they impress others with their creativity." In their book *The Creativity Infusion*, R. Donald Gamache and Robert L. Kuhn declare, "Most new ideas are presented in such an amateurish way that only an idiot or a genius would be willing to invest his or her time, money, or career in them." David Ogilvy offers that, "Management cannot be expected to recognize a good idea unless it is presented to them by a good salesman."

When you have ideas that your organization needs to know about, be a maverick: Speak up! Let the strength of your convictions match the quality of your ideas. Think through your proposal, consider all the possible positive and negative ramifications, document your case and present it with passion.

A solution unexpressed solves no problems. Share your good thinking with a world that so desperately needs it.

Afterword

We've got to find ways to encourage everybody to have ideas, and reward them, and recognize them. We can do it with a system where people are encouraged to contribute their ideas whether they're in the mailroom, on the assembly line, in the executive suite, or wherever.

Marsh Fisher

Every creator expresses a unique, recurring view of reality—as it is or could be—through his or her creations. For the painter, it's beauty; the sculptor, form; the musician, rhythm; the architect, balance; the scholar, wisdom; the engineer, structure; the soldier, security; the merchant, abundance; the athlete, strength; the lawyer, justice; the teacher, potential; the doctor, well-being; the accountant, order; the inventor, possibilities; the social worker, help; the farmer, renewal; the nurse, care; the salesman, influence; the writer, relationships; the traveler, wonder; the clergy, hope; the executive, prosperity; the volunteer, compassion; the scientist, knowledge; the statesman, harmony; the parent, love; the laborer, purpose. At various times in our lives, we are all of these.

In creating this book, I've tried to write of hope for commercial relationships based on enterprise, not greed; trust, not manipulation; freedom, not control; merit, not muscle; expression, not constraint.

The greatest challenge to progress, I believe, is not adversity or even failure. It is success—when it is easy to justify a static status quo, and easy not to seek, push, or demand better. Complacency, the maverick knows, is stagnation and soon destruction.

I undertook this project as a learning experience. And that it has been. My learning is not complete. I would like to know how the agenda I described in these pages works for you, and what works for you that isn't inscribed here.

I invite your correspondence to:

Box 791
Princeton Junction, NJ 08550

Donald W. Blohowiak

Maverick Resources

American Compensation Association

14040 N. Northsight Blvd.
Scottsdale, Arizona 85260
602/951-9191
The ACA is a membership organization which sponsors research projects on compensation and benefit issues, and offers educational opportunities for compensation professionals.

American Productivity and Quality Center

123 North Post Oak Lane
Houston, Texas 77024
713/681-4020. FAX: 713/681-8578
This nonprofit organization provides advisory, research, and information services to improve productivity, quality, and quality of work life. It issues a variety of publications, conducts public seminars, and offers research, reference, and individualized services.

Malcolm Baldrige National Quality Award Office, U.S. Dept. of Commerce

National Institute of Standards & Technology, Administration Building
Gaithersburg, Maryland 20899
301/975-3972
Provides information on the rigorous requirements for the prestigious prize for quality.

Business Incentives

7630 Bush Lake Road
Edina, Minnesota 55439
612/835-4800
This privately held company with 850 employees provides performance incentive services—research, communications, training, measurement, travel and merchandise awards, meeting services—to a Fortune 500 client base.

Center for Creative Leadership

Box 26300
Greensboro, North Carolina 27438-6300
919/ 288–7210. FAX: 919/ 288–3999
The Center is an international, nonprofit educational institution. It is one of the largest leadership research and training organizations in the world. More than 16,000 executives attended its programs worldwide in 1990. It conducts research and produces publications in many areas including leadership development, creativity and innovation, diversity in the work place, education and nonprofit leadership.

The Council for Exceptional Children

1920 Association Drive
Reston, Virginia 22091-1589
FAX: 703/ 264–9494
This organization operates as a clearinghouse for information on gifted and handicapped children.

Creative Learning International

68 East Wacker Place, Suite 800
Chicago, Illinois 60601
312/ 853–4748. FAX: 312/ 782–7367
The company provides creativity training and consulting to a diverse client base, and sells thinking tools (including Pocket Innovator, Idea Volley Bulb, and creativity software); it publishes a helpful newsletter called *The Innovator*.

Creative Realities

17 Arlington Street
Boston, Massachusetts 02116
617/ 247–1313. FAX: 617/ 247–7438
This consulting firm bills itself as "an idea development company." The principals have experience with new product development and an extensive blue-chip client roster.

DuPont Center for Creativity & Innovation

1007 Market Street, Room 6009
Wilmington, Delaware 19898
302/ 773–0232
Innovative DuPont employees assembled short essays on creativity with cartoons to publish an entertaining and enlightening book called *Are We Creative Yet?* A single copy costs $14.90 plus applicable tax; discounts are available for multiple copies.

Fisher Ideas Systems

2222 Martin Street, Suite 110
Irvine, California 92715

714/ 474–8111. 800/ 289–4332. FAX: 714/ 757–2896
This company makes the *IdeaFisher* software, profiled in Chapter 10, for both
DOS and Macintosh personal computers.

Genesis Training Solutions

23 Skyland Place
The Woodlands, Texas 77381
713/ 364–7739
Principal Ray Slesinski is an author, innovation consultant, and keynote speaker
on corporate creativity topics.

The Ned Herrmann Group

2075 Buffalo Creek Road
Lake Lure, North Carolina 28746
704/ 625–9153. FAX: 704/ 625–2198
Author of *The Creative Brain*, Herrmann produces the Herrmann Brain Dominance Instrument which profiles one's thinking styles and preferred ways of
knowing.

Hewitt Associates

Offices worldwide
Founded in 1940, this international consulting firm specializes in the design,
financing, communication, and administration of employee benefit and compensation programs. Consultants and actuaries will evaluate programs, design new
ones, provide cost projections for existing and new programs, assist with plan
implementation, develop employee communications, conduct research and
surveys.

Institute for the Development of Educational Alternatives (IDEA)

Box 1004, Mower County
Austin, Minnesota 55912
This nonprofit, educational corporation publishes a bimonthly, brain-teasing
newsletter called *Provoking Thoughts*.

InnerTrack, Inc.

800/ 274–4334
The company makes and sells the WayToGo card line to express your appreciation to colleagues in a businesslike way.

INNOTECH

2285 Reservoir Ave.
Trumbull, Connecticut 06611
203/ 371–0191. FAX: 203/ 371–6253
Founded in 1969, this international specialty consulting firm helps companies
grow new businesses or revitalize existing ones. It maintains a computerized
database of nearly 4,000 specialists who lend their knowledge to client projects.

Macro Thinking

99 Wrexham Road
Bronxville, New York 10708
914/337–4454. FAX: 914/337–4474
Principal Robert Zadek consults organizations on applying technology to accelerate idea generation for product development, naming, and other applications. Zadek is an accomplished *IdeaFisher* user and consultant.

National Association of Suggestion Systems (NASS)

230 N. Michigan Ave. Suite 1200
Chicago, Illinois 60601-5910
312/372–1770. FAX: 312/372–7723
NASS is a not-for-profit association of administrators of suggestion systems. It provides education to its members (including printed materials and conferences), explores trends in all types of employee involvement programs, and keeps statistics on employee suggestion systems.

Sibson & Co.

Chicago: 312/580–7770; Los Angeles: 213/556–3277; New York: 212/891–9800; Princeton: 609/520–2700; San Francisco: 415/989-2517; Toronto: 416/867–4500.
This management consulting firm, a part of Johnson & Higgins, specializes in compensation management, executive compensation, sales management, human resource and organization effectiveness, employee communications, and surveys.

Jeremy P. Tarcher, Inc.

5858 Wilshire Blvd., Suite 200
Los Angeles, California 90036
800/288–2131
Publisher of a line of books on creativity.

Roger von Oech

Box 7354
Menlo Park, California 94026
415/321–6775. FAX: 415/321–0609
Mr. von Oech is said to be an entertaining speaker and workshop leader. He also offers his books (*A Whack on the Side of the Head*, and *A Kick in the Seat of the Pants*) as well as his *Creative Whack Pack*.

References

Preface

Page

viii   Leonard Ackerman wrote "Whose Ox Is Being Gored," *HRMagazine*, February 1991, p. 96.

viii   DePree made his observation in his book, *Leadership Is an Art* (New York: Doubleday, 1989), p. 46.

ix   From the *Tao Te Ching*, passage 63, translated by R. L. Wing in *The Tao of Power* (New York: Doubleday, 1986).

Introduction

Page

2   The quote from *Fortune* was written by Thomas A. Stewart in the special edition, New American Century, 1991, p. 21.

2   Ray Slesinski's quote from an interview with me.

2   John Hoerr's quote taken from "Sharpening Minds for a Competitive Edge," *Business Week*, December 17, 1990.

3   The transcript of the "Industrial Revelation" commercial, produced by the Los Angeles office of the BBDO advertising agency, is printed here with the kind permission of Apple Computer. Chris Wall, BBDO/LA's associate creative director, wrote the spot.

4   Norton Paley, president of Alexander-Norton, Inc., wrote "Monday Morning Marketing Memo," in *Marketing Forum*, published by the American Management Association, January 1991, p. 4.

4   Rick Going's great observation about change from his speech to the Sales and Marketing Executives symposium in New York City, March 1991. Text provided by Avon.

4   Edward L. Hennessy's remarks from "Meeting the Global Challenges of the '90s," a speech presented to the International Industrial Conference in San Francisco, September 18, 1989. Text provided by Allied-Signal.

Page

4   Quote from *Machine Design,* October 12, 1989, in "Brainstorming Software Unlocks Creativity," by Nancy E. Rouse, p. 100.

4   The failure of computers to improve productivity from "Heads that Roll if Computers Fail," by Glenn Rifkin, *New York Times,* May 14, 1991, p. D6.

5   John Sculley's remark on the old work model from a speech he made to the Software Publishers Association Spring Symposium, San Francisco, March 1991. Text provided by Apple Computer.

6   Markovits is quoted in "The Power of the Patent Portfolio," in *Think,* IBM's employee magazine, no. 5, 1990, p. 10.

6   Marsh Fisher's comments from an interview with me.

7   Mark Sebell's comments from an interview with me.

8   Virgil Barry of A. T. Kearney quoted in "Now Capital Means Brains, Not Just Bucks," *Fortune,* January 14, 1991, p. 31.

8   *Time* magazine's declaration of ideas as wealth from "Whose Bright Idea?" by Thomas McCarroll, June 10, 1991, p. 44.

8   The ad for Perdue chicken was created by Scali, McCabe, Sloves Advertising in New York, and received an Athena award from the Newspaper Advertising Bureau.

8   *Capitalis* defined by *Webster's New Twentieth Century Dictionary,* (New York: Simon & Schuster, 1983), p. 268.

8   Research and Development spending figures reported in "America's Hot Young Scientists," by Gene Bylinsky, *Fortune,* October 8, 1990, p. 56.

8   Lawsuit statistics from "Whose Bright Idea?" *Time,* June 10, 1991, p. 44.

9   Alvin Toffler's quote from his book *Powershift* (New York: Bantam Books, 1990), p. 173.

9   Microsoft statement from its 1989 annual report, p. 16.

9   "BrainPower" by Thomas A. Stewart, *Fortune,* June 3, 1991, p. 45.

9   John Sculley's remarks on creativity from *Odyssey,* his book written with John A. Byrne (New York: Harper & Row, 1987), p. 184.

10   Gamache and Kuhn wrote of managerial ignorance in their book, *The Creativity Infusion* (New York: Harper & Row, 1989), p. 15.

Page
11   Robert Waterman's comment from his book *The Renewal Factor* (New York: Bantam Books, 1987), p. 99.

11   Robots in fast-food restaurants reported by Michael Lev in "Raising Fast Food's Speed Limit," *New York Times*, August 7, 1991, p. D1.

12   Tom Stewart made the remark about bodies and brains in an interview with me.

12   Manufacturing job estimate from Table no. 651, Employment by Selected Industry, 1970 to 1988, and Projections, 2000, *Statistical Abstract of the United States*, Washington, DC, 1990, p. 395.

12   "It's no accident . . ." Tom Stewart wrote in "Now Capital Means Brains, Not Just Bucks," *Fortune*, January 14, 1991, p. 32.

12   Mercer survey reported in *Personnel Journal* and cited in *Boardroom Reports*, June 15, 1991, p. 15.

12   "Seven of 10 companies," survey by Roseland, N.J. law firm of Grotta, Glassman & Hoffman, reported by *The Wall Street Journal*, November 7, 1990, p. B1.

13   Peter Gelfond cited in *Boardroom Reports*, February 15, 1991, p. 15.

13   Michael LeBoeuf's observation from his book *The Greatest Management Principle in the World* (New York: Berkley Books, 1989), p. 5.

13   Service complaint research reported in *Total Customer Service* by William H. Davidow and Bro Uttal (New York: Harper & Row) cited in *The Competitive Advantage*, November 1990, p. 1.

13   Gallup poll cited in *The Journal of Business Strategy*, July/August 1990, p. 8.

14   Wyatt Company survey cited in *Boardroom Reports*, August 15, 1990, p. 15.

14   Roy Chitwood made his remark while running a workshop at the National Association of Legal Vendors symposium in San Diego, October 26, 1990.

Chapter One

Page
16   M. Scott Peck's quote is from *The Road Less Traveled* (New York: Simon & Schuster, 1978), p. 285.

Page

16 Warren Bennis's observation about nonconformists is from *Why Leaders Can't Lead* (San Francisco: Jossey-Bass, 1990), p. 124.

16 Roger von Oech's quote is from *A Whack on the Side of the Head* (New York: Warner, 1983), p. 113.

16 Jack Welch's quote from "GE Keeps Those Ideas Coming," *Fortune*, August 12, 1991, p. 41.

18 Buck Rodgers is quoted in "An Upbeat Message for American Management," *Executive Excellence*, June 1987, p. 16.

18 Dr. Markowich reported on his studies in "Is It Risky to Give the Boss a Good Idea?" *Management Review*, October 1990, p. 28.

19 Alvin Toffler, *PowerShift* (New York: Bantam Books, 1990), p. 179.

19 Toffler quotes Lenin in his book, *The Third Wave* (New York: William Morrow & Co., 1980), p. 56.

19 Robert Levering's remark about management elite is from *A Great Place to Work* (New York: Avon Books, 1988), p. 106.

20 Harvey Cox is quoted from his book, *The Seduction of the Spirit* (New York: Simon & Schuster, 1973), p. 49.

21 The General O'Donnell story was recalled by Gerald A. Johnston in commencement remarks at the UCLA School of Engineering, and reported in *The Executive Speaker*, September 1990, p. 1.

21 Bob Doyle's remark appeared in *Inc.*, September 1982, p. 54.

21 Chuck Reaves's remark from his book, *The Theory of 21* (New York: M. Evans & Co., 1983), p. 13.

21 Hank Johnson's comment on a few things going right quoted in *Boardroom Reports*, October 15, 1990, p. 5.

22 DeBono's "blocked by the adequate" from his book, *Lateral Thinking* (New York: Harper & Row, 1970), p. 267.

22 Skyscraper story from *Lateral Thinking*, p. 36.

22 DeBono's remark on history and validity from DeBono, *Lateral Thinking*, p. 91.

22 Ezra Pound's quote was found in Jaques Elliott, *Creativity and Work* (Madison, Wisc.: International Universities Press, 1990), p. 176.

22 Elizabeth Bailey related the Mrs. Edison story in a discussion recorded in *New Directions in Creative and Innovative Management*, edited by Yuji Ijiri and Robert Lawrence Kuhn (Cambridge, Mass.: Ballinger Publishing Company, 1988), p. 323.

Page

23   Ogilvy tale from Stephen R. Fox, *The Mirror Makers* (New York: William Morrow and Co., 1984), p. 234. The chapter notes indicate the material was drawn from *Advertising Age*, May 13, 1957.

23   Bennis, *Why Leaders Can't Lead*, p. 15.

23   Ray Slesinski's clever turn of phrase from his booklet, "Creative Personality Traits," Genesis Training Solutions, p. 31.

24   Lao Tzu from R. L. Wing *The Tao of Power* (New York: Doubleday, 1986), passage 57.

24.   The concept of boredom at work equating with death derives from Elliott Jaques, *Creativity and Work*, p. 186.

24   Rolf Landauer is quoted in "Not Just Another Quality Program," *Think*, no. 5, 1990, p. 51.

25   Ed McCabe quoted in "Talking Ed," *Advertising Age*, March 1989, p. 10.

25   Tom Stewart's remarks from an interview with me.

25   Robert Levering's observation on management literature is from the preface to *A Great Place to Work*, p. x.

26   Ken Matejka, *Why This Horse Won't Drink* (New York: AMACOM, 1991), pp. 141–54.

26   Peter M. Senge wrote *The Fifth Discipline* (New York: Doubleday, 1990), p. 44.

Chapter Two

Page

28   Irving Thalberg's comment on Margaret Mitchell's *Gone with the Wind* recorded in Christopher Cerf and Victor Navasky, *The Experts Speak: The Definitive Compendium of Misinformation* (New York: Pantheon Books, 1984).

30   History of the term "maverick" from *The Oxford English Dictionary*, Second Edition, Volume 9, (Oxford, England: Clarendon Press, 1989), p. 494. If the guy's name had been Blohowiak, Czymworitz, or Haghawagawagh, do you think it would have entered the language?

31   James Dunlap's remarks about the dollar bill are from a speech he gave to a meeting of Texaco Jobbers, quoted in, "Imaginative People at Work," *The Executive Speaker*, March 1991, p. 7.

Page

31   Galileo's imprisonment from Arthur E. Bostwick, *Pivotal Figures of Science* (Chicago: American Library Association, 1928), p. 15.

31   The presumed insanity of gifted people noted by Linda Kreger Silverman, citing writings from the late 19th century, in her essay, "Issues in Affective Development of the Gifted," in *A Practical Guide to Counseling the Gifted in a School Setting*, edited by Joyce Van Tassel-Baska (Reston, Va.: The Council for Exceptional Children, 1990), p. 20.

31   Invention as a recently encouraged endeavor reported in the *Academic American Encyclopedia*, (New York: Grolier Electronic Publishing, Inc., 1990) accessed on Prodigy Interactive Personal Service.

31   M. Scott Peck's comment about Adam and Eve from *The Road Less Traveled* (New York: Simon and Schuster, 1978), p. 272.

32   Hero's water dispenser chronicled in David MacCauley's *The Way Things Work* (Boston: Houghton Mifflin, 1988), p. 359.

33   Pascal's invention described in MacCauley, *The Way Things Work*, pp. 372–73.

33   Costs and weight of the first electronic calculators from Sheridan M. Tatsuno, *Created in Japan* (New York: Harper & Row, 1990), p. 120.

33   Kaempffert's comment from his book *Invention and Society* (Chicago: American Library Association, 1930), p. 12.

34   Marsh Fisher's comment from an interview with me.

34   Neil Postman's remark appears in Roger von Oech's *Whack on the Side of the Head* (New York: Warner, 1983), p. 22.

35   Charles Garfield made his plea in his book *Peak Performers* (New York: Avon Books, 1986), p. 33.

35   Rene Dubos's comment on being free to choose, from his book *Celebrations of Life* (New York: McGraw-Hill, 1981), p. 117.

35   The problems of mavericks in school drawn in part from Miriam Adderholdt-Elliott, *Perfectionism: What's Bad About Being Too Good* (Minneapolis: Free Spirit Publishing, 1987), pp. 16 and 53.

36   Honda's comment reported in his obituary in the *New York Times*, August 6, 1991, p. A15.

36   William Gates as Harvard dropout from "Mr. Software" by Fred Moody, *New York Times Magazine*, August 25, 1991, p. 56.

Page

36   Abraham Lincoln held a patent on a boat designed to float over obstacles, according to Thomas P. Carney in his book *False Profits* (Notre Dame, IN: University of Notre Dame Press, 1981), p. 164.

36   James Delisle's comments from "The Emperor Still Needs Clothes," *TAG Update*, Spring 1991, p. 1.

37   The study on earnings of MBAs and other executives was reported in the article "Myth of the Well-Educated Manager," by J. Sterling Livingston. It originally appeared in the *Harvard Business Review*, January–February, 1971. While that study might seem quite dated, the principle is more evergreen. My copy of the article is included in a book published by Harvard Business Review, Boston, Mass. in 1983, *Paths Toward Personal Progress: Leaders Are Made, Not Born*, p. 64.

37   "Positive maladjustment" attributed to K. Dabrowski, *Positive Disintegration* (Boston: Little, Brown, 1964), and other psychological works.

38   Chester Carlson's story from *The Innovators* by John Diebold (New York: Truman Talley Books/ Plume, 1991), pp. 88–108.

38   Honda's great story told by David E. Sanger in "Soichiro Honda, Auto Innovator Is Dead at 84," *New York Times*, August 6, 1991, p. A1, A15.

38   Riggs' observation from his book *Managing High Technology Companies* (Belmont, Calif.: Lifetime Learning Publications, 1983), p. 280.

39   Rosabeth Moss-Kanter wrote about the quiet entrepreneurs in her book *The Change Masters* (New York: Simon & Schuster, 1983), p. 210.

39   Professor Gary A. Steiner made these observations about attitudes of highly creative individuals toward authority in *The Creative Organization*, which he edited (Chicago: University of Chicago Press, 1965), p. 8.

39   Chuck Reaves made his comment on rules in *The Theory of 21* (New York: M. Evans & Co., 1983), p. 95.

39   The ad for the new Porsche 911 Carrera 2 Coupe as prepared by ad agency Fallon McElligott in Minneapolis; Creative Director, Pat Burnham; Copywriter, John Stingley.

40   Sculley's remarks about anarchy from his book written with John Byrne, *Odyssey* (New York: Harper & Row, 1987), p. 186.

Page

46 Gardner's observation is noted in *Fire in the Crucible* by John Briggs (Los Angeles: Jeremy P. Tarcher Inc., 1990), pp. 233 and 364.

46 Sandra Hale's tale from "25 Who Help the US Win," in New American Century issue of *Fortune*, 1991, p. 36, and "Sandra Hale's Expose of Good Government" in Fred Jordan, *Innovating America* (New York: Ford Foundation, 1990) pp. 28–49.

47 Information on the Army truck-fix from materials provided by the National Association of Suggestion Systems, dated Sept. 25, 1990.

47 Fahey's landfill mining reported by Carol Steinbach in *Innovations in State and Local Government 1990* (New York: Ford Foundation, 1990), p. 10.

47 Tacoma program for the homeless, Steinbach, *Innovations*, p. 30.

47 Georgia dry hydrants, Steinbach, *Innovations*, p. 27.

48 Arcata, California, waste-water treatment system reported in Fred Jordan, *Innovating America*, (New York: Ford Foundation, 1990), p. 14.

48 Newport News police training, Steinbach, *Innovations*, pp. 29–30.

48 Franklin Thomas wrote his remarks in the foreword to *Innovating America*, p. 5.

Chapter Three

Page

50 Albert J. Bernstein and Sydney C. Rozen quote from their book *Dinosaur Brains* (New York: Ballantine Books, 1989), p. 198.

50 Warren Bennis quote from *Why Leaders Can't Lead* (San Francisco: Jossey-Bass, 1990), p. 29.

50 Dr. Piechowski's quote from his essay, "Emotional Development and Emotional Giftedness," in *Handbook of Gifted Education*, edited by Nicholas Colangelo and Gary A. Davis (Boston: Allyn & Bacon, 1991), p. 287.

51 Linda Kreger Silverman is director of the Gifted Child Development Center in Denver. Her remarks from Joyce VanTassel-Baska's *Practical Guide to Counseling the Gifted* (Reston, Virginia: The Council for Exceptional Children, 1990), p. 19.

Page

51 William Gates's prodigy from "Mr. Software" by Fred Moody, *New York Times Magazine*, August 25, 1991, p. 56.

51 I became exposed to the gifted children literature while my wife, Susan, worked on her masters degree in special education. She detected some striking parallels between my life and work experiences and those attributed to the children under study. I am grateful to Susan for insisting that I read that fascinating information; without question, it has helped to change my life for the better.

52 John Briggs, from his *Fire in the Crucible* (Los Angeles: Jeremy P. Tarcher Inc., 1990), p. 201.

53 Dr. Gallagher's comment from "Issues in the Education of Gifted Students," *Handbook of Gifted*, p. 14.

53 Tannebaum's rebuke of the straight A student from "The Social Psychology of Giftedness," *Handbook of Gifted*, p. 29.

53 Gardner's multiple intelligence theory from *Frames of Mind: The Theory of Multiple Intelligences* (New York: Basic, 1983).

54 Von Oech's comment on patterns from *Whack on the Side of the Head* (New York: Warner, 1983), p. 45.

54 Garfield, *Peak Performers* (New York: Avon Books, 1986), p. 52.

54 Prof. Steiner's assessment of a creative man recorded in *The Creative Organization* (Chicago: University of Chicago Press, 1965), pp. 257–59.

55 Wareham's comment on *fingerspitzengefuhl* from his *Secrets of a Corporate Headhunter* (New York: Atheneum, 1981), p. 105.

55 Sternberg's insights on practical giftedness from "Giftedness According to the Triarchic Theory of Human Intelligence," *Handbook of Gifted*, pp. 46, 50.

55 Isaac Bashevis Singer quoted by Israel Shenker in a tribute to the recently-deceased writer, "The Man Who Talked Back to God," the *New York Times Book Review*, August 11, 1991, p. 11.

56 Arthur Bostwick's comment about scientists' curiosity from his *Pivotal Figures of Science* (Chicago: American Library Association, 1928), p. 18.

56 Leslie Kaplan's observation from "Helping Gifted Students with Stress Management," *ERIC Digest* no E488, The Council for Exceptional Children, 1990, p. 1.

Page

56   Philip Perrone's list of attributes appears in "Career Development," *Handbook of Gifted*, p. 326.

57   Chet Holmes used the phrase *nut case believers* in personal correspondence.

57   Riggs' quote from his *Managing High-Technology Companies* (Belmont, Calif.: Lifetime Learning Publications, 1983), p. 279.

57   Steve Jobs and his "reality distortion field" from the *New York Times*, September 19, 1990, p. D5.

59   Dr. Donall Thomas's story from "Two American Transplant Pioneers Win Nobel Prize in Medicine," *New York Times*, October 9, 1990, p. C3; and "Nobel: The Story Behind the Prize," *Sky*, October 1991, p. 76.

59   Marsh Fisher's idea for an idea storage system from a personal interview with him.

60   Honda's idea bank from "Create and Survive," *Economist*, December 1, 1990, p. 77.

60   Sam Walton's strategy from Vance H. Trimble, *Sam Walton* (New York: Dutton, 1990).

60   Tannenbaum on risk taking, *Handbook of Gifted*, p. 36.

60   Dean Simonton's remarks from "Original Spin" by Lesley Dormen and Peter Edidin, *Psychology Today*, July/August 1989, p. 49.

60   Robert J. Sternberg's comment on genius from *The Nature of Creativity*, edited by Dr. Sternberg (Cambridge, Mass.: Cambridge University Press, 1988), p. 422.

60   J. Briggs' observation on creators and chance from *Fire in the Crucible*, p. 278.

61   The discovery of Nutra-Sweet was related by Moshe F. Rubinstein of the UCLA School of Engineering and Applied Science in remarks to the Town Hall of California, recounted in "Seeing What Others Do Not See," *The Executive Speaker*, February 1991, p. 5.

63   John Markoff wrote about Steve Jobs and Next Inc., in "Nextstation's [sic] Future Hinges on Software," *New York Times*, August 11, 1991, p. F8.

64   Professor Argyris, "Teaching Smart Managers to Learn," *Boardroom Reports*, August 1, 1991, p. 5.

Page
65   The screenplay for *Star Trek V* was written by David Loughery, copyright 1989 by Paramount Pictures Corp.

67   Dr. Silverman's assessment of gifted children's confounding emotions from her essay, "Issues in Affective Development of the Gifted," in *Practical Guide to Counseling the Gifted in a School Setting*, edited by Joyce VanTassel-Baska (Reston, Va.: Council for Exceptional Children, 1990), p. 16.

67   Larry Smarr's story from "A Citizen-Scientist Spreads Supercomputer Power," The New American Century, *Fortune*, special issue, Spring/Summer 1991, p. 45.

68   Dr. Longfellow's insights from *Beyond Success*, audio tape, 1988.

69   Dr. Piechowski's stinging comments from *Handbook of Gifted*, p. 293.

69   Gifted adults are overexcitable, *Practical Guide to Counseling the Gifted*, p. 24.

70   M. Scott Peck on Christ's loneliness from *The Road Less Traveled* (New York: Simon & Schuster, 1978), p. 288.

70   Garfield observation from *Peak Performers*, p. 79.

71   Andrew Harvey quoted in a review of his book, *Hidden Journey*, in the *New York Times Book Review*, August 11, 1991, p. 23.

71   James Delisle, Kent State University, wrote about underachievement in "Underachieving Gifted Students," *ERIC Digest* no. E478, The Council For Exceptional Children, 1990, p. 1.

Chapter Four

Page
74   Honda's quote from the *New York Times*, August 6, 1991, p. A15.

74   Albert J. Bernstein and Sydney C. Rozen quote from their book *Dinosaur Brains* (New York: Ballantine Books, 1989), p. 225.

74   Lumsden quote from his article, "Management Lessons Learned from the War in the Gulf," *Sales and Marketing Executive Report*, April 10, 1991, p. 8.

74   Robert Lawrence Kuhn's quote from his essay, "Personality and Innovation: How Creative Types Think and Act," in *Frontiers in Creative and Innovative Management*, which he edited (Cambridge, Mass.: Ballinger Publishing Co., 1986), p. 167.

Page

76   Steelcase survey reported by *Inc.* magazine and cited in *Boardroom Reports,* May 1, 1991, p. 2.

77   Survey by the American Productivity and Quality Center, reported by Caleb S. Atwood and Rolf C. Smith in the Center's newsletter, *Consensus,* December 1990, pp. 1–2.

77   Wyatt Co. survey reported in *Communications Briefings,* May 1991, p. 3.

79   Carl Ally quote from Stephen R. Fox, *The Mirror Makers* (New York: William R. Morrow & Co., 1984), p. 316.

80   Harvey Cox, *Seduction of the Spirit* (New York: Simon & Schuster, 1973), pp. 319–20.

80   Paul Allaire was quoted in "The Bureaucracy Busters" by Brian Dumaine, *Fortune,* June 17, 1991, pp. 46 and 50.

80   Lao Tzu from R. L. Wing, *The Tao of Power* (New York: Doubleday, 1986), passage 3.

81   Peter Senge's comment on leadership from *The Fifth Discipline* (New York: Doubleday, 1990), p. 360.

81   Goings made this declaration in remarks to the Sales and Marketing Executives meeting in March 1991, New York.

83   Fr. Bartel's comment on competence from his interview with Peter F. Drucker in Dr. Drucker's book *Managing the Nonprofit Organization* (New York: Harper-Collins, 1990), p. 164.

83   Alfred Nobel's pursuits from "Nobel: The Story Behind the Prize" by Walter Roessing, *SKY,* October 1991, pp. 76–82.

84   J. B. Fuqua remark on giving people authority from *Boardroom Reports,* March 1, 1991, p. 6.

84   Andrall Pearson's comment on innovation from his essay, "Tough-Minded Way to Get Innovative," *Harvard Business Review,* May–June 1988, p. 100.

85   The story of Mary Ayres, from "Careers at SSC&B," a brochure produced by SSC&B: Lintas Worldwide, New York, 1987.

87   Max DePree's comment from his *Leadership Is an Art* (New York: Doubleday, 1989) p. 23.

87   John Sculley's remark about hierarchy from his speech to MacWorld, Tokyo, Japan, February 1991; text provided by the company.

Page

89   Riggs' comment on justifying the rejection of ideas from *Managing High-Technology Companies* (Belmont, Calif.: Lifetime Learning Publications, 1983) p. 279.

90   Zemke's recommendation from his article "The Dirty Word," *Incentive*, June 1990, p. 6.

90   Dr. Mecca's conclusion on self-esteem in *Toward a State of Esteem*, (Sacramento: California State Dept. of Education, 1990), p. vii.

90   Bob Waterman's comment on self-confident employees from "The Pygmalion Effect," *Success*, October 1988, p. 8.

92   The shrinking white male work force statistic from "What's All This About a Labor Shortage," by Dave Jensen, *Management Review*, June 1991, p. 44.

92   James Houghton made his remarks about cultural diversity to the Conference Board in New York, May 4, 1988. Text provided by Corning.

92   Gamache and Kuhn, *The Creativity Infusion* (New York: Harper & Row, 1989), p. 18.

92   Hanley Norins made his comment about ideas and tension in his book, *The Young & Rubicam Traveling Creative Workshop* (Englewood Cliffs, N.J.: Prentice Hall, 1990), p. 4.

93   Stephanie Tolan's comments on the gifted from the pamphlet she wrote, "Helping Your Highly Gifted Child" (Reston, Va.: The Council for Exceptional Children, 1990), p. 4.

93   T. J. Rodgers' sign reported in *Fortune* magazine's New American Century, 1991, p. 40.

94   Melissa Lande's comment from personal correspondence.

94   M. Scott Peck, *The Road Less Traveled* (New York: Simon & Schuster, 1978), p. 76.

95   Kahlil Gibran's ode to work from his book *The Prophet* (New York: Alfred A. Knopf, 1979), p. 28.

Chapter Five

Page

96   Charles Garfield quote from *Peak Performers* (New York: Avon Books, 1986), p. 17.

96   Rick Goings quote from his address to the Sales and Marketing Executives, March 1991.

Page

96   Michael LeBoeuf quote from his book, *The Greatest Management Principle in the World* (New York: Berkley Books, 1989), p. 110.

96   Honda quoted in *New York Times*, August 6, 1991, p. A15.

96   René Dubos quote from *Celebrations of Life* (New York: McGraw-Hill, 1981), p. 73.

97   Survey results cited in *Boardroom Reports*, March 15, 1991, p. 15.

99   R. L. Wing, *The Tao of Power* (New York: Doubleday, 1986), p. 12.

100   *Incentive* magazine's comment about money's modest motivational value from "Special Report: 1990 Facts Survey," December 1990, pp. 40–41.

100   Yankelovich survey reported in "Is the Work Ethic Dead?" by Michael Rozek, *Incentive*, October 1990, p. 65.

100   Richard Bartlett was quoted by *Incentive*, June 1990, p. 16.

100   Jude Rich's comment from "Coping with Work Force Inadequacy," *Chief Executive*, reprint, provided by Sibson & Co.

102   Rob Henderson's 30-60-10 rule from *Boardroom Reports*, April 15, 1991, p. 15.

103   Roger Milliken quoted in "At Milliken & Co., Quality Is a Matter of 'Divine Discontent,' " in IBM's *Think* magazine, no. 1, 1990.

103   Paul Cook made his comment about personal recognition in an interview published in the *Harvard Business Review*, March/April 1990, p. 99.

103   James Quinn presented his observations on the power of recognition at a symposium sponsored by the Sales and Marketing Executives of New York, March 1991.

103   The number of Baldrige Award applications reported in *Incentive*, April 1991, p. 33.

104   R. M. Kanter, *The Change Masters* (New York: Simon & Schuster, 1983), p. 151.

104   Hanley Norins made his point about unsigned creative works in his *The Young & Rubicam Traveling Creative Workshop* (Englewood Cliffs, N.J.: Prentice Hall, 1990), p. 10.

105   Lester Krogh's comments on awards from remarks he made to Canada United States Law Institute, Case Western Reserve University School of Law, April 14, 1989. Text provided by 3M.

106   Paul Cook's "Not Invented Here Award," *Harvard Business Review*, March/April 1990, p. 102.

Page

106 3M's policy on freedom to pursue pet projects verified by correspondence with the company.

111 Former football great Fran Tarkenton's comments from an interview in *Personal Selling Power*, May/June 1991, p. 17.

112 Richard Gurin and Crayola Crayons from an AP story in *The Times*, Trenton, NJ, July 8, 1991, p. B1.

112 Prof. Isen quoted in "Funny Business," by M. S. Allison, *Incentive*, March 1991, p. 42.

113 On extrinsic rewards actually diminishing creativity: Teresa Amabile of Brandeis has published widely on this phenomenon. A good summary of research supporting this finding can be found in "The Conditions of Creativity," by Beth A. Hennessey and Teresa Amabile, in *The Nature of Creativity* (Cambridge, Mass.: Cambridge University Press, 1988), pp. 11–38.

114 Northwest Airlines anecdote from "Is the Work Ethic Dead," by Michael Rozek, *Incentive*, October 1990, p. 65.

115 R. M. Kanter, *The Change Masters*, p. 151.

Chapter Six

Page

116 William Shockley's quote from *Creative Organization* (Chicago: University of Chicago Press, 1965), p. 97.

116 Pat Choate's quote from "Today's Worker in Tomorrow's Workplace," *The Journal of Business Strategy*, July/August 1990, p. 7.

116 Quote from Buck Rodgers, former VP of marketing for IBM, from his book, *Getting the Best Out of Yourself and Others*, with Irv Levey (New York: Harper & Row, 1987), p. 136.

116 Tom Stewart's quote from my interview with him.

116 The fascinating look at the variety of annual pay from "What People Earn," by Michael Vermeulen, *Parade Magazine*, June 23, 1991, pp. 4–8.

117 Data on income for lawyers from "What Lawyers Earn," *National Law Journal*, May 6, 1991 pp. S3–6.

117 CEOs make 85 times the wages of typical factory worker, from "The Flap Over Executive Pay," *Business Week*, May 6, 1991, p. 90.

Page

118   Dr. Sternberg's observation about the controlling nature of monetary rewards from the *Nature of Creativity*. (Cambridge, Mass.: Cambridge University Press, 1988), pp. 24, 405.

119   The idea of a pay gap being motivational is derived from Elliott Jaques' essay "The Work-Payment-Capacity Nexus," in his book, *Creativity and Work* (Madison, Wisc.: International Universities Press, 1990), pp. 191–207.

121   White-collar earnings vs. that of skilled tradespeople from "Sharpening Minds for a Competitive Edge" by John Hoerr, *Business Week*, December 17, 1990.

123   Income and debt statistics from "Where We Stand," by Thomas A. Stewart, in The New American Century, *Fortune*, 1991, pp. 16–17.

124   The insightful comments from Victor Rodriguez are from an interview with me.

124   Henry Riggs, *Managing High-Tech Companies* (Belmont, Calif.: Lifetime Learning Publications, 1983), p. 288.

127   Kenneth Mason's comments on executive compensation from his article "Four Ways to Overpay Yourself Enough," *Harvard Business Review*, July-August 1988, pp. 71–72.

128   The Sibson & Company survey results provided by the company.

128   Paul Cook's comments from "The Business of Innovation: An Interview with Paul Cook," *Harvard Business Review*, March/April 1990, p. 100.

128   John L. Frost of General Mills, quoted in "A Company of Champions," by Stephenie [sic] Overman, *HRMagazine*, October 1990, pp. 58–60.

128   Rick Chandler wrote about his Cellular Infrastructure Group in "Timely Strategy is Timeless Approach to Success," Motorola's *Impact* journal, May–June 1991, pp. 7–9.

128   Victor Kiam discussed his incentive program at the Sales and Marketing Executive's symposium in New York, March 26, 1991.

131   Merck's employee stock option plan reported in "Employees Offered Stock," *The Times*, Trenton, N.J., September 12, 1991, p. D1.

131   Biomet's stock option plan for employees reported in "Pay that Was Justified—And Pay that Just Mystified" by Geoffrey Smith and James E. Ellis, *Business Week*, May 6, 1991, p. 92.

Page

132   Benefit costs from U.S. Chamber of Commerce statistics cited in "Did You Know That . . ." *Boardroom Reports*, June 15, 1991, p. 15.

133   Federal Express's awards from *Blueprints for Service Quality* (New York: American Management Association, 1991), pp. 34–35.

133   The Philadelphia VA office's spot awards reported in "Applause, Applause," *Incentive*, July 1991, p. 34.

134   Fran Tarkenton spoke of Knowledgeware's Sterling Club in "Fran Tarkenton: Knowledgeware's $60 Million Champion," *Personal Selling Power*, May/June 1991, p. 16.

Chapter Seven

Page

136   Syd Kershaw quoted in "Suggestions Pay Off for Companies, Workers in Savings and Bonuses," by Rebecca Yerak, *Cleveland Plain Dealer*, January 22, 1991.

136   James Canada quoted in "Employers Reap Rewards from Employee Suggestions," *Employee Benefit News*, April 1990.

136   Cynthia McCabe is 1991 president of the National Association of Suggestion Systems. Her quote was provided by that organization.

136   Howard Schimerling quoted in "Employees' Ideas Mean Big Savings," *San Diego Tribune*, October 1, 1990, p. AA–1.

137   Rebecca Yerak penned the words about dusty suggestion boxes in "Suggestions Pay Off for Companies, Workers in Savings and Bonuses," for the *Plain Dealer's* January 22, 1991, edition.

138   Information on William Connor and Kodak suggestion program from "Diamonds in the Rough," *Democrat and Chronicle*, Rochester, N.Y., April 19, 1987, p. 1F, and "Employees Are Ideas Waiting to Be Tapped," *San Diego Daily Transcript*, September 28, 1990.

138   Kaiser's new perinatal center reported in "Employee Suggestion Programs Boost Morale and Bottom Line," *Hospitals*, May 20, 1991, p. 46.

138   The U S West success story from "The Modern Suggestion Box," by Janet Bronck, *Colorado Business Magazine*, September 1990.

138   Joseph Grisbach's story from "It Pays to Listen" by Peter H. Frank, *The Baltimore Sun*, January 22, 1990.

Page

139   Information on Stephen Schroeder's computer database provid-
           ed by NASS, and from "Employees Are Ideas Waiting to Be
           Tapped," by Herbert Lockwood, *San Diego Daily Transcript*, Sep-
           tember 28, 1990, and "Employees' Ideas Mean Big Savings," by
           Michael Kinsman, *San Diego Tribune*, October 1, 1990.

139   The ten NASS tips reprinted by permission of National Associa-
           tion of Suggestion Systems.

140   Modern of Marshfield's reward system from "Ideas that Pay
           Off," by Skip Berry, *Nation's Business*, April 1991.

145   Information on Ritz-Carlton's employee suggestion system from
           conversations with hotel officials, and materials provided by the
           company.

145   Milliken suggestion system described in "At Milliken & Co.,
           Quality Is a Matter of 'Divine Discontent,' " *Think*, Number 1,
           1990, p. 5.

145   The GE Work-Out program described in "GE Keeps Those Ideas
           Coming" by Thomas A. Stewart, *Fortune*, August 12, 1991, pp.
           41–49.

146   Information on Boardroom's suggestion program provided by
           the company.

147   Insights on incentives, cash versus merchandise, drawn from
           my personal experience, and "Do You Favor Money as an Incen-
           tive?" by Mark Blessington and Jack D. Daniels, *Business Market-
           ing*, March 1991, pp. T10, T12; information provided by Business
           Incentives, Minneapolis; and *"How to Run an Incentive Program,"*
           a booklet by Todd Englander and Bruce Bolger, published in co-
           operation with *Incentive* magazine, the Maritz Motivation Com-
           pany and the American Productivity and Quality Center, 1990.

148   Chuck Loose of Briggs & Stratton quoted in "Good Idea!" by
           Anita Bruzzese, *Employee Benefit News*, April 1990.

148   James Houghton's stirring testimony to employee involvement
           from his address to The Economic Club of Detroit, October 1,
           1990. Text provided by Corning.

149   For a more complete explanation of *kaizen* and Japanese employ-
           ee suggestion systems, consult Yuzo Yasuda, *40 Years, 20 Million
           Ideas*, (Cambridge, MA: Productivity Press, 1991), and *Kaizen* by
           Masaaki Imai (New York: McGraw-Hill, 1986).

149   Thinking training in Japanese companies from *Kaizen*, pp. 111–14.

Page
150   Data comparing Japanese and U.S. suggestion systems from
           "Power of Suggestion Stronger in Japan," *The Wall Street Journal*,
           October 19, 1989, p. B1, and *1990 Annual Statistical Report*, Na-
           tional Association of Suggestion Systems, Chicago, Ill., 1991, p.
           vii.

Chapter Eight

Page
152   Robert Pirsig quote from a remark he made to Roger Cohen in
           "Motorcycle of 'Zen' Goes in the Other Direction," *New York
           Times*, October 8, 1991, p. C18.

152   Peter Senge quote from his *Fifth Discipline* (New York: Double-
           day, 1990), p. 239.

152   Charles Garfield quote from *Peak Performers* (New York: Avon
           Books, 1986), p. 190.

152   Tom Stewart's quote from an interview with me.

152   Ray Slesinski's quote from an interview with me.

152   Paul Cook's quote from "The Business of Innovation: An Inter-
           view with Paul Cook," *Harvard Business Review*, March/April
           1990, p. 98.

154   Edward Hennessy's comments on American competitiveness
           from remarks he made at Northeastern University, Weston, MA,
           June 6, 1989. Text provided by Allied-Signal; emphasis in
           original.

154   Donald Gamache's comment on companies' steady state orienta-
           tion from his essay "Planned Growth," in *New Directions in Crea-
           tive and Innovative Management*, by Yuri Ijiri and Robert L. Kuhn
           (New York: Ballinger Publishing, 1988), p. 255.

155   M. L. Caravatti wrote of her study in "Business Needs More
           'Dull' R&D," *New York Times*, October 6, 1991, p. F13.

155   Sun Tzu, from *The Art of War*, translated by Samuel B. Griffeth
           (London: Oxford University Press, 1963), p. 77.

156   Paul Cook on making ideas practical, from *Harvard Business Re-
           view*, March/April 1990, p. 98.

156   Wal-Mart information from "Leaders of the Most Admired" by
           Sarah Smith, *Fortune*, January 29, 1990.

Page

158   Merck information from company reports and "America's Most Admired Corporations" by Alison L. Sprout, *Fortune*, February 11, 1991, and "Brain Power" by Thomas A. Stewart, *Fortune*, June 3, 1991, pp. 44–60.

158   Information on 3M drawn from company documents unless otherwise noted.

158   The 70 percent of sales from worker-generated products from *John Naisbitt's Trend Letter*, September 27, 1990, p. 2.

158   Lewis Lehr's comment about the mother of invention from his article, "The Care and Flourishing of Entrepreneurs at 3M," *Directors and Boards*, Winter 1986, p. 18.

159   3M's many job applicants from "Why 3M Values 'Intrapreneurship'," by Charles J. Murray, *Design News*, July 4, 1988.

159   A. F. Jacobson made his remarks about innovation to the Automotive News World Congress, Detroit, July 29, 1987. Text provided by 3M.

159   Corning information provided by the company, and from "Corning's Class Act," *Business Week*, May 13, 1991, p. 70.

159   Information on IBM obtained from materials provided by the company.

161   Isamu Kuru's comment on organizational support for achievement from Nippon Motorola newsletter *Motrend*, March 1991, p. 6.

161   Ijiri and Kuhn wrote in *New Directions in Creative and Innovative Management*, p. 328.

161   Robert M. White's comment delivered as the Inventors Day Address, Allied-Signal Corp., Morristown, N.J., April 18, 1990.

162   The *Management Review* article was "Whose Problem Is It Anyway?" by Martha H. Peak, in the May 1991 edition, p. 1.

162   Ritz-Carlton information provided by the company and from "Ritz-Carlton: Elegance with Feeling" by Lincoln Avery, *Hotel & Resort Industry*, August 1989.

163   Honda engineers' education from "Create and Survive," in the *Economist*, December 1, 1990, p. 77.

163   Motorola's training information from information provided by the company; and "Motorola U: When Training Becomes an Education" by William Wiggenhorn, *Harvard Business Review*, July–August 1990, pp. 71–83; and "Brain Power," *Fortune*, June 3, 1991, p. 54.

Page

163   William Wiggenhorn's comment from his *Harvard Business Review* article.

163   Arthur Andersen information from "Training for a 'One-Firm' Philosophy," *New Accountant*, September 1991, p. 15.

164   *Six Thinking Hats* by Edward DeBono (Boston: Little, Brown, 1985).

164   Frito-Lay's creative problem solving from "Creativity Training," by Charlene Marmer Solomon, *Personnel Journal*, May 1990, pp. 67–69.

164   Du Pont information from an interview with, and materials provided by, Dave Tanner.

166   Lewis Lehr's observation on priorities from his article in *Directors and Boards*, p. 20.

167   Peter Senge on corporate religiosity, quoted in "Should Your Company Save Your Soul?" *Fortune*, January 14, 1991, p. 33.

167   Robert Kuhn posed his questions in *New Directions*, p. 334.

167   Kodak closes ventures from "Kodak Folds 'Intrapreneur' Program" by Kate Bertrand, *Business Marketing*, December 1990, p. 53.

169   Information on Federal Express's SFA from information provided by the company, and *Blueprints for Service Quality*, American Management Association, New York, 1991, pp. 36–42.

169   Ray Slesinski's comment from an interview with me.

169   William Miller's creativity goals from his book *The Creative Edge* (Reading, Mass.: Addison-Wesley, 1987), p. 185.

171   E. L. Hennessey's comments on organizational barriers from his remarks to the Math and Simulation Sciences Conference, Madison, N.J., October 23, 1990. Text provided by the company.

171   R. M. Kanter's comment from *The Change Masters*, p. 221.

172   Derwynn Phillips wrote his comment on performance and expectation in *The Creativity Infusion* by R. Donald Gamache and Robert L. Kuhn (New York: Harper & Row, 1989), p. 42.

172   Motorola's team competition from company-provided documents.

172   Peter Senge's comment on cause and effect from *The Fifth Discipline*, p. 63.

172   Avon statistics provided by the company.

Chapter Nine

Page

174   Chinese philosopher Chuang-tzu lived in the third century B.C.

174   Edward DeBono quote from his *Lateral Thinking* (New York: Harper & Row, 1970), p. 9.

174   Ray Slesinski's quote from my interview with him.

174   Tom Stewart's quote from my interview with him.

175   John Akers' remarks quoted in "IBM Chief Gives Staff Tough Talk," by John Markoff, *New York Times*, May 29, 1991, p. D1.

175   Conflict is energy: a concept I picked up from Thomas F. Crum's *The Magic of Conflict* (New York: Simon & Schuster, 1987), pp. 25, 47.

176   Survey by the American Productivity and Quality Center reported in "Autonomy Is Widespread, Members Say, but Feedback Is Scarce," in its newsletter *Consensus*, September 1990, pp 1–4.

176   The Federal Express statement from its Leadership Evaluation and Awarenes Process (LEAP) program, quoted in *Blueprints for Service Quality*, 1991, pp. 22, 24.

176   Dick Garwin's statement on candor from "Not Just Another Quality Program," by Mason Southworth, *Think*, no. 5, 1990, p. 49.

179   John Kiel's remark on emotion from his book, *The Creative Mystique* (New York: John Wiley & Sons, 1985), p. 200.

179   Donald Gamache's thought on the erector set and combinations from his essay, "Planned Growth," in *New Directions in Creative and Innovative Management* (New York: Ballinger Publishing, 1988), p. 258.

179   The "wildcards" in INNOTECH's discussions from a personal interview with Kurt Eastman, president of INNOTECH; and from *The Creativity Infusion* (New York: Harper & Row, 1989), a book co-written by its chairman, R. Donald Gamache.

180   Roger von Oech from *Whack on the Side of the Head* (New York: Warner, 1983), p. 26.

180   Edward DeBono's observation from *Lateral Thinking*, p. 42.

181   IBM's computerized meeting centers from "How to Have an 'Electronic' Brainstorm," by Mason Southworth, *Think*, no. 1, 1990.

Page

181   Aristotle's judgment on judgment from his Psychology Book III, translated by J. A. Smith, in *The Pocket Aristotle*, edited by Justin D. Kaplan (New York: Pocket Books, 1958), p. 89.

182   Hanley Norins, *The Young & Rubicam Creative Workshop*, (Englewood Cliffs, NJ: Prentice Hall, 1990), p. 56.

182   Mark Sebell's "war games" remark from my interview with him.

183   R. Donald Gamache's comment on phantom criteria from his essay "Toolbox for Practical Creativity," in *Handbook for Creative and Innovative Managers*, edited by Robert L. Kuhn (New York: McGraw-Hill, 1988), p. 105.

183   Henry Riggs, *Managing High-Tech Companies* (Belmont, CA: Lifetime Learning Publications, 1983), p. 279.

Chapter Ten

Page

184   René Dubos's quote from his book *Celebrations of Life* (New York: McGraw-Hill, 1981), p. 251. Emphasis in the original.

184   Robert Sternberg's quote from *The Nature of Creativity* (Cambridge, Mass.: Cambridge University Press, 1988), p. 11.

184   Marsh Fisher's comments from a personal interview.

186   David Ogilvy's comment from his essay, "The Creative Chef," in *The Creative Organization* (Chicago: University of Chicago Press, 1965), p. 206.

186   DeBono on logic, from *Lateral Thinking* (New York: Harper & Row, 1970), p. 48.

186   Roger von Oech wrote about right answers in *Whack on the Side of the Head* (New York: Warner, 1983), p. 21.

186   John Briggs, *Fire in the Crucible* (Los Angeles: Jeremy P. Tarcher Inc., 1990), p. xiii.

187   René Dubos's comment from his *Celebrations*, p. 28.

188   Thomas Carney wrote his tribute to creativity in *False Profits* (Notre Dame, IN: University of Notre Dame Press, 1981), p. 172.

189   The AP dispatch on IBM and Apple's historic cooperative pact was carried in *The Times*, Trenton, NJ, July 4, 1991, p. D1.

189   Hanley Norins wrote of openness and serendipity in *The Young & Rubicam Creative Workshop* (Englewood Cliffs, N.J.: Prentice Hall, 1990), p. 50.

Page

189   The birth of Scotchgard® drawn from materials provided by 3M.

190   John Cleese on creativity as behavior from his essay, "And Now for Something Completely Different," in *Management Review*, May 1991, p. 50.

191   Joseph Campbell was quoted by Clara Pierre in *The Times*, Trenton, NJ, February 24, 1991, p. BB4.

191   Hockey players' quick perceptions from a speech given by SRI Senior Vice President Jim Sorenson to the National Association of Legal Vendors, San Diego, CA, October 1990.

195   John Briggs discusses some research on behavior and neural patterns in *Fire in the Crucible*, pp. 48–66. A reading of scientific and popular journals suggests that much less is known about the brain's neural networks than is known, but theories abound.

196   Thelonius Monk is said to have said, "Sometimes I play things I never heard myself."

198   The term *OmniMedia* is from my first book, *NO COMMENT! An Executive's Essential Guide to the News Media* (New York: Praeger Publishers, 1987), pp. 4–5.

198   DeBono on a mind switch from *Lateral Thinking*, p. 18.

200   Les Brown's comment from a video-taped speech run on WHYY-TV, Philadelphia.

200   Failure versus feedback, inspired by this line from R. Donald Gamache and Robert L. Kuhn in their book *The Creativity Infusion* (New York: Harper & Row, 1989), p. 54: ". . . explore the difference between *mistake* (an emotional, bad word) and *feedback* (an intelligent, good word)." [emphasis in original]

200   Peter Senge wrote about constraints in *The Fifth Discipline* (New York: Doubleday, 1990), p. 353.

201   Joseph Brodsky wrote "The Best Way Out Is Always Through," *Career Insights Law*, 1989, p. 63.

201   M. Scott Peck's words on wisdom from *The Road Less Traveled* (New York: Simon & Schuster, 1978), p. 51.

202   The tale of Banc One's financial marketplace from "The Best Little Bank in America," by Steve Lohr, *New York Times*, July 7, 1991, pp. F1, F4.

203   Quotes from Marsh Fisher, and information about him drawn from an interview with Mr. Fisher, and information provided by the company. I use *IdeaFisher*; it's a great tool.

Page

204   Information about *Pocket Innovator* provided by its manufacturer, Creative Learning International, and my own experience with the device.

205   SCAMPER is from the book *Scamper* by Robert Eberle (Buffalo, NY: DOK Publications); cited in *Idea Management* by Charles H. Clark (New York: AMACOM, 1980), p. 16.

206   Elliott Jaques wrote of better alternatives in his *Creativity and Work*, p. 129.

206   The costs of creativity drawn from my personal experience, and from *Idea Management* by Charles H. Clark, pp. 53–54.

207   Bertolt Brecht's line on peace is from *Mother Courage and Her Children*, Act I.

207   Robert Sternberg's comment on creativity as a persuasive act is from *Nature of Creativity*, p. 386.

207   Gamache and Kuhn from *Creativity Infusion*, p. 12.

207   David Ogilvy, *The Creative Organization*, p. 207.

Afterword

Page

208   Marsh Fisher's poignant comment from an interview with me.

ACKNOWLEDGMENTS

I am in the debt of many, including many whose names don't appear here or in the text. I salute all those for whom I've worked and those who have or do work with me; you have been my teachers about the awesome responsibilities of management, the joy of creative work, and the need for self-expression on the job. And I am grateful.

To all who gave of their time, their files, their ideas, I say thank you for helping me to find some answers and more questions. The generosity of people I contacted for help has been inspiring. My thanks to Ken Wilkie for his creative vision; his delightful cartoons more than capture the essence of what I struggled to say.

I especially want to thank Chet Holmes, who encouraged this project from the very start when it was only an idea for a speech; his enthusiastic support makes him the project's patron. Jeffrey Krames, a resident maverick at Business One Irwin immediately latched onto the concept; I thank him for recognizing its potential, and Cindy Zigmund for patiently shepherding it through to completion.

While this work was in progress, I was aided by the well-stocked marketing library at my employer, Matthew Bender & Co. (which has encouraged my personal creative growth immensely under the supportive leadership of Pam Sallander). I received help from the Petrozzini and Martino families who generously (and literally) gave this book a home when it desperately needed one. Thanks, Doug and Mary, and Kathy and Phil, I appreciate it.

Long before this project formally began, my parents enthusiastically encouraged my insatiable curiosity, even when that must have been maddening; later, Ken Eckhardt wisely urged me to pursue a generalist's path in business; and a few years back, Rick Mitchell encouraged me to write about management matters because "business needs more philosophers." Thank you all.

Writing a book is joyous torture for me; this book required an extraordinary sacrifice by my family. They arranged their schedules, creatively invented excursions to allow me some quiet time, and freely gave of themselves to accommodate my need to spend every waking moment out of the office for more than a year working on this task. We have many, many occasions to catch up on with family and friends. I am deeply touched and grateful for your selflessness.

I especially want to thank Susan, my friend and partner, whose own intellectual pursuits contributed immensely to the formation of the theses in this book; and whose patience, support, and understanding over the years have contributed profoundly to my emotional and intellectual growth.

Index

A

Absorbing, creative behavior, 192
Accepting, creative behavior, 200–201
Achievement specialists, 103
Achievers-in-waiting, defined, 11
Acting, creative behavior, 201
Adams, Henry, on influence of teachers, 83
Administration, of suggestion box systems, 140
Adventuring, creative behavior, 193
Allaire, Paul, concerning the line manager, 80
American Compensation Association, 122
American Productivity and Quality Center, 77, 176
American Psychological Association regarding focus on the gifted, 51
Annual personal performance review, 93
Anticipating, creative skill, 188–189
Antistenes, Cynic school of philosophy, 26
Apple Computer, and industrial revelation, 2–3
Are We Creative Yet?, DuPont publication, 165
Argyris, Chris, concerning defensiveness of accomplished individuals, 164
Aristotle on thinking and judgment, 181
Armstrong, John, on source of ideas at IBM, 160–161
Army Ideas for Excellence Program, 47
Arthur Andersen (accounting firm), spending on professional education, 163
Artificial innovation, 24–25
Association for the Gifted, 36, 71
Associative, state of problem solving, 202
Average award to employees, suggestion program, 149
Average savings, from suggestion programs, 149
Avon, 4
  reaction to changes in the market, 172–173
Awards schedule, suggestion box system, 140–141
Ayres, Mary, and Noxzema skin products, 85–86

B

Baby boomers, need for recognition, 103
Bailey, Elizabeth, on reactions to new ideas, 22
Balancing, creative behavior, 193
Barron, Frank, on creative people, 55
Barry, Virgil, on business advances, 8
Bartel, Father Leo, on education and motivation, 83
Base pay, control of, 126

Bennis, Warren, on the effects of routine work, 23
Boardroom, Inc., new ideas system, 146–147
Bodily-kinesthetic intelligence, 53
Bolger, Bruce, on incentive plans, 129
Bonaparte, Emperor Napoleon, on motivation, 99
Bonuses, criteria for good ideas, 182
Boredom, mavericks reaction to, 56
Borrowing, creative behavior, 199
Bostwick, Arthur E., describing great scientists, 56
Brain power, as competitive weapon, 8
Brains, pay for, 120–122
Brainstorm, term, 181
Bravo Zulu, spot award, 133
Breaking habits, creative behavior, 194–195
Brecht, Bertolt, 207
Briggs, John
  on creativity and conflict, 175
  on creators and chance, 60–61
  on geniuses, 187
Brown, Les, on importance of taking risks, 200
Budget, for incentive compensation, 131–132
Bureaucracy busting, 168–173
Business achievement awards, and performance expectations, 106
Business creativity, 6–10
Business risk, and variable compensation plans, 126–128
Business skills, creative, 188–201
Business success, correlation with formal education, 37
Byron, Lord
  on adversity and truth, 174
  concerning creative instincts, 24

C

Campbell, Joseph, concerning gurus, 191
Caravatti, Marie–Louise, study of funding for innovation, 155
Carlson, Chester, and Xerox Corporation, 38
Carlton Society, at 3M, 105
Carney, Thomas P., on the act of creativity, 188
Cash awards, for innovation, 148–149
Challenging the status quo, by mavericks, 59
Chandler, Rick, on skill-based pay and merit pay, 128
Characteristics, of mavericks, 54–62
Chartier, Emile, on single ideas, 186–187
Cheerleading
  forms of, 90
  manager's role, 89–93
Chitwood, Roy, concerning employee potential, 14

Churchill, Winston
    school career of, 35
    on workplace environment, 171–172
Cleese, John, on creativity, 190–191
Commuting time, use as meditating time, 197
Company performance variable, 130–131
Compensation
    and choice of occupation, 116–120
    and incenting mavericks, 116–124
Compensation budget, and thank-you
        gestures, 108
Compensatory management directive, 83–84
Compliments, as motivation technique,
        107–108
Conflict
    bosses and, 176
    creativity and, 174–183
    in judgment, 181–183
Confrontation, and creativity, 174–183
Connor, Tim, on investing in learning, 196
Consultants, use of, 171
Control freaks, 64–65
Controlled anarchy, 40
Conversation Ball, use in meetings, 180
Cook, Paul
    on innovation, 156
    and Not Invented Here awards, 106
    regarding individual recognition, 103
    on use of bonuses, 128
Corning, Inc.
    job-related training, 162
    on organizing for innovation, 159
    recognition for innovation, 148–149
Corporate contrarian, 38–40
Corporate environment, and open
        communication, 77
Costs of creativity, 206–207
Cover Girl cosmetics, 86
Creative acts, components of, 52
Creative assets, as competitive weapon, 8
Creative Realities, consulting firm, 7
Creative Whack Pack, creative tool, 205
Creatives. See Mavericks
Creativity
    business skills, 188–201
    business success and, 186–187
    communicating and presenting, 207
    and conflict, 174–183
    costs of, 206–207
    as a learned skill, 187
    result from meditating, 197–198
Cultural diversity, and company tolerance, 92
Culture of discovery, 166
Cumming, Charles, on incentive plans, 129
Curiosity, as intelligence, 53
Customer service complaints, levels of, 13
Cynic school of philosophy, 26

D

DeBono, Edward

DeBono, Edward—continued
    on creativity and open discussions, 180
    on intuitive thinking, 186
    on resistance to change, 21–22
    six hat thinking method, 164
Decision Support Centers, IBM, 181
Delegation of assignments, 90
Delisle, James R.
    on gifted children, 36–37
    on underachievement, 71
Department, term, 171
Desirables, criteria for good ideas, 182
Development of human potential, Franklin A.
        Thomas, 48
Difficult employees, managing, 25–26
Direct personal communication, importance
        of, 90
Discovering, creative skill, 189
Discovery, culture of, 166
Divine discontent, 37
Doyle, Bob, concerning big companies and
        new ideas, 21
Dubos, Rene
    on human creativity, 35
    on human potential, 187
Dunlap, James L., concerning currency and
        the maverick ethic, 30–31
DuPont, Center for Creativity and
        Innovation, 164–166

E

Eastman Kodak
    early suggestion box programs, 137–138
    intrapreneur programs, 166–167
Edison, Mrs. Thomas, phenomenon, 22
Edison, Thomas, on other people's ideas,
        199
Egalitarian democracy, in companies with
        fewer managers, 87
Einstein, Albert
    on feeling and desire, 99
    school career of, 35
Eligibility to participate, suggestion box
        programs, 144
Embellishing, creative skill, 190
Emotions, in mavericks, 65–71
Employees, constraint in performance of
        tasks, 19–20
Employees, view of management, 76
Enthusiasm, literal meaning, 115
Epiphanic, state of problem solving, 202
Equality versus meritocracy, 124
Evaluating
    managers, 169–170
    suggestions, 168
Even-handed debate, for controversial
        proposals, 180
Expertise, of staff members, 88
Extra Step award, Veterans Administration,
        Philadelphia, 134

F

Face-to-face communication, importance of, 107–108
Facilitator, role in open discussion, 179
Failure, need to acknowledge, 111–112
Favorite phrases, of mavericks, 62
Fear, as motivation, 99
Federal Express
    Bravo Zulu spot awards, 133
    effective managers, characteristics of, 176–177
    evaluation of managers, 169–170
    Golden Falcon program, 133
Financial compensation, psychic motivator, 119–120
Fingerspitzengeful, 55
Fisher, Marsh
    converting ideas to finished products, 7
    on creative tools, 205
    on creativity and art, 184–185, 184–186
    creativity as a learned skill, 187
    IdeaFisher software, 203–204
    importance of ideas, 6
    on need for education and training, 162
    need for system to capture, store, and retrieve ideas, 59–60
    on schools and creativity, 34–37
Fixed merit budget, 124
Fixed pay, fixed performance, 122–123
Flat-pay system, and purchasing power, 123
Focusing, creative skill, 190
Ford Foundation, Innovations in State and Local Government Awards Program, 47
Fox, Stephen R., on David Ogilvy, 22–23
Franklin, Benjamin, belief in imagination, 31
Frito-Lay, Inc., and problem-solving training, 163–164
Frost, John L., on employee awards, 128
Fulfillment, as motivator, 100
Fun, as motivation, 112-113
Fuqua, J.B., on giving people authority to act, 84

G

Gallagher, James J., concerning intelligence tests, 53
Gamache, R. Donald
    on business executives and creativity, 9–10
    on formality and insecurity, 92
    on innovation, 154
    on the phantom criterion, 183
    on presenting new ideas, 207
    on thought provokers, 179
Gardner, Howard, and seven types of intelligence, 53–54
Garfield, Charles
    on the dual needs of autonomy and affiliation, 70
    on peak performers, 54

Garfield, Charles—*continued*
    on systematic study of human achievement, 35, 51
Garwin, Dick, on handling of problems, 176–177
Gates, William H.
    first two companies, 52
    school career of, 36
Gelfond, Peter, concerning poor management, 13
General Electric, Work-Out meetings, 145–146
General Mills, incentive based compensation programs, 128
Genesis Training Solutions, consulting firm, 23
Genius
    akin to insanity, 31
    in Roman mythology, 115
Gifted children, 51
    emotional development of, 67–70
    raising, 92–93
Giving, creative behavior, 199
Goethe, Johann Wolfgang von, defining the perfectionist, 63
Goings, E. V. "Rick"
    on change, 4
    on changes at Avon, 173
    on leadership, 81–82
Golden Falcon, Federal Express program, 133
Groupthink, 177
Growth, as motivator, 109
Gurin, Richard S., regarding fun, 112–113

H

Hale, Sandra, procurement operation in Minnesota, 46–47
Harvard Advanced Management Program impact on salary levels, 37
Harvey, Andrew, 70
Hawthorne Effect, 114
Hay Group, human resource consultants, 13
Henderson, Rob, on work force productivity, 102–103
Hennessy, Edward L.
    on American complacency, 154
    on departments, 171
    on markets and ideas, 4
High-achievers, 51–52. *See also* Mavericks
Holmes, Chet, regarding need to effect change, 57
Holmes, Justice Oliver Wendell, on new ideas, 178
Honda, Soichiro
    founder Honda Motor Company, 38
    school career of, 36
Honda Motor Company
    idea bank, 59–60
    new hires training, 163
Hoping, creative behavior, 200
Houghton, James R.

Houghton, James R.—*continued*
  on Corning, Inc. recognition programs,
    148–149
  on cultural diversity, 92

I

IBM
  Decision Support Centers, 181
  and innovation, 159–161
Idea
  criteria for good ideas, 182
  epicenters, in U.S., 12
  generating, 201–206
  Idea bank, Honda Motor Company, 59–60
  implementation, 168–173
  judgement of, 181–183
Ideafeast, term, 181
Ideafest, term, 181
IdeaFisher, computer software, 203–204
Idea Inertia (I - I) syndrome
  description of, 21–22
  and market research, 24–25
  and variable pay for select few, 125
Ideas for Excellence Program, U.S. Army, 47
Ignoring, creative behavior, 198–199
Incentive magazine,
  on basic compensation and motivation, 100
Ijiri, Yuji, on teamwork, 161
Imagining, creative behavior, 201
Impact on society, need of mavericks to
    make, 57
Imposter syndrome, 71–72
Impulsing, creative behavior, 197
Incentive compensation, 128–129
  budget for, 131–132
  professional help for, 129
  rating variables for, 130–132
Incentive increases, 123–125
Independence and motivation, 111
Informing employees, on suggestion box
    program, 141
InnerTrack, Inc., 106–107
Innovation
  and corporate policies, 155–161
  encouraging, 152–153
  rewarding, 147–149
  and teamwork, 161–162
Innovations in State and Local Government
    Awards Program, Ford Foundation, 47
Inquiring, creative behavior, 194
Inspiring, creative skill, 189
Intellectual capital, as competitive weapon, 8
Intellectual freedom, in progressive
    companies, 77
Intelligence, seven kinds of, 53–54
Intelligence tests, 53
Intention state, of problem solving, 202
Interest, as motivation, 99
Interpersonal intelligence, 53
Intrapersonal intelligence, 53

Intrapreneur programs, at Kodak, 166–167
Intuitive thinking, 186
Investigation, of suggestion box ideas,
    143–144
IQ test, high score on, 53
Isen, Alice M., on people's moods, 112–113

J

Jacobson, A. F., on organizing for innovation,
    159
Job satisfaction, as motivator, 100
Job well-done letter, motivation technique,
    106–107
Johnson, Hank, on resistance to change,
    21–22
Johnston, Gerald A., concerning the
    yes–man, 20–21

K

Kaempffert, Waldemar, concerning new
    inventions, 33
Kaizen ethic, in Japan, 149–150
Kanter, Rosabeth Moss
  on dynamics of change, 39
  on ideas for innovation, 171
  on performance, 115
  on recognition, 104
Kaplan, Leslie S., concerning reaction to
    boredom, 56
Keeping up, responsibility for, 88
Kiam, Victor, and incentive pay plans,
    128–129
Kiel, John M., on meeting leadership, 179
Knowing, creative behavior, 199
Knowledge of self, 53
Krogh, Lester C., on peer recognition, 105
Kuhn, Robert L.
  on business executives and creativity,
    9–10
  on formality and insecurity, 92
  on presenting new ideas, 207
  on the purpose of business enterprise, 167
  on teamwork, 161

L

Landauer, Rolf, 25
Lande, Melissa, on avoiding leniency, 94
Lao Tzu
  concerning leadership, 80
  concerning prohibitions on thought, 24
Laughing, creative behavior, 201
Leadership, inadequacies of, 81–82
Leadership Index, Federal Express, 169
Learning, creative behavior, 196–197
Learning company, description of IBM, 160

LeBoeuf, Michael
   concerning poor management, 13
   Imagineering, book, 191
Lehr, Lewis W.
   on innovation, 166
   on invention, 158
Lenin, on the management class, 19
Levering, Robert
   on employee viewpoint of management, 19
   on management literature, 25
Limits, setting and communicating, 94–95
Linguistic intelligence, 53
Listening, importance of, 107–108
Logic, confining nature of, 186
Logical-mathematical intelligence, 53
Longfellow, Layne, on life skills, 68
Long-term variable, 131

M

McCabe, Ed, on noncreative people, 25
Machine Design magazine
   regarding new product introduction, 4
MacKay, Harvey, concerning incompetence,
   13
Management
   ability to manage people, 79–81
   as a class, 19–20
   and managerial effectiveness, 80
   rewards of constriction, 23–24
Management Review, American Management
   Association report on training
   expenditures, 162
Managing difficult employees, 25–26
Mann, Horace, on blind impulse, 197
Market research, and innovation, 24–25
Markoff, John, regarding NeXt Inc, and
   perfection, 63
Markovits, Gary, on world-class
   manufacturing and marketing, 5–6
Markowich, Dr. Michael, on employee
   attitudes and making suggestions, 18
Marquis, Don, on manager's operative
   thinking, 19
Marveling, creative behavior, 192–193
Mastery in work, need of mavericks, 57
Matejka, Ken, regarding managing difficult
   employees, 25–26
Maverick, Samuel A., symbol for
   nonconformity and individualism, 30
Maverick culture, evolving, 152–153
Maverick managers
   as cheerleader, 89–93
   and the communication equation, 90–91
   and conflict, 176–177
   educator role, 83–89
   and evaluation of ideas, 183
   importance of listening, 107–108
   as learner, 86
   quality assurer role, 93–95
   requesting ideas from staff, 85–86

Maverick managers—*continued*
   responding to ideas, 89
   use of face-to-face communication, 107–108
   use of meetings, 87–88
Mavericks
   and American industry, 31
   challenging the status quo, 59
   champions of change, 37–38, 40
   common characteristics of, 50–72
   and compensation, 116–124, 125–129
   creative business skills, 188–201
   and emotions, 65–71
   favorite phrases, 62
   impact on society, desire for, 57
   mastery in work, need for, 57
   motivation of, 96–115
   natural condition of, 34–37
   news junkies, 56
   in not-for-profit organizations, 46–48
   other names for, 31, 52
   and the perfection infection, 62–65
   in pursuit of goals, 58–59
   as risk takers, 60–61
   sense of social responibility, 61–62
   view of authority, 39
   work ethic of, 56-57
   work style, 54–62
Mecca, Dr. Andrew M., on the four primary
   ingredients of self-esteem, 89–90
Mechanical intelligence, 53
Meditating, during commuting, 197
Melville, Herman, on originality and
   imitation, 199
Mencken, H. L., on doubt, 177
Merck, culture of innovation, 156–158
Meritocracy versus equality, 124
Micromanagement, 14
Miller, William
   on creativity, 93
   on rating managers' innovation
      contribution, 169
Milliken & Co.
   and Malcolm Baldridge Quality Award, 103
   quality improvement suggestions, 145
Milliken, Roger, on applause, 103
Minnesota Mining and Manufacturing. See
   3M
Mitchell, Maria, on learning to see, 200
Moderator, role in open discussion, 179
Money, and motivation, 118–120
Moonlighting and motivation, 111
Morale and motivation, 97–98
Moral intelligence, 53–54
Motivation, factors in, 96–115
   role of money, 118–120
Motivation gap, 12–14
Motorola
   intracompany competition, 172
   and the Malcolm Baldrige Quality Award,
      172
   merit raises and performance bonuses, 128
   Motorola University, 163
   Six Sigma manufacturing goal, 163

Musical intelligence, 53
Musts, criteria for good ideas, 182

N

National Association of Suggestion Systems,
    138
National Science Foundation, on nonmilitary
    research and development spending, 8
Negative communicator, 91
New hires, and internal operations, 85
General Index for Blohowiak: Managing
    Mavericks
Noncash awards, for innovation, 147–148
Nonmilitary research and development
    spending, 8
Nonmonetary compensation, 101–102
Norins, Hanley
    on creative people in advertising, 104
    on generating new ideas, 92
    on idea selection, 182
    on luck and serendipity, 189
    on work as education, 115
Not-for-profit maverick, 46–48
Noxzema skin products, role of Mary Ayres,
    85–86
Nurturing intelligence, 53

O

Oech, Roger von
    concerning the right answer, 186
    Creative Whack Pack, creative tool, 205
    on creativity and open discussions, 180
    intelligence as pattern recognition, 54
    A Whack on the Side of the Head, book, 191
Ogilvy, David, advertising executive, 22–23
    on presenting new ideas, 207
    on the tyranny of reason, 186
On-the-Spot awards, Veterans
    Administration, Philadelphia, 134
Open communication, and the corporate
    environment, 77
Opposing conformity, an American tradition,
    30
Orchestrating dissent, techniques for, 178–181
Osborn-Parnes method, of problem solving,
    164

P

Paley, Norton, on motivating staff, 3–4
Paralysis of procedure, and management
    control, 23
Pasteur, Louis, on the prepared mind, 199
Payroll, percent spending on training, 162
Pearson, Andrall E., on innovative leaders, 84

Peck, M. Scott
    contemplation of anti-authority, 31
    on importance of decisiveness, 94
    on need for action, 201
Perceiving, creative behavior, 191–192
Perfection infection, and mavericks, 62–65,
    93–95
Perfectionists, as managers, 63–65
Perrone, Philip A., characteristics of
    giftedness, 56–62
Personal performance variable, 130
Personal projects, as motivation, 110–111
Phantom criterion, 183
Philips, Derwyn, on organizational
    performance, 172
Picasso, Pablo
    creation as act of destruction, 31
    school career of, 35–36
Piechowski, Michael M., on gifted children,
    69
Player/coaches, managers as, 107
Pocket Innovator, creativity device, 204–205
Pondering, creative behavior, 198
Positive maladjustment, 37
Postman, Neil, on schools and creativity, 34
Practical giftedness, 55
Praise, as motivational technique, 102–113
Presentation of awards, suggestion box
    programs, 143
Problem-solving process, stages, 201–202
Process innovation, spending on, 155
Process productivity, at 3M, 158–159
Product innovation, spending on, 155
Project deadlines, importance of, 88
Psychic paychecks, 96–115
Psychic productivity, 6
Public recognition, motivator, 104–106
Public school system
    impact on creativity, 34–37
    need to stimulate children, 36–37
Purchasing power, of workers in flat-pay
    system, 123

Q

Quality, and competitiveness, 6
Questioning, creative behavior, 200
Questors, mavericks as, 56
Quiet entrepreneurs, 39
Quinn, James E., regarding individual
    recognition, 103

R

Reaves, Chuck
    on maverick's view of authority, 39
    regarding obstacles to new ideas, 21
Reciprocal motivation deficit, 98–101

Recognition
    as feedback, 113
    incentive for innovation, 148
    motivation technique, 103–104
    and spot bonus, 133–134
Recording, creative behavior, 194
Record keeping, suggestion box programs, 142–143
Reflecting, creative behavior, 197–198
Rejection of promising ideas, 89, 94
Relaxing, creative behavior, 193
Research and development spending, nonmilitary, 8
Resolution, of suggestion box ideas, 144
Responding
    to ideas from co-workers, 89
    to suggestion box program, 141–142
Reverse Hawthorne Effect, 114
Reverse yes-man mentality, 22–23
Rich, Jude, on employee motivation, 100
Riggs, Henry
    on compensation systems, 124
    on founders of high-technology companies, 38
    on need to champion new ideas, 57
    on rejection of ideas, 89, 183
Risk, and new ideas, 17–18
Risking, creative behavior, 200
Risk takers, mavericks as, 60–61
Ritz-Carlton Hotels
    employee training, 162
    Quality Network, 145
Rodgers, Buck, on bosses and status quo, 18
Rodriguez, Victor
    on managers making performance distinctions, 123–124
    on use of spot bonus, 133
    on variable compensation plans, 126–127
Russell, Bertrand
    on importance of insight, 197
    on types of work, 120–121

S

Sales compensation plans, no-cap, 119
SCAMPER, idea generating technique, 205
School aptitude tests, 53
Sculley, John
    on anarchy, 40
    on management and creativity, 9, 86
    on network as metaphor, 87
    on white collar productivity, 5
Sebell, Mark
    on anarchy, 40
    on business creativity, 7, 87
    on idea selection, 182
Seeking, creative skill, 189
Self-esteem, as motivator, 100
Senge, Peter M.
    on changing corporate culture, 172
    on corporate mission, 167

Senge, Peter M.—*continued*
    on natural leadership, 81
    on nature of structure in human systems, 26
    on working within constraints, 200
Set-increase compensation system, and competitiveness, 124
Sharing, creative skill, 190
Sibson & Company, human resource consultants, 128
Sifting, creative skill, 190
Silent ballot, conflict resolution technique, 180–181
Silverman, Linda Kreger
    on emotional development of gifted children, 67
    on gifted adults and overexcitability, 69
    regarding focus on the gifted, 51
Simonton, Dean, on geniuses and mistakes, 60
Singing, creative behavior, 201
Six sigma, manufacturing goal, 160, 163
Six Thinking Hats, book, 164
Slesinski, Raymond A.
    on bosses' intransigence, 23
    on rating managers' innovation contribution, 169
Social conformity, 20–21
Social responsibility, sense of, 61–62
Social skills, 53
Spatial intelligence, 53
Speaking originally, creative behavior, 196
Special project, as motivator, 110
Spirited group discussions, for constructive conflict, 178–180
Spot bonus, recognition award, 133–134
Standards of performance, 172–173
Steiner, Gary A.
    on maverick characteristics, 54–55
    on maverick's view of authority, 39
Sternberg, Robert J.
    creativity as act of persuasion, 207
    on geniuses, 60
    on individual's ability to shape an environment, 55
    regarding monetary rewards, 118–119
Stewart, Tom
    on management vs. creative guys, 25
    and worker as thinker, 11–12
Street smarts, as intelligence, 53
Stress, internalization of, 177–178
Suggestion box systems
    administration of, 140
    average award value, 149
    average savings from, 149
    awards schedule, 140–141
    early history of, 137–138
    eligibility to participate, 144
    examples in use, 138–139
    General Electric, 145–146
    investigation of ideas, 143–144
    Milliken & Co., 145
    and the National Association of Suggestion Systems, 138
    presentation of awards, 143

Suggestion box systems—*continued*
  publicizing, 141
  record keeping, 142–143
  resolution of pending suggestions, 144
  responding to suggestions, 141–142
  Ritz-Carlton Hotels, 145
  top management and, 139–140
Sun Tzu, on organization and management, 155
Surfacing, creative skill, 189
Survey-Feedback-Action program, Federal
    Express, 169–170
Sustaining rewards, 113
Symbolic work, 12

T

Talking Stick, use in meetings, 180
Tannenbaum, Abraham J.
  concerning success in school, 53
  describing mavericks' risk inclination, 60
Tanner, Dave, regarding recognition awards,
    105
Tarkenton, Fran, concerning time off, 111
Teaching opportunity, as motivator, 109
Team performance variable, 130
Teamwork, and innovation, 161–162
Thank-you gestures, motivation technique, 108
Think, IBM employee magazine, 160
Thinking, creative behavior, 194
Thomas, Franklin A., on development of
    human potential, 48
360-degree vision, 56
3M
  Carlton Society, 105
  discovery of Scotchgard fabric protector, 189
  and failures, 112
  and innovation, 158–159
  and personal projects, 110–111
  and process productivity, 158–159
Time away from work, 111
Time sensitivity, as intelligence, 53
Times Mirror Cable Television, recognition
    program, 105
Toffler, Alvin
  on breaking with formal procedures, 19
  regarding turbulent environments, 8–9
Tolan, Stephanie S., on raising gifted
    children, 92–93
Top management, and suggestion systems,
    139–140
Training expenditures, 162
Trust barrier, 76–78
24 hour drawer, use of, 91

U

U.S. Constitution, conceived by mavericks, 30
U.S. Office of Consumer Affairs findings
    regarding customer service, 13

V

Variable pay
  and business risk, 126–128
  and the I-I syndrome, 125
Veteran Administration Philadelphia office,
    spot awards, 134
Visibility, as motivator, 108–109

W

Walking, creative behavior, 200
Wallace, Marc J., Jr.
  on incentive plans, 129
  reporting on pay scales, 121–122
Wal-Mart, entrepreneurial environment, 156
Ward, Professor Lewis B., findings on salaries
    of Harvard MBA holders, 37
Wareham, John, on intuition, creativity, and
    judgement, 55
Waterman, Bob, on importance of self-
    confidence, 90
Waterman, Robert H., on creativity, 11
Way to Go Cards, motivation tool, 106–107
White, Robert M., on organization support to
    inventors, 161
White collar productivity, 4–5
Whitehead, Alfred North, on effective ideas,
    177
Wiggenhorn, William, on Motorola's
    commitment to education, 163
Wildcard participants, in discussion groups,
    179
William M. Mercer, Inc., benefit consultants,
    12
Wing, R. L., on fear, 99
Wondering, creative skill, 190
Workaholic, description of, 65
Workers, as thinkers, 11–12
Work ethic, of high–achievers, 56–57
Work force, motivation and innovation, 6
Work-Out meetings, at General Electric,
    145–146
Work team, term, 171
World-class manufacturing and marketing,
    5–6
Wyatt Company, survey regarding
    motivation, 13

Y

Yes-man, proverbial, 20–21

Z

Zemke, Ron, on managers as cheerleaders, 89

Second to None
How Our Smartest Companies Put People First
Charles Garfield

Discover how you can create a workplace where both people and profits flourish! *Second to None* by Charles Garfield, the best-selling author of *Peak Performers*, gives you an inside look at today's leading businesses and how they became masters at expanding the teamwork and creativity of their work force. Using this unique mix of practical strategies gleaned from our smartest companies, you can respond to the challenges of today's global marketplace, provide superior service to your customers—and your own employees, maintain a competitive edge during times of rapid transition and restructuring, and much more! *ISBN: 1-55623-360-4*

Workforce Management
How Today's Companies Are Meeting Business and Employee Needs
Barbara Pope

Provides practical advice for organizations struggling to respond to ongoing change. Pope shows how to integrate business and employee needs in order to recruit and retain the best employees. She shows how you can manage work force problems before they become critical, work collaboratively to develop human resource programs and policies that match business plans, jobs, and people, and much more! *ISBN: 1-55623-537-2*

Team-based Organizations
Developing a Successful Team Environment
James H. Shonk

Shonk shows you how to structure and manage an organization that is built around teams versus forcing a team approach into an existing structure. He identifies the advantages and challenges associated with team-based organizations so that you'll be prepared to deal with and resolve any issues that arise. You'll find valuable planning tools to assist you in implementation and help you avoid wasted time. *ISBN: 1-55623- 703-0*

Survive Information Overload
The 7 Best Ways to Manage Your Workload by Seeing the Big Picture
Kathryn Alesandrini

Gives you a step-by-step action plan to survive the information onslaught and still have time to effectively manage people, increase productivity, and best serve customers. You'll find innovative techniques, such as Priority Mapping, Context Analysis, Visual Organization, and the use of a Master Control System to manage details by seeing the big picture.   *ISBN: 1-55623-721-9*

Continuous Improvement and Measurement For Total Quality
A Team-Based Approach
Dennis C. Kinlaw
Copublished by Pfeiffer & Company/Business One Irwin

You'll find the tools, processes, and models for success that assist you in measuring team performance, improving customer satisfaction, and solving unique challenges your company faces. No matter if you're a team member, manager, or consultant, Kinlaw gives you valuable insight so your organization can benefit from teams!   *ISBN: 1-55623-778-2*

Action:

_____

_____

Action:

_____

_____

Action:

_____

_____

Action:

_____

_____

Action:

_____

_____

Action:

_____

_____

Action:

_____

_____

Action:

_____

_____

Action:

_____

_____

Action:

_____

_____

Action:

_____

_____

Action:

_____

_____

Action:

_____

_____

Action:

_____

_____

Action:

_____

_____

Action:

_____

_____

Action:

_____

_____

Action:

_____

_____

Action:

_____

_____

Action:

_____

_____

Action:

_____

_____

Action:

Action:

Action:

Action:

Action:

Action:

Action:

Action:

_____

_____

Action:

_____

_____

Action:

_____

_____

Action:

_____

_____

Action:

_____

_____

Action:

_____

_____

Action:

_____

_____

Action:

_____

_____

Action:

_____

_____

Action:

_____

_____

Action:

_____

_____

Action:

_____

_____

Action:

_____

_____

Action:

_____

_____

Action:

_____

_____

Action:

_____

_____

Action:

_____

_____

Action:

_____

_____

Action:

_____

_____

Action:

_____

_____

Action:

_____

_____

Maverick Action Planner

Ideas to Pursue/Actions to Take
Indicate the who, what, where, when, why, and how

Action:

_____

_____

Action:

_____

_____

Action:

_____

_____

Action:

_____

_____

Action:

_____

_____

Action:

_____

_____